The Revelation

The Revelation

by

JJ Winston

Published by Wins Consulting

www.NovelistJJWinston.com

ISBN: 978-1-7350903-9-9

Cover Design Robins Gregson and Kozkura

Editor: Eryka Parker of Legacy Book Coaching & Consulting | Michael C. Payne

Interior Formatting: Eryka Parker

Printed in the United States of America

First Edition: 2025

For permissions, inquiries, or bulk orders, contact:

www.NovelistJJWinston.com

This book is dedicated to my mother, son, granddaughter Amaya and most of all my husband. Their encouragement, love and sacrifice have allowed me to be of service to the behavioral health, sickle cell and human trafficking communities and without them, there would be no me. They are the wind beneath my wings. I hope my words as told by my characters inspire the world to donate their time, money, resources and service to causes that make our world a better place to call home.

Table of Contents

Prologue

W*hat do you do when the truth threatens to destroy your Kingdom?*

Juliette stood at the front of the church next to her sister-in-law, Greta, who looked stunning in her off-white Vera Wang wedding gown. The sweet fragrance of fresh-cut roses and lilies mingled with the light musk of polished wooden pews. Ribbons of satin in soft cream and gold were draped along the sides of the pews, gently knotted to hold bunches of baby's breath and roses, adding a delicate touch to the beautiful scene. Juliette scanned the faces of the family and friends who were scattered around the pristine church when her eyes caught Grandville's, and her heart smiled. He looked dapper in his black tuxedo with hunter green accents and she felt like the happiest woman on earth. She was already married to her king, and she blushed when she thought about what she would do to him when they were alone tonight.

As Greta, Grandville's twin sister's matron of honor, she was happy that Greta and Derek's wedding was occurring without a hitch. Everything had started on time and Juliette was looking forward to the reception that she had helped Greta painstakingly plan. There were only fifty wedding guests, but Greta had gone all out for the reception, which would take place at the famed five-star Cleveland Clinic Intercontinental Hotel. Greta said that her first wedding to BBA Star Rayshawn Robinson was a large affair. For her second wedding she wanted a small, intimate affair. The menu included filet mignon, sushi, lemon chicken and a variety of side dishes and salads—just thinking of the tasty meal made Juliette's stomach growl. She remembered that she had skipped breakfast and resolved to make up for it at the reception. She palmed Derek's wedding band, anticipating when Greta would slide it onto his finger, signifying to the world that he was spoken for.

"If anyone knows a reason why these two should not be joined in holy matrimony, speak now or forever hold your peace," the minister said.

Juliette was already imagining where she would hang Derek and Greta's beautiful wedding portraits in her home when a disturbance at the back of the church caught her attention. A loud voice screamed, "I protest!"

Juliette couldn't believe her ears. Her eyes focused across the church, landing on the source of the voice: a fair-skinned woman with long hair, dressed in a black pantsuit, with Rayshawn at her side. Juliette looked at Greta and Derek, both of whom seemed equally confused.

"Did you think you could sleep with me, get me pregnant, and leave me? No, I don't think so. You will not ride off into the sunset with another woman. Does she know about the baby?!" the woman yelled, her words echoing throughout the church.

Before Derek could respond to the woman, Grandville shouted, "Rayshawn, what are you doing here? Who is this woman, and why are you crashing my sister's wedding?"

"Don't even try to play me because you and I both know that you could never forget Katilina," the woman continued.

Ignoring the woman, Grandville asked again, "Rayshawn, why would you bring her here?"

Rayshawn, who was wearing a shocked expression that matched everyone else's, finally said "Grandville, she took advantage of me. She asked me to accompany her to her cousin's wedding here in Cleveland. She said she'd never been here before and wanted to see the sights. I had no idea that this was Greta's wedding, or I never would have come!"

Greta was beyond angry . She turned to the groom, her voice shaking, "Derek, what is she talking about? Who is she and why is she here? Is it true? Did you sleep with her and get her pregnant?" Greta angrily questioned.

"Sweetheart, I don't know what she's talking about. I didn't get her pregnant," Derek replied.

"But did you sleep with her?" Greta asked while their wedding guests looked on.

"Greta, this should be a private discussion. Please, babe; we're getting married," Derek pleaded.

"No, we're not," Greta declared, her voice cold as she turned and stomped off, leaving Derek standing at the altar and her guest stunned. Greta picked up the hem of her dress and headed towards the church's office.

"Rayshawn, get this trick out of here right now!" Grandville yelled.

Katilina sneered, dropping her hands to her curvy hips. "No, you didn't just call me a trick! I wasn't a trick when you were trying to play hide the banana with me. I don't know why everyone's so in love with your sister and that you all feel the need to protect her. Playa, you should have taken me up on my offer—you have no idea what you missed out on. If you don't believe me, ask your boys Rayshawn and Derek about me."

Juliette's veins surged with pure fury. This woman, who she did not know, seemed overly familiar with her man, and Juliette forgot where she was when she yelled, "Grandville, how do you know this slut?"

"Who are you calling a slut? Bitch, you don't want it with me! Pregnant or not, you've got one more time to call me out of my name!" Katilina said, charging towards Juliette.

Juliette's mother, her aunt, and her very pregnant cousin, Melinia, jumped up, ready to meet Katilina halfway down the aisle, when Grandville rushed over and took control.

"Rayshawn, I said get her out of here now! Everybody else, please try and relax. Come on, fam, sit down and remember that we're Christians, and we're in a church," Grandville said in an even but forceful voice.

"Katilina, let's go," Rayshawn said as he grabbed her arm and pulled her towards the door.

Katilina struggled but couldn't escape Rayshawn's strong grip. As he dragged her away, Katilina yelled, "You skanks better be glad that I'm pregnant or I'd show you how a slut from LA gets down. I don't care if it *is* three of you. I'll show you how I use my black belt in Taekwondo."

"Really? Well, we have black and blue belts in kicking natural ass, and if you don't get to stepping, we'll show you just how Cleveland girls get down!" Samantha, one of Juliette's best friends, yelled standing up.

Grandville reattempted taking control of the situation. "Alright, everybody. Please just sit tight. We'll resume soon."

Once Rayshawn managed to remove Katilina from the building, Juliette headed towards the office to find Greta. Samantha and Maria, who was far along in her pregnancy, jumped up and followed her. When they all got to the office, they found Greta sitting on the couch crying. Juliette was furious and wanted to snatch that tramp for ruining Greta's beautiful day, she knew she needed to try to calm the situation.

"Hey girl, I know it looks bad, but this is probably all just a big misunderstanding," Juliette said soothingly.

"Yeah, girl. It may not be what it seems," Sabrina added. "At least talk to Derek before calling the wedding off."

The Revelation

With tears streaking down her face, Greta slumped her shoulders and shook her head. "I think this is God and the universe telling me not to marry Derek. What I can't understand is why God keeps sending me cheating men. Why am I not enough? What's wrong with me!?"

"Wait a minute, just because this woman came in here uninvited making these claims doesn't make them true. You've heard of innocent until proven guilty, right?" Samantha, an attorney and firm believer in due process, asked.

Loud banging on the office door interrupted their discussion. "Greta, let me in. I need to talk to you," Derek pleaded.

"Derek, please leave me alone. I don't want to see you," Greta shouted with tears ruining her makeup.

"I'm sorry Greta, but I have to open the door," Maria said, looking down.

"Girl, this isn't the time to play peacemaker. Greta doesn't want to see him right now," Samantha scolded.

"I know and I'm so sorry, but my water just broke. I'm in labor," Maria announced.

Chapter 1

If I Ever Feel Better

Juliette gazed at the computer monitor taking in her beautiful little goddaughter, Martinez, as she cooed into the screen, melting Juliette's heart. Martinez was two months old and just starting to smile and show her little personality. Born on Valentine's Day, she was a sweetheart, and Juliette wanted nothing more than to kiss her sweet face but this would not happen—at least, not right

and into Montell's car. They ran out of the church to assist getting Maria to the hospital as quickly and safely as possible. Grandville had been tasked with telling the guests that there would be no wedding, but that everyone was still invited to the reception at the hotel. The food and DJ were non-refundable, and Greta wanted her guests to have a good time, especially since they'd come to see a wedding but ended up witnessing drama.

Juliette's family and friends who had attended the party said it was an epic event, and it made her sad to know she had missed it. Now she wouldn't be attending any parties, at least not for the foreseeable future. Within a blink of an eye, everything had spiraled out of control, and Juliette struggled daily to come to terms with it all. The fear of catching the COVID-19 virus kept her on edge, and she struggled not to let the anxiety overwhelm her. She was constantly worried about Grandville and the kids catching the virus, especially thinking about what it could do to her daughter, Jolene, who suffered from sickle cell disease.

Greta was temporarily residing with her and Grandville, which was great for them because she was instrumental in helping them run their household. With little to no warning, all four of their children had gone from leaving the house daily to attend school to learning virtually from home. Juliette hadn't realized teaching would be so hard, and with Greta there, she had a second set of eyes to help her manage the kids' schoolwork.

The Zoom call was their first time seeing each other since the pandemic began. They had only spoken by phone since Maria had the baby, and their conversations were centered around Martinez, Maria and Montell's new bundle of joy. Maria had shared how long it had been since they'd had a baby in their home and how they were experiencing the joys and challenges of parenting an infant.

"Hey girl, are you even listening to a word that I am saying?" Maria asked.

"Girl, not really and I'm so sorry. I guess getting overwhelmed by all the Zoom calls and I'm starting to zone out. I really wish I could be there with you, holding my goddaughter in person. But, I'm downright petrified to leave the house. I love my family, and I feel blessed that I don't have to be completely isolated, but we're having way *too much* family time," Juliette complained.

"Girl, don't I know it. The last time I saw anyone besides Monty, Montell, and the baby was when I gave birth. I miss my girls. I wish we could all get together," Maria's voice was wistful.

"I'm going to see if we can arrange a Zoom girls' night. That would be a great way for us to connect and it would also cheer Greta up. She's really down. She refuses to take Derek's calls and has blocked him, so he calls here a thousand times a day. It's hard to believe that he cheated on her with that skank," Juliette declared.

"Well, Rayshawn was with her at the wedding. Do you think Rayshawn could have set Derek up?" Maria asked.

"I don't know," Juliette said. "Rayshawn seemed surprised by it all. But I'm hoping Grandville will find out what really happened. Grandville also blocked him but, after months, Grandville finally took his call. He found out Rayshawn is in town this weekend and agreed to meet him in person. they're together right now."

"I'm glad Grandville is meeting with Rayshawn. Despite everything, they have been friends for years. How did Rayshawn convince Grandville to meet with him after all this time?"

Juliette shook her head. "Rayshawn said if they didn't meet now, he wasn't sure when they'd be able to see each other again. The Black Basketball Association (BBA) and his team are going into something called a bubble—all the teams will live in one complex to reduce the risk of catching the virus. Once Rayshawn goes in, he won't be allowed to leave. I think deep down, Grandville really wanted to talk to him but needed time to process everything. Grandville hasn't physically met with anyone except Franklin, his business partner, since the pandemic began. But Rayshawn is constantly tested and they are wearing masks and socially distancing,"

"That's good. You can't be too careful these days. How's Melinia?"

"She and the baby are doing great. Rafael is ecstatic to be a big brother, and my aunt is spoiling the baby rotten," Juliette said.

Maria placed the baby on her shoulder and gently patted her back to burp her. "Did her friend Julio get here yet?"

"Yes, he got a job as the manager of my male boarding home, A New Beginning. He was with Melinia when she delivered the baby, and he's ecstatic to be living here in the States. We were so lucky to get him here right before everything locked down," Juliette said.

"That's fantastic. How's he doing at his job?" Maria asked.

"Great. He spends all day cooking and cleaning, and the house is so spotless that you can literally eat off the floor. I appreciate him so much because I'm barely able to visit my boarding homes, trying to limit contact, and he's been holding things down at A New Beginning," Juliette said.

"Oh, I'm glad to hear that. Do you think he and Melinia have been dating?" Maria asked.

"I'm not sure. Melinia said she named the baby Jesus because he saved her and Rafael's lives. When Julio is around, he acts like he's both the boys' biological father, but Melinia won't say anything about their father's identity," Juliette disclosed.

"Well, I'm glad Greta's there with you guys," Maria said.

"Me too. I worry about her but the kids keep her busy. I'm just glad we can keep an eye on her—" Juliette began, but before she could complete her thought, she heard, "I'm doing fine. You guys don't have to worry about me."

Juliette swallowed hard, realizing Greta had heard her every word.

Chapter 2

Please Do Not Lean

Melinia sat in her drug counselor Ms. Zenobia King's office, silently thanking God.

"Melinia, I have great news," Zenobia began. "Your housing application has been approved. The agency was able to secure funding for a three-bedroom apartment for you and your sons."

Melinia could barely contain her excitement, but then she remembered that she didn't have any money to furnish her new home or even pay for basic necessities. Zenobia quickly followed this up with more good news.

"Also, the board members of both The Monarch Program and Jordan House have great sympathy for your ordeal, and they want to help you recover from everything that you've endured. So, they've arranged for you to receive a grant of up to thirty-five hundred dollars for new furniture and appliances." Zenobia's voice was full of compassion.

"Oh my God, are you for real?" Melinia asked, her expression serious. "Ms. Zenobia, I don't know what to say. But why?"

"I'm not sure what you mean," Zenobia responded with curiosity.

"I don't mean to seem skeptical, but for years no one has done anything for me unless there's something in it for them. So, I can't help wondering what will be expected of me in return for all this?"

Zenobia gave a warm smile. "That's a fair question, Melinia. I can personally relate to some of what you've experienced. I, too, was addicted to heroin and was forced to support my habit by using my body. All we want is to see you turn your tragedy into success. When you're ready, my cousin, Reverend Dr. Mixon and I hope that you'll work with us to help other survivors."

Melinia knew that Reverend Dr. Mixon was the owner of the Christian-based mental health and addiction agency that employed Zenobia, but she didn't realize he knew anything about her or her story.

"I don't understand why anyone would listen to me. I'm so messed up that I'm in no position to advise anyone," Melinia declared solemnly, dropping her head to hide the tears welling in her eyes.

Zenobia reached across the desk and gently touched her hand. "Melinia, you may not feel strong right now, but over time, with the right support, you will find your strength. I see myself in you. I want you to be reassured, because now I'm now working on my Ph.D. in addiction to help others. I believe God has a purpose for me, and that includes using my journey to help others. He wants that for you too. You're in a different position than the young ladies I usually work with."

Melinia looked up with a sarcastic smirk. "I'm pretty sure I'm stupider than your usual clients."

"No, Melinia, you're far from stupid. Actually, I think you're very bright, and you've done something that many women in your position wish they could do."

"What's that? Have illegitimate kids whose future is bleak due to my stupidity?" Melinia shot back, her voice full of bitterness.

Zenobia shook her head. "Never forget that you made it out. Did you know that it's estimated that 20 to 40 million people are victims of human trafficking, or as some know it, modern-day slavery? We don't even know if those numbers are accurate, as so many cases go undetected, and we don't know how many victims die in captivity. Some overdose, some are killed by their captors or their johns, and many commit suicide. Not only did you make it out alive, but with a child and another on the way. Do you understand how amazing that is? God has a plan for you that will come to fruition in time, but for now, we need to start where you are and focus on getting you settled in your new life," Zenobia said, her voice filled with quiet strength.

Melinia thought for a moment, then took a deep breath. "Thanks, I really appreciate everything you're doing for me Ms. Zenobia. But I need to get back home because my mother has my kids, and with the baby being so small, I don't like being away for too long."

"That's understandable." Zenobia nodded. "But before you go, let's discuss your cravings. Are you still experiencing them?"

Melinia looked away for a moment, before answering honestly. "Yes, sometimes."

"Melinia, this is a dangerous time in your recovery. When you feel those cravings, occupy yourself and don't hesitate to call your sponsor. Many relapse and overdose after entering recovery because the disease tricks them into thinking they can handle it. It's the devil trying to deceive you, so when you're feeling weak, pick up your Bible which is the foundational text for Alcoholics Anonymous, also known as the Big Book. Don't ever forget to call on God. I'll see you in two weeks at your usual time," Zenobia said gently but firmly.

"Thank you, Ms. Zenobia," Melinia replied.

Melinia left the office feeling energized. Zenobia had played a huge role in helping her transition back into the world, and she felt grateful. But, she also felt a twinge of guilt for lying about why she needed to leave. She didn't need to get home right away; she was actually going to see Julio. She had mapped out the bus route and couldn't wait to share the news about her apartment.

Julio was her only connection to her old life as a human trafficking victim aboard the La Barca—the boat where she'd been held captive by the Sandego Crew. Julio hailed from the same Dominican Republic village as Rique, the leader of the crew, and many of its members. Julio had joined the crew despite knowing that his brother had sexually assaulted Rique's sister, Romanita, leaving her incapable of bearing children, and had also killed her fiancé. Although Julio had no part in these crimes, Rique and the crew were after him. Julio acted as if he knew nothing of his brother's crimes and willingly joined the crew, putting himself in extreme danger. The members of the Sandego Crew underestimated him—Julio had used the crew to achieve his goal of coming to the US and becoming a citizen.

Julio arrived in the US on March 1st, just before the borders were closed due to the pandemic. Julio showed his gratitude by cooking and cleaning with zeal, and both Juliette and Grandville often complimented his hard work. He was the only person who truly understood what it had been like to be a captive on La Barca. As Melinia transferred from bus to bus, she thought of her friend Mimi, a fellow captive.

Melinia and Julio saw an opportunity to escape when the crew sailed to the Bahamas during a hurricane to rescue Rique's sister, Romanita. Rique had dropped Melinia, Julio, and Mimi off in the Bahamas before taking the boat back out to sea to save it. Once on the island, Melinia and Julio made the heartbreaking decision to leave Mimi behind. At the time, Mimi was addicted to heroin. Melinia had intentionally gotten pregnant with Remy— Rique's brother's—baby, knowing that Rique would help wean her off the drug for the sake of the unborn child. Melinia and Julio were concerned that if Mimi attempted to withdraw cold turkey, she would eventually give in to desperation and contact Rique without their knowledge. They couldn't take the risk of her jeopardizing their escape. Some days, the guilt over leaving Mimi behind ate at Melinia, but most days, she was too busy caring for her two sons to think about it.

Melinia stood at the bus stop at the Windermere stop, waiting for the bus that would drop her right in front of A New Beginning. The station was bustling with people rushing to and from their destinations. Out of the corner of her eye, she could have sworn she saw Remy, her infant son's father. She shook her head—surely it was just her imagination.

Remy Sandego had no idea that she had become pregnant with his child, and the authorities believed that he and the rest of the crew were lost at sea during the hurricane. No trace of La Barca or its crew was ever discovered. While she was confident that if any of them had survived, they wouldn't be looking for her, the thought of it still made her nervous. Just as she was about to board the bus, someone tapped her on the shoulder. She quickly turned around, but there was no one there. Melinia felt her stomach twist with unease. As she stepped onto the bus, she couldn't shake the feeling that her good fortune might be short-lived.

Chapter 3

Bad Habits

Grandville walked through the lobby of the Ritz Carlton Hotel in pursuit of Rayshawn's room and the truth. He was doing his best not to allow his anger to overtake him, focusing on his breathing and resigning himself to hearing Rayshawn out. Everything in his life had been looking up since he and Juliette had come to terms with the fact that their daughter was suffering from sickle cell disease. He had forgiven Juliette for sleeping with a total stranger after he had accidentally caused their oldest daughter, Jessica's tragic death. Juliette had experienced a mental health breakdown after learning about their child's condition and fearing she might have gotten pregnant from the one-night stand. After Juliette came clean about her infidelity while being involuntarily committed to a mental health hospital, their relationship survived. It was even stronger now that they both had revealed their most intimate secrets. A weight had been lifted, and Grandville felt even closer to Juliette than ever before.

He wanted Greta, his twin, and only sibling, to experience what he and Juliette had, and he was happy that she was marrying Derek, who appeared to be a genuinely nice guy. Things were looking up, but as usual in his life, their world took another tumble after Rayshawn and Katilina's actions left his sister emotionally devastated and embarrassed. To make matters worse, the world had come to a standstill due to the pandemic.

It had taken months for Grandville to overcome his rage and bring himself to answer Rayshawn's calls. He still couldn't understand how Derek could have cheated on Greta because he genuinely seemed to be in love with her. Grandville was reminded that things were not always what they seemed. Derek had confided in Grandville that some of his friends from the LA's front office had met in Los Angeles two months ago for an impromptu bachelor party. Before moving home to Cleveland, Derek had worked with the LA's basketball team in a management role. Derek admitted that Katilina was part of the entertainment arranged by his friends and colleagues from the LA's front office, but he was adamant that he did not sleep with her—though he admitted that he couldn't remember part of the evening. Grandville still struggled to make sense of what he'd been told, it was all just… weird.

It didn't take long for Grandville to locate Rayshawn's room. Before he could knock the door opened and a huge, bald, Black man with bulging muscles beckoned him inside.

"Mr. Stubbs, Mr. Robinson is waiting for you. Please come in," the large man said in a soft, polite voice that surprised Grandville.

Grandville walked into the spacious suite and marveled at its beauty. Since entering the BBA, Rayshawn had always stayed in the best hotels, ensuring that if he had to be away from home, he did so in luxury.

Rayshawn carried his tall, muscular frame out of the connecting room to the large open living area, which was equipped with a 55-inch flat-screen TV. His face was masked, but Grandville could clearly see that it was his old friend and ex-brother in law.

"Hey, fam. Thanks for agreeing to see me," Rayshawn said. "I know that you're really upset with me, and I appreciate you giving me a chance to explain."

"Yeah, I'm here. So get to explaining," Grandville said. "I want to know how you ended up at Greta's wedding with one of the women you cheated on her with—and to top it off, neither you nor Katalina were invited."

"Grandville, why do you always get straight to the chase?" Rayshawn asked. "Sit down and have a drink with me. Do me the honor of some small talk for a few minutes. I haven't seen or talked to you in months. Tomorrow I'm headed to the BBA bubble, and I won't be seeing anybody outside of my fellow BBA players, coaches and trainers."

Grandville relaxed his shoulders a bit and sank back into the soft leather couch. "Okay, man. You have a point, I'll chill. Tell me more about this bubble."

"The league wants to house all the players and coaches in one facility because they think it's the best way to allow the BBA to play and reduce the risk of catching COVID."

Grandville nodded. He hadn't seen anyone outside of Juliette, his children and Franklin since the pandemic began. Having a beer with Rayshawn suddenly seemed like a really good idea.

"Alright, I'll have one nonalcoholic beer, if you have it. I'm driving and it's not a good idea for me to mix alcohol with my meds," Grandville admitted.

"I understand. I'll send one of my bodyguards down to the hotel bar to grab us a few," Rayshawn said as he headed to the huge kitchen attached to the suite where another one of his bodyguards was sitting.

Grandville pulled out his phone as he waited. Soon, Rayshawn returned with a platter overflowing with assorted wings and sandwiches.

"I hope you're hungry, fam," Rayshawn said, grinning. He went back into the kitchen and returned with another tray filled with cheese cubes, crackers, veggies, and dip.

Grandville heard his stomach grumble, realizing he was starving.

"Thanks, man. But while I'm making my plate, you can start answering my questions," Grandville said, sanitizing his hands before picking up a paper plate and loading it with food.

"Okay, Grandville, I get it. I know I owe you an explanation, but all I can say is Katilina played me. I hadn't been in touch with her since I started my sex addiction recovery. I needed to make amends, and that's why I reached out. I had no idea she would set me up like that."

Katilina was one of Rayshawn's groupies. Grandville had encountered her years before when she tried to get him to have sex with her while simultaneously giving Rayshawn head. Grandville had refused, and after that meeting, he hadn't seen her again.

"What did you do to her that made it necessary to make amends?" Grandville asked, crunching on a carrot stick.

"Man, the things I made that girl do to my body… it was criminal. I now realize that Katilina has her own issues, and I should have been helping her, not exploiting her," Rayshawn admitted, his shoulders slumping.

"Okay, but you had a problem too," Grandville replied.

"I did, and while I'm trying to get better, I owe it to the people I hurt to make things right," Rayshawn confided. "That's why I reached out to Katilina. But I recently found out she's been holding a grudge."

Their conversation was interrupted by one of Rayshawn's bodyguards, who walked in holding a brown paper bag.

"Mr. Robinson, I have the nonalcoholic beer you requested. Would you like a glass for the beer?" he asked Grandville.

"Nah, I'm good. Thanks for getting the beer," Grandville said, reached for the frosty bottle and taking a long sip.

"I think I'll have one too. I've given up alcohol until after the season to stay in shape. Every year it gets harder to compete against these rookies," Rayshawn said, chuckling.

They sat in silence for a few minutes before Rayshawn spoke.

"I want you to know that after leaving Greta's wedding, I let Katilina have it. You may not believe it, but I heard Greta, and I had resigned myself to the fact that what we had was over. I was at peace knowing that she had moved on with someone who made her happy. I was ready to move on myself and let the past stay the past," Rayshawn said.

"What do you mean you *were* ready?" Grandville asked in between bites of food. "It's over. You don't have a choice in the matter."

"I'm saying what happened is a sign from God," Rayshawn declared. "I mean, I know a little about your almost brother-in-law, Derek, and honestly, if Greta was going to marry someone like him, she might as well have stayed with me."

Grandville studied him for a moment in shock. "What the hell is that supposed to mean? You had hoes in every area code all over the globe, and you're trying to throw shade on Derek?" Grandville retorted, his tone laced with sarcasm.

"Okay, you might be right, but none of my so-called hoes could ever say it was anything but an oral. Last time I checked, it's impossible to have a spit baby, so no one could ever say I got them pregnant. Can your boy Derek say the same?"

"Just because no one's accused you doesn't mean you don't have a child out here," Grandville said, scoffing. "I know you, Rayshawn, and despite what you say, I know you've slipped up and raw-dogged a random chick at least once."

"Hey, Grandville, no disrespect, but I don't need to lie to you. What does it matter now? Greta and I are divorced, so I don't need to convince you or anyone of anything. I only slipped up once, and that was after the divorce—which I regret it to this day."

Grandville noticed the tremble in his voice, but he wasn't buying it. "Oh, come on Rayshawn. I know how you roll. It couldn't have been that bad."

"It was. I told you about what happened with Juliette's cousin, Melinia. What I didn't tell you was she was the one chick that got me."

"What do you mean, 'she got you?'" Grandville asked, putting down his wing and leaning forward at the mention of his wife's cousin.

"She was the one I had unprotected sex with. I knew she was hooked on smack. Hell, I'm lucky I didn't catch anything. Having unprotected sex with Melinia is partly why I decided to get help. I didn't want to end up with some incurable disease like some of the greats. I mean, I'm one of the G.O.A.T.s in the BBA, and I realized my actions were destroying my future. I was so hurt and angry that Greta divorced me—maybe on some level, I was trying to get back at her. I was drunk, high, and emotionally done. I just wish I'd had that revelation before Melinia got me on tape. I'm still afraid she might release it."

"You know, I promised Juliette that I'd talk to you about Melinia's situation, but before I could, you and that broad Katilina crashed my sister's wedding. Don't think I forgot the reason I'm here," Grandville said with an edge in his voice.

"I know I fucked up, but before we get into that, I'ma need you to get back to Melinia," Rayshawn said.

Grandville took a sip of his beer to cool down. "Okay, man. You need to speak to Lovelle and find out how much Melinia owes. Whatever it is, I'll cover it."

"Why? What's going on?" Rayshawn asked.

"We found Melinia a few weeks before Greta's wedding. She was being held captive by a human trafficking ring run by some Dominican thugs," Grandville said.

Rayshawn jumped to his feet. "What?! Why am I just now hearing about this?"

Grandville looked up at him. "Hey, man, you need to pipe down. You have a lot of nerve. First, I was barely speaking to you at the time. And if you had been paying attention, you would've seen Melinia at the wedding. She was pregnant and holding her son sitting on her lap. We found her right before the wedding, not that I owe an explanation. After we got her back, my intent was to call you the day after Greta's wedding, but we both know how that went," Grandville scoffed.

The color drained from Rayshawn's face. "Melinia has kids?"

"Two sons," Grandville responded, draining his beer and reaching for another one.

"I distinctly remember her telling me she didn't have any kids," Rayshawn stated.

"When she became a trafficking victim, she didn't have any. She had the oldest while in captivity, and she was pregnant when we found her," Grandville explained it to Rayshawn like he was a toddler.

"Did she mention who their fathers are?" Rayshawn inquired.

"No, and this discussion about Melinia is over. You know why I'm here," Grandville said.

"You're right." Rayshawn's eyes darted to the floor, his hands clasping together tightly, "But can you at least tell me their ages?"

"Rafael is four, and the baby is only a few months old."

"Oh my god, what if Rafael's mine?" Rayshawn wailed, sinking down on the couch. He put his head in his hands.

"Hey, slow down, bruh. Melinia has been out here doing all kinds of things—some she consented to, and most she didn't." Grandville said, scooting to the edge of his seat. "Nothing indicates that Rafael is your son. There's no telling who his father is, given what she's been through."

"What has she been through?" Rayshawn asked.

"Before I get into all that, you need to go first. Tell me about Katilina's grudge against you that made you two crash my sister's wedding," Grandville demanded.

"When I called her to make amends, she told me she was going to a wedding in Cleveland and begged me to go with her," Rayshawn explained. "I hitched a ride with LBJ on his private jet because he had business here in Ohio, and I let her tag along. I figured I could use the trip to smooth things over with her. Plus I wanted to tell her about the Sex Addicts Anonymous program."

Grandville nodded, urging him to continue.

"On the flight, Katilina told me she'd always been in love with me. She thought since I was divorced, I'd be with her. I don't know why she thought I'd want her, when I know how she gets down. After everything happened, I made some calls and found out she used to have a huge crush on Derek. Apparently, they slept together back when he was in LA. When she found out about the wedding, she deliberately set out to ruin the day. She blames Greta for taking both Derek and me away from her."

"What else did you find out?" Grandville inquired.

"That when Derek went to LA for his bachelor party, he and Katilina went into a bedroom alone. I don't know if you're aware, but for a time, Derek had a bad reputation for sleeping with the groupies the players no longer wanted."

It was Grandville's turn to stand. He rubbed his hand down his face. "Nah, man. I didn't know that."

After a few moments of silence, Grandville sighed and sank back into the couch, knowing that he was in for a long afternoon.

Chapter 4

Jolene

Juliette walked from room to room, observing her children doing their schoolwork. She paused in each doorway, quietly taking in their faces, the way they focused—some more intensely than others. She had placed each child in a separate room, allowing them to connect to their classrooms remotely and giving them the space and opportunity to learn without distractions from one another. Grandville had boosted the high-speed internet in their home. He had also put parental controls on each device to monitor what the children were viewing since they were spending more time on their devices. After what Melinia had endured, Grandville and Juliette wanted to ensure that their children didn't fall victim to online predators.

As Juliette headed towards the kitchen, she collided with Greta, who was walking swiftly, her eyes wide with urgency.

"Hey, sis. You okay?" Juliette asked, her heart already quickening in response to Greta's frantic expression.

"Juliette, come quick, it's Jolene," Greta said, her voice barely above a whisper, trembling.

Juliette felt her stomach drop, her whole body going cold. Without a word, she quickly followed Greta to the kitchen, where she found Jolene on the floor, writhing in pain. Seeing her daughter like this filled Juliette with an overwhelming sense of helplessness, her chest tightening as if she couldn't draw a full breath.

"Mommy, it hurts so bad," Jolene cried out, her small face contorted in agony, tears streaking down her cheeks. "I tried to walk over to get you and I fell!"

Juliette knelt beside her, trying to remain calm despite the frantic beat of her heart. "Okay, sweetie. Let's get you off the floor," she said softly, trying to keep her voice steady. Her hands were trembling slightly, but she scooped Jolene up, feeling her daughter's weight so fragile in her arms, and placed her gently onto a barstool chair in front of the breakfast bar.

"Okay, sweetie, let's do some breathing exercises together," Juliette said, drawing in a deep breath herself to show Jolene how. "Come on, do them with me. Deep breath in… let's hold it… now let's blow it out." Juliette's voice remained calm, but inside she felt the fear clawing at her composure.

After what felt like an eternity, but was only just a few minutes, Jolene's sobs evened into gentle breaths. But her tears were still flowing. Juliette stroked her daughter's hair, her heart aching with each pained sob.

"Okay, can you tell Mommy what's hurting? Try to describe the pain," Juliette said, her eyes searching Jolene's for any sign of comfort.

"It's my leg, Mommy," Jolene whimpered. "It feels like someone's stabbing it with a knife."

Juliette swallowed hard, her throat suddenly dry. She had to stay strong for Jolene, but every word felt like a punch to her chest. She forced herself to smile reassuringly. "Okay, I'm going to give you some medicine, and we're going to stop school for now so we can elevate your leg."

"And I'm going to bring you lunch in bed. Won't that be fantastic?" Greta added, her voice overly cheerful, clearly trying to lighten the mood. She gave Jolene a bright smile, but Juliette could see the worry lurking in her eyes.

"Okay, Aunt Greta," Jolene replied, wiping her tears. Here voice was small and her eyes were tired.

"Can you walk up to your room on your own?" Juliette asked.

Jolene nodded.

"Okay, lay down on your bed and I'll be right there," Juliette instructed.

"But I have a test this afternoon."

"I'll talk to your teacher and have it reset for later this week," Juliette assured her, brushing a tear from Jolene's cheek. "I don't want you to worry about that right now. Go on ahead to your room, and I'll be there in a few minutes."

Jolene slid off the chair and slowly hobbled towards her room, her small body looking frail. Juliette watched her go, her own chest aching, her eyes welling up before she turned away and wiped them quickly. She couldn't fall apart now. Greta, who had been standing quietly beside her, broke the silence once Jolene left the room.

"What should we do?"

Juliette took a deep breath, trying to calm the frantic thoughts racing through her mind. "I guess we should take her temperature, and if it's elevated, that's probably an indicator of an infection or maybe a virus," Juliette said, rubbing her forehead.

Greta nodded, but her eyes never left Juliette's face. "Okay, Juliette. I can tell by your face that you're worried, but Jolene's going to be fine. You get the thermometer and her meds, and I'll make the kids some lunch."

"Yes, okay. Let me get everything together," Juliette muttered to herself.

The tightness in her chest didn't ease as she tried to focus on what Jolene needed. Juliette zipped around gathering her supplies, fighting against the panic building inside of her, her breaths shallow. She'd been diagnosed with an anxiety disorder and PTSD—receiving Jolene's sickle cell disease diagnosis and watching her oldest daughter, Jessica, die in her arms after Grandville's tragic accident seven years before haunted her still. The images flashed through her mind now, her heart pounding painfully against her ribs. She had to constantly remind herself that this was different—Jolene was still here, she was breathing, she was alive. She just needed to be cared for.

She hoped that whatever was ailing Jolene was something she could treat at home so she wouldn't have to take risk a trip to the hospital amidst the growing pandemic—it felt like a death sentence waiting to happen. Once she had gathered the thermometer, water, and Jolene's medicine, Juliette was sure of one thing—she needed Sabrina.

Sabrina was a lifeline. She was Franklin's fiancée, who had quickly become one of her closest friends. Franklin had kept his relationship with Sabrina a secret for years, but upon their first meeting, it felt like Juliette had known her forever. Sabrina, a psychiatrist, had helped her through the nightmare of Jolene's sickle cell diagnosis, as well as her recent anxiety diagnosis, providing the support and understanding that Juliette hadn't known she needed. She would be giving her friend a call shortly.

Soon, she was in the twins' bedroom where Jolene had obediently gotten into bed. Her face was scrunched in discomfort, her small body trying to curl up into itself.

"Okay, sweetie, sit up. I have your meds," Juliette said, her voice soft as handed Jolene the water and opened her hand, showing her the pill. Jolene swallowed the children's Tylenol. Juliette gently kissed her warm forehead.

"Now, let's take your temperature." She placed the thermometer in Jolene's ear. After a few moments, the blinking numbers on the digital screen read 99.9. Not dangerously high, but enough to make her stomach clench in worry. Juliette could only pray that whatever was causing her elevated temperature could be treated with over-the-counter medication.

Seconds later, Greta entered, carrying a tray with a bowl of chicken soup, a grilled cheese sandwich, and orange juice. "Okay, Jolene, it's time for lunch," she announced.

"I'm not hungry, Aunt Greta," Jolene said, frowning.

"I know, but I want you to try to eat a little bit," Greta coaxed. "Juliette, you go ahead and have lunch with the kids. I'm going to visit with Jolene for a bit."

Juliette hesitated, her instincts screaming at her not to leave. But Greta's eyes were steady and reassuring. "Thanks, sis. I appreciate you. But please come and get me if she gets worse."

As Juliette left, she cast one last look at her daughter, seeing how small and vulnerable she looked. She found the strength to walk out, knowing her other children needed her. Approaching the kitchen table where her children were seated, Juliette noticed Jabari was staring at his food, a frown tugging at his lips, and she felt the tension in the room. Already stressed out about Jolene, she decided to ignore Jabari for the moment. She sat down and silently thanked God for Greta who had successfully managed her household in Juliette's absence. Her sister-in-law had made them all the same lunch, and though her appetite was all but gone, she took a bite of her grilled cheese sandwich.

"Mommy, where's Jolene?" Jenae Jolene's fraternal twin, asked. Her eyes were wide and worry was etched across her young face.

"She's not feeling well, so she's lying down," Juliette replied in a light voice, while eating a spoonful of soup. "She may have picked up a bug, so I want you kids to stay away until she feels better so you don't get sick too."

Jabari let out a loud sigh. "Mom, when is this pandemic going to be over? I want to have Monty over so we can play video games in person."

Juliette felt the weight of his frustration, understanding it all too well.

"Listen, I want this pandemic to be over, too," she said, setting down her sandwich. She could feel her patience being tested, but she had to be strong for them. "But despite what I want, COVID is still here. If we all do what we're supposed to, we can minimize the risk of getting sick. You know your sister has an underlying illness and we have to be extra careful for her sake."

Jabari's face hardened. "I know you're worried about Jolene, Mom, but what about the rest of us?" Jabari snapped, his frustration spilling over his flushed face.

Juliette folded her arms across her chest, her expression stern. "What kind of question is that? We're talking about your little sister, and I'm going to need you to behave like you're the oldest."

Jabari looked down at his plate, his shoulders slumping. "Mom, I'm sorry, but I'm going crazy being stuck in this house," he said, his voice breaking slightly. "We never go anywhere, and we don't ever do anything. I feel like a prisoner. I love Jolene and don't want her to get sick, but I literally feel like the walls are closing in on me."

Juliette released a slow breath, her heart aching. She reached across the table and rested her hand on his. His fingers twitched, but he didn't pull away.

"I hear you, sweetheart," she said softly, her voice filled with empathy. "I know this has been so hard on you. On all of us. But I need you to be strong just a little longer. Your sister needs us to be strong for her, and I need my big boy to help hold things together. In the meantime, I'm going to talk to your father, and we'll figure out a family outing that we can all do together."

Jabari looked up, his eyes glistening slightly, his lips trembling. He nodded slowly, the weight of her words settling on him.

"Okay, Mom. But please talk to Dad about us doing something fun, because we're dying of boredom over here," he said.

Juliette smiled, giving his hand a quick squeeze. "I promise we'll figure something out. And tonight, after dinner, I want all of you to meet me and your dad in the family room. We're going to have a Stubbs Family night."

Jabari's eyebrows raised with curiosity. "What are we going to do?"

"You'll find out this evening," Juliette said. " Now, how did your morning classes go?"

"They went okay. I miss attending class in person."

"Yeah, we miss our friends and our teachers," Jonah, her second eldest son chimed in.

"I know you do, but we have a huge backyard. So, when you finish your homework, go outside and play like I used to do with my siblings," Juliette advised.

"I'm too old to play, Mom. I want to hang out with kids my age," Jabari argued.

"Okay, kids. Put your dishes in the sink and get back to your computers. Class will be resuming soon."

As she watched her children walk over to the sink, Greta came into the kitchen with Jolene's tray. Juliette spied the half-eaten sandwich, a half-empty bowl of soup, and a mostly empty glass of OJ.

"Greta, you're an awesome aunt. Thanks for getting Jolene to eat. How's she doing?" Juliette asked.

Greta gave a small smile, though her eyes held the same worry that was constantly gnawing at Juliette. "She's asleep. I put a pillow under her leg to elevate it and she was out like a light. You go ahead and get some rest. I'm going to clean the kitchen. It's important for me to stay busy."

"Okay. The kids are back in class, so I'm going to my bedroom to give Sabrina a call," Juliette said.

"Okay, tell her I said hello," Greta replied as she started to run water into the sink.

Juliette headed upstairs to call Sabrina. She was anxious, but did her breathing exercises to calm herself. The phone rang three times before a breathless Sabrina picked up.

"Hello."

"Hey, Sabrina, how are you?"

"I'm over here going through it," Sabrina admitted.

"Really? Well, what's wrong?"

"My mother has been in the nursing home for years. I'm bringing her here to live with me to prevent her from getting COVID. She's only in her late sixties and is in reasonably good health, despite her mental health issues. The nursing home is trying to prevent me from removing her, but Franklin was just able to get me an order from Probate Court granting me the authority to take her. I'm moving her in tomorrow."

"Oh my God! That's fabulous news," Juliette exclaimed.

"Yes, I'm excited, but also nervous. She can be a handful, but I'm seeing my clients virtually from home, so I'll be here with her," Sabrina explained.

"I'm glad you'll be making the best of the pandemic by spending time with your mother. How do Franklin and George feel about everything?" Juliette inquired about her fiancé and son.

"Franklin has been awesome. He moved me and George into his house. We're planning to sell both of our homes and buying a bigger house with a mother-in-law suite once the pandemic ends. After all this, I'm not sure if I'll be comfortable sending my mother back to the nursing home."

"I surely hope that we're close to the end of this," Juliette replied.

"According to some of my classmates and colleagues, we'll be dealing with the pandemic for a while. However, my contacts tell me that there are great strides being made towards the creation of a vaccine. But once it is done, I'm sure there will be resistance from the public about taking it."

"Did your contacts share whether that vaccination will be suitable for kids?" Juliette questioned.

"Probably not. They usually start with adults. Why? What's wrong?"

"It's Jolene," Juliette sighed. "She's saying her leg hurts and I took her temperature, and it is 99.9. I'm so scared that she's picked up the virus somehow."

"Well, just relax because it's more likely that she picked up a bug," Sabrina explained. "So many people assume that if they're sick, it's COVID. But there are several other issues that can cause a temperature."

"I sure hope you're right, Sabrina."

"Juliette, please do me a favor," Sabrina said.

"What?"

"Try not to worry, because everything will be alright in the end."

"I'll try," Juliette said as she attempted to shake the bad feeling that had suddenly overcome her.

Chapter 5

Let's Fall in Love

"Chica, it is so good to see you," Julio gushed as he hugged and kissed Melinia on the cheek, pulling her into a tight embrace. His warmth and the scent of freshly cooked food surrounded her, and for a moment, she felt the weight of her past lift slightly.

"It's great to see you too, Julio," Melinia replied, sinking into the comfort of his arms. The familiarity of his presence set her at ease.

"I'm cooking lunch and dinner, and I made enough for you to eat with me. Come into the kitchen," Julio suggested, his eyes lighting up with excitement.

Melinia followed Julio into the kitchen, marveling at how well he looked—happier and healthier than she could ever remember. She sat down at the small table that took up most of the space in the kitchen, her eyes tracking Julio as he moved around, whipped between cabinets and stovetops with practiced ease.

"So, how is everything going over here?" Melinia asked, trying to push aside the small bit of nervousness twisting in her stomach.

"It's going better than good. I'm putting the finishing touches on lunch, and I can't wait for you to taste what I made," Julio said, grinning as he began preparing four plates.

"Is someone joining us?" Melinia asked, her brows furrowing.

"All of us are going to have lunch together," Julio replied casually as he scooped food from several dishes.

"Exactly who is 'all of us?" Melinia asked using air quotes.

"Melinia, I have to serve lunch to the residents, and I thought it would be nice if we could all eat together. I talk about you so much that my new friends are anxious to meet you."

Melinia sighed in frustration. "Julio, I really wanted to spend time alone with you. I miss you. Besides, I don't really feel like socializing."

"Chica, I missed you too," Julio said with a wide smile. "The guys will probably only be at the table for a few minutes. These guys are huge and they tend to inhale their food. I made tuna melts for lunch, and I'm planning tuna casserole for dinner with the leftovers. I also made fruit salad and freshly squeezed lemonade." He paused, the passion evident in his voice. "I really love making food that the guys love. I've been watching the Food Channel on the TV. Big Joe even showed me how to use On Demand to watch any episode I want. You wouldn't understand, but I'm the happiest I've ever been. There's so much knowledge at our fingertips." His eyes gleamed with excitement. "I know you don't feel like seeing anyone, but please, let me share you with my new friends."

Melinia shrugged, forcing a small smile. She didn't have the heart to disappoint him. "Julio, I'm happy that you're doing so well, and I'm okay with having lunch with the guys."

The truth was, she felt nervous. Except for her male relatives and Julio, she hadn't been around any men since escaping from captivity. She took a deep breath, trying to quell the unease building inside her.

Julio smiled, clearly delighted, and soon he placed a full plate in front of her. "Chica, let me get the guys, and then we can say grace," Julio beamed, rushing up the stairs.

Melinia sat quietly, her fingers twisting in her lap. She jumped slightly when she heard a booming voice behind her.

"Melinia, it's so good to finally meet you! Julio talks about you all the time," the man's voice echoed in the intimate space.

Melinia looked up to see a massive man—bald, with bulging muscles stretching beneath his white t-shirt. His broad smile was genuine and kind, and it eased her nerves, if only a little.

"Hello, you know my name, but I don't know yours," she said, trying to sound more confident than she felt.

"Sorry about that! Being in the big house can mess up your manners." The man let out a hearty laugh. "My name is Joe, but my friends call me Big Joe. Julio is getting Kane—he was probably asleep, but Julio makes sure that we all get up and eat. And he also makes sure we take our meds. He's been a blessing and because of Julio, Kane and I are breathing free air."

Melinia nodded, maintaining her gentle smile.

A few moments later, Julio returned to the kitchen with another hulking man in tow. He had long blond hair, and a thick beard, and piercing blue eyes. Beneath all the hair, Melinia could tell that he had strong, attractive features.

"Gentlemen, let me introduce you to my dear friend Melinia," Julio said, gesturing toward her. "Melinia, meet Big Joe and Kane. Now, let's say grace." Julio immediately bowed his head. "Dear Lord, thank you for giving us the opportunity to share a meal together. Thank You for providing us with all we need including our freedom. Amen."

Everyone echoed amen.

Melinia picked up her sandwich and took a bite, her eyes widening in surprise. The food practically melted in her mouth. "Oh my God, Julio, this sandwich is amazing. What's in it?"

Julio chuckled, his eyes twinkling. "A whole lot of love."

"Well, your love is hella good," Melinia said, laughing softly. For a moment, her mood lightened.

"Thank you, Chica."

"Julio, are we still on for playing chess later on this evening?" Joe asked in between bites of the tasty food.

"Sure. If you and Kane can clean the kitchen for me after you finish your lunch, we'll have more time to play," Julio replied, winking at Joe.

"No problem. You also need to spend some time with your lady friend." Joe smirked. "Don't forget to tell her how much you love her." Joe made a smooching sound.

"What, you got some girl in the neighborhood or something?" Melinia asked, a hint of sarcasm in her voice.

"I'm talking about you, Ms. Melinia. You must know how this guy feels about you," Joe said.

Melinia turned her gaze to Julio, her face filled with curiosity. "Julio, what is he talking about?"

"Ms. Melinia, Julio is too scared to tell you on his own," Joe said, shaking his head.

"Julio, you're too scared to tell me something?" Melinia's voice carried an edge of irritation now, her patience wearing thin.

Julio sighed, rubbing the back of his neck, all earlier signs of joviality gone. "Joe, please cut it out."

"No, really. What is it?" Melinia demanded. "You know I hate riddles. I want to know exactly what Joe's talking about."

The Revelation

Julio hesitated for a moment, then looked directly at her, his eyes softening. "Okay, if you must know, I'm in love with you," he declared, his voice steady. "Soon—very soon—I'll be making you my wife."

Melinia blinked, stunned into silence. The room stilled around them as Big Joe and Kane exchanged knowing glances, their eyes fixed on Julio. Julio looked at her, a gentle smile on his face, as if waiting for her response.

But words failed her. All she could feel was her heart thudding in her chest, caught between the fear of the past and the hope of something new.

Chapter 6

I Love You

Grandville drove through the streets of Cleveland in a daze, overwhelmed by all the information that Rayshawn shared. Rayshawn had asked his cousin Lovelle for his price to remove the bounty on Melinia's head. However, before Lovelle would accept the money, he demanded that all copies of the sex tape that Melinia had secretly recorded with him and Rayshawn be delivered to him.

The situation was tricky for Grandville. Melinia wasn't aware that Grandville even knew about the tape. Additionally, he had never told Juliette that while he was in Oakhill, he had hired a private investigator and found out that there was a bounty on her head. Then there was the matter of Melinia's son, Rafael. Once Grandville thought about it, he realized that the child was the spitting image of Rayshawn. He could only hope and pray that his suspicions were unfounded, as the news would undoubtedly disrupt his peaceful home. He had to inform Melinia of Lovelle's conditions, but he had not seen her since the pandemic had begun. As he tried to figure out how to approach the problem, his phone rang. He glanced at the console and realized that it was Juliette trying to reach him.

"Hello," he answered.

"Hey, sweetie," Juliette greeted, her voice playing in his ear like a lullaby. "I hate to bother you, but I was hoping you could stop at the drugstore on your way home."

"Sure. Anything for you."

"Well, if that's the case, I should forewarn you that I promised the kids that we would do something fun after dinner tonight. I was hoping we could play some board games."

"Yeah, that's a great idea. You know, I think now would be a good time to plan a family outing with some extended relatives," Grandville proposed, nodding his head to himself.

"That sounds good. Whatever we plan, it should probably be outdoors, at a roomy space that allows social distancing," Juliette advised.

"We have a large backyard, so we can host it at our house."

"Alright, let's plan it when you get home. Did everything go okay with Rayshawn?"

"Yes, and I must admit, I had a good time with him," Grandville replied. "I'm almost certain that Rayshawn was set up. He was unaware he was attending Greta's wedding."

"Really? How horrible. Why would that woman do such a thing?"

"She's a groupie who's been following Rayshawn around for years. She knows Derek from his time in LA and has a crush on him, along with a vendetta against Greta," Grandville explained.

"A vendetta? But why?"

"According to Rayshawn, she believes Greta is the reason he and Derek never chose her," Grandville answered honestly.

"Well, it sounds like she's a hoe and a homewrecker. You also seemed familiar with her. Do you have history with her too, Grandville?"

"No, never that. I only met her one time before she crashed Greta's wedding, and I turned down her proposition because she wasn't my type. Honestly, I find her to be loose, and at that point in my life, I was no longer engaging in meaningless sex. But I'm not going to pass judgement on her. Before you, I treated women in ways that I'm not proud of," Grandville soberly responded.

"Well, it doesn't matter because that was yesterday, and today you're my man, so let's leave the past behind us, where it belongs.," Juliette said, her voice lifting.

Smiling, Grandville said, "Agreed. What do you need from the drugstore?"

"Jolene is sick and running a fever. I gave her Tylenol and we're almost out. I also need you to pick up a heating pad. Her leg hurts and we're trying to treat her issue at home. The last place she needs to be is in the emergency room right now."

"Okay, I'm on my way to drugstore, and then I'll be right home. Please try to relax until I get there. Jolene will be just fine," Grandville soothed.

"Grandville, I'm not going to lie, I'm scared. Suppose Jolene catches COVID, she might not survive it," Juliette said, her voice tinged with fear.

"Don't underestimate our Jolene. She's strong and no matter what happens, we're going to be alright. We've survived a lot and, if necessary, we'll survive more. Whatever we do, we'll be doing it together."

"I love you, Grandville. Hurry home for game night, and once the kids are asleep, we'll have a special game of our own," Juliette teased in a breathy voice.

A grin stretched across his lips and he licked them. "Promises that I intend to make sure you keep."

The Revelation

"Mommy!" Jolene cried out so loudly that Grandville heard it through the phone.

"Honey, what's wrong?" Grandville asked, his heart suddenly thumping.

"It's Jolene. I need to go. Please, hurry home," Juliette said, and the line went dead.

Suddenly, Grandville had a bad feeling. He gripped the steering wheel tighter, the anxiety seeping into his veins. He had to get home fast.

Chapter 7

I Want You Around

Melinia looked around her new apartment, beaming with pride. Zenobia had helped her locate the three-bedroom apartment, which featured a large bathroom and kitchen, in a building near a playground on a quaint residential street. She straightened the pillows on her new sofa. The furniture, purchased for her by the Monarch Project, was sturdy yet fashionable, and her mother had given her a small kitchen table and a television. While she still had some decorating to do, things were starting to look up for her, and she was even considering attending graduate school online. She really wanted to work, but with two small children at home since daycares and schools were closed due to the pandemic, she figured it was best to stay home and focus on her sons.

Julio was coming over to see her new apartment, and she felt excited and terrified at the same time. Their interactions had become somewhat awkward ever since Julio had declared his love for her. They still talked on the phone daily, but their conversations felt strained. Melinia had no idea that Julio had romantic feelings before her visit to A New Beginning. And she wasn't sure if she felt the same about him. Julio was extremely attractive, and she didn't have to explain her recent complicated past to him. However, she was still figuring out how she felt about him.

The Revelation

The kids were napping, and she was deep in thought when she heard the doorbell ring. She immediately hit the buzzer to allow access to her locked building. She was so excited to see Julio, she didn't bother looking through the peephole when she heard a knock at her door. Heart pounding with anticipation, she threw open her front door, her smile still forming—but it froze midway. The man standing in front of her was not Julio. Instead, she found herself face-to-face with an unfamiliar, very tall African American man, with a medium build, steel grey eyes that seemed to pierce right through her, and dreadlocks framing his round face. The man stared at her, his eyes cold and assessing.

Melinia's heart sank as her thoughts immediately flicked to her sleeping children just one room away. Unease crept through her body and her instinct screamed at her that something was wrong.

"Hello, can I help you with something?" Melinia asked, her voice slightly shaky, trying to mask her growing anxiety.

The man's lips curled into a sneer, his gaze unwavering "No, I think I have the wrong apartment," he said, his sinister tone making her stomach tighten.

Melinia swallowed hard, her fingers trembling as she tried to push the door closed. "Okay," she said, but before the door could latch, the man moved his foot between the doorframe and the door, halting her attempt to shut him out.

Fear spiked through her, and her breath caught in her throat. She tried to be brave as her heightened pulse roared in her ears. Her voice wavered as she tried to sound firm. "Excuse you! I'm closing the door now."

The man leaned closer, his steel-grey eyes narrowing as a dangerous smirk spread across his face. "You know, the next time I show up, I might find myself at the right apartment," he said, his voice low and threatening. Then, just as quickly as he had appeared, he turned and walked away, leaving Melinia standing in the doorway, stunned and shaking.

She closed the door and locked it quickly, trying to still her hands long enough to slide the deadbolt. Her mind was spinning, and her legs felt weak beneath her. She backed away from the door, her heart pounding in her chest. Who was he? What did he want? The fear clawed at her insides, a knot tightening in her stomach.

Melinia sank onto the couch and put her head in her hands, taking deep breaths to calm herself, but the anxiety remained, gnawing at her. She was confused and afraid for herself and kids. She jumped when she heard the doorbell again and was unsure whether she should hit the buzzer to unlock the front door or ignore it. The doorbell rang several times, but she was still frozen with fear, scared that the strange man had returned. The sound echoed throughout the apartment, each chime sending a fresh jolt of panic through her.

Seconds later, her cell phone began to ring, breaking the tense silence. She grabbed it quickly, and she answered it without looking at the screen.

"Hello," she said, her voice barely a whisper.

"Melinia, I'm standing outside your apartment building," Julio's familiar voice came through, filled with warmth and concern. "Are you home?"

Relief flooded her so intensely that tears sprang to her eyes. "I'm here. Buzzing you in right now." Melinia spoke into her phone, her voice cracking slightly. She pressed the buzzer, and in less than three minutes, Julio was standing in her living room.

"Chica, your apartment is as beautiful as you are," Julio said cheerfully, his presence instantly easing the tension in her chest. "Please, give me the tour."

"It is nice, but there really isn't much to see," Melinia said, said managing a weak smile, though her heart was still racing.

Julio's eyes narrowed as his brows pinched together, concern etching his face. "What's wrong? You seem a little down."

"Did you see a guy walking out when you entered the building?" Melinia asked.

"No, I didn't see anyone. Why?"

"Some guy knocked on my door, and I opened it thinking it was you," she explained.

Julio nodded, his handsome face marred by a slight frown. "What did he want?"

"He said he was at the wrong apartment."

Julio's face softened a little. "Okay, that happens. I'm hungry. What do you have to eat?" Julio asked as he headed to the kitchen, but Melinia could see the tension in his shoulders. He was trying not to worry her further, but she knew what she'd shared with him had him concerned.

"I have chips, fruit, and deli meat. Let me make you lunch. I've already eaten and the boys are napping right now, but they'll be up soon."

Melinia moved around the kitchen, putting together lunch for Julio, her mind in a whirl. She felt safe with Julio there, but she knew that at some point, he would have to leave to return to A New Beginning.

Before long, she placed a plate in front of him.

"Melinia, this looks great. Thank you," Julio said, happily taking a bite of his sandwich.

"You're welcome. Would you like iced tea or bottled water?"

"Bottled water would be great."

When Melinia placed it in front of him, he said, "Okay, can you please tell me why you seem so tense?"

"I have a lot of people after me," Melinia admitted after a brief pause.

Julio lowered the sandwich and held his gaze on her. "Do you think that guy's connected to Rique or the Sandego Crew?"

"Goodness, Julio, I don't know," she sighed, shaking her head. "When I was with Rique and the crew, I knew for certain that no one would hurt me."

"Yeah, because they *were* the ones hurting you," Julio said, his voice dripping with sarcasm.

Melinia threw her hands up in the air and sucked her teeth. "Aww, come on, Julio, it wasn't all bad. I mean, if it weren't for Rique and the Crew, I would've never met you."

"Yes, coming to America is the only good thing that happened because of him. But honestly, they all treated you and Mimi badly. I fell in love with your strength, Chica, and you don't have to worry about anything because I'm going to take care of you and your sons."

"Julio, I don't need you or any other man to take care of me," Melinia stated firmly. "According to my drug counselor, people in recovery shouldn't begin romantic relationships until after they've achieved at least a year of sobriety. You deserve the opportunity to explore dating here before deciding if you want to be with someone like me."

"I know what I want, Chica, and it's you. I understand you have strong feelings for someone else, but I'm telling you here and now that one day we will be together," Julio said with a confident smile.

"Julio, you don't really know me. I'm going to level with you. I also joined Rique and the Crew willingly because I was trying to get out of here to save my life."

Julio frowned, shaking his head slightly. "What happened?"

"I owe money to some bad people here in Cleveland," she explained. "I knew that when I was with Rique, the enemies I had made along the way couldn't touch me. Now that I'm back, I'm not sure if those people are still after me."

"How much do you owe? I'll work harder to pay off your debt."

She reached across the table and covered his hand. "Julio, please. I appreciate the offer, but unfortunately, you don't make enough to pay back what I owe, and honestly, it isn't your problem. You have parents and sisters back in DR who need your money, so send what you can to them and don't worry about me."

Julio placed a hand on top of hers and smiled. "Chica, I'll work a second job to pay off your debt. You've been through so much, and I want you to know how proud I am of you for getting off drugs and doing better for yourself and your sons."

Melinia's heart warmed at his kind words. She knew he meant each of them. "Thank you, Julio."

"Just make one promise to me, Chica."

"Okay, what?"

"That no matter what, you won't go back to drugs and that you'll seriously consider me as your man."

"Okay, I promise," Melinia said, silently hoping she could live up to her words.

Chapter 8

Breathe

Juliette looked down at her beautiful daughter's sleeping face and sighed with relief. It had been touch and go for a while, but Jolene seemed to have turned a corner and was now resting comfortably. The Stubbs family had enjoyed a fun-filled evening of charades, and the game had helped take Jolene's mind off her pain. It wasn't long before she was laughing along with her siblings, her giggles lighting up the room and easing Juliette's worry.

Afterward, Juliette gave both her daughters a bath, adding Epsom salt and lavender to Jolene's bath water to help soothe her pain. Once they were dressed for bed, she gave Jolene more children's Tylenol, which put her out like a light. Standing there in the dim light of her room, Juliette whispered a silent prayer of gratitude, her heart still heavy with worry and hope. She was hoping for an exciting, quiet night with Grandville, and her body tingled at the thought of what he would do to her, a rare spark of excitement she allowed herself amidst the tension of the day.

She slipped into their bedroom to find Grandville waiting for her in bed, his eyes softening at the sight of her.

"Come on, girl, you made me a promise and I intend for you to keep it. Get on in this bed," Grandville said seductively, biting his lip.

Juliette giggled, her heartbeat quickening, and said, "Boy, give me a few minutes. I need to get myself ready, but I intend to keep my promise and make some new ones."

With a devilish grin, he said, "Okay, I'll be waiting."

Juliette went into their attached bathroom to prepare herself for an exciting night. After removing her makeup and brushing her teeth, she entered her closet and took out a red negligee. She felt a thrill as she smoothed the fabric over her curves, and it wasn't long before she was sashaying across her bedroom to join Grandville in bed.

"Girl, you look beautiful and certainly worth the wait," Grandville complimented, his eyes roving all over her body with desire as he reached for her.

"Thank you. You know I'm a woman of my word. Now, what exactly was it that I promised to do to you?" Juliette asked, batting her eyelashes as she slowly gyrated her hips, her voice low and teasing.

"You promised to do this," Grandville said as he pulled her close and kissed her lips passionately. His hand slipped around her waist, pulling her down onto the bed, and she let herself melt into his embrace. The world outside of their bedroom fell away, the worries, the fears—all of it replaced by the warmth of his touch.

She was so entranced by his kisses that she thought she was hallucinating when she heard a knock on the bedroom door. Her brows furrowed in confusion, and her body went rigid in Grandville's arms.

"Who is it?" she asked, trying her best not to sound irritated by the interruption.

She heard Jenae's voice say, "Mommy, it's me."

Both she and Grandville quickly adjusted their positions on the bed, Grandville pulling up the blanket to cover them as Juliette took a deep breath, smoothing her hair and giving the okay for Jenae to enter.

Jenae walked in, her small face a mirror of worry. Her eyes, just like Grandville and Greta's, were wide and filled with concern.

"Sweetheart, why aren't you in bed?" Grandville inquired, sitting up and leaning forward.

"Daddy, Jolene's crying," Jenae said in shaky voice.

Juliette's heart clenched. Panic rushed in, as she exchanged a quick glance with Grandville. Both of them moved at once, almost knocking each other down as they rushed toward the twins' bedroom. The urgency pounded in her veins, her mind filling with flashes of Jessica—how helpless she had felt then, how she couldn't let anything happen to another one of her children.

When they entered the room, they found Jolene curled up in a fetal position on her bed, moaning in pain, her small frame trembling. The sight sent a chill down Juliette's spine. She swallowed hard, forcing herself to remain calm.

She leaned down and gently touched Jolene's shoulder. "Jolene, what is it? Where's the pain?" she asked softly.

"Everywhere, Mommy," Jolene whispered, tears streaming down her pretty little face. Her voice was so weak, it made Juliette's heart break all over again.

Grandville placed his hand on Jolene's forehead, his face hardening as he felt the heat radiating off her. "Juliette, she's burning up with fever. We need to get her to the hospital," he said, his tone leaving no room for argument. He looked down at his daughter, his eyes filled with love and determination. "You get Jolene ready."

He turned to Jenae, who still stood in the doorway, watching. "Jenae, you were a good sister for getting us when your sister was ill and needed help. When we get back home, I'll let you pick out a gift on Amazon," he promised with a soft voice. He picked Jenae up, kissed her on the cheek, and gently placed her back in her bed. "Now, I want you to get back in bed and think about what you want to order, and try to go back to sleep."

Juliette could feel her breathing become uneven, the panic rising as her throat seemed to close up at the thought of taking her baby to the hospital. She gritted her teeth, trying to force herself to focus on what she needed to do.

After a quick glance at her, Grandville straightened his shoulders and knelt down to face Juliette, still seated on the side of Jolene's bed. "Sweetheart, focus on your breath and remember it's going to be all right," he said. "Go take your medicine and let Greta know we're leaving. I'll get Jolene ready," he added with a gentle voice.

Juliette nodded, her head feeling light as she walked out the room in a daze. Her whirling thoughts consumed her as her feet moved almost of their own accord. In her bedroom, she gripped the Valium bottle with shaky hands. She took a pill, swallowing it down with a gulp of water. As she tried to gather her thoughts, she heard Greta's voice., cutting through the fog of her panic

"Juliette, what's going on?" Greta's voice was filled with concern, and it brought Juliette back to the present.

"It's Jolene. We need to get her to the hospital. She's burning up with fever, even after I gave her Tylenol. I need you to stay with the kids."

Greta nodded, her face softening. "Okay, no problem. It's not like I have anywhere to go." Greta stated, trying to inject a bit of lightness into the situation, though her eyes betrayed her worry.

Juliette couldn't believe how her night had taken such a sudden turn. Juliette moved around the room in a rush, desperately searching for something to wear to the hospital, her mind racing. Greta's voice pulled her back to reality.

"Juliette, I know you're worried, but you need to calm down. What are you looking for?" Greta asked gently, her tone a grounding presence.

"Something to wear to the hospital," Juliette replied, her voice barely above a whisper.

"Okay, here's a sweatsuit you can wear," Greta said, handing Juliette a pink sweatsuit from her closet with their sorority letters on the front. Juliette took it and went into the bathroom to change. When she emerged, Grandville was standing in their bedroom, fully dressed with keys in hand. His face was set in determination.

"I have Jolene settled in the car. Are you ready?" Grandville asked, with a hint of impatience in his voice.

"Yes," Juliette replied, nodding as she followed Grandville out of their bedroom.

"Greta, we'll be in touch as soon as we have news," Grandville said, his voice softening as he addressed his sister.

Greta nodded, her eyes meeting Juliette's. "Take care of her, mama," she whispered, her voice filled with emotion.

Grandville drove fast, his hands gripping the wheel tightly as he expertly weaved in and out of traffic. Juliette kept her eyes on Jolene, who was strapped in her car seat, her little face flushed with fever. The fear of the unknown gnawed at Juliette's insides, but she put on a small smile for Jolene. It wasn't long before they were sitting with masks on their faces in an isolated corner of the emergency room, waiting for Jolene's name to be called.

The Revelation

Gently holding Jolene in her lap, Juliette laid her head on Grandville's shoulder, her eyes stinging with unshed tears as she silently prayed for Jolene. She could tell that Grandville was trying his best to hold it together, taking in his clenching jaw and tapping foot. The waiting room was cold, the air smelled sterile, and the beeping machines and hurried footsteps added to her anxiety. It felt like hours passed before she heard a familiar voice.

"Oh my God, Grandville and Juliette! Is Jolene okay?" she asked.

Juliette looked up to a woman standing about six feet away and wearing a mask with her sorority letters on it. Despite the mask, Juliette knew it was Sabrina. Seeing her was a calming comfort that she sorely needed.

"Hey Sabrina. Jolene was burning up with a fever and is in a lot of pain. I think she's having a sickle cell crisis. I'm surprised you recognized me with this mask on. What are you doing here" Juliette asked.

"Aww, poor baby. I hope she feels better soon. I saw your jogging suit and your box braids. Even with the mask, I'd recognize you anywhere. Anyway, Franklin's really sick," Sabrina said sadly, her eyes glistening with worry.

"What's wrong with him?" Grandville inquired, concerned.

"They're not sure yet. He's being examined by the ER doctors. I was on my way to get bottled water," Sabrina said.

Grandville frowned. "Okay, well, what are his symptoms?"

"He started coughing uncontrollably and said he couldn't breathe. I thought he may be having a heart attack, so I called an ambulance. They gave him oxygen, and he seemed to feel a little better, but I'm concerned," Sabrina admitted.

"You're a doctor; what do you think it is?" Juliette asked, rubbing Jolene's back.

"I hope I'm wrong, but it could be COVID. The doctors are waiting for the test results," Sabrina said, her eyes filling with tears.

"Oh my God. Poor Franklin! I hope that's not what Jolene has," Juliette said, her voice barely audible.

"Let's not jump the gun, Juliette," Grandville said, squeezing her hand gently. "There's no indication that Franklin or Jolene have caught the virus." His words were steady, but she could see that his jaw was still clenching.

Juliette and Grandville looked up when a nurse called Jolene's name. The sound seemed to echo through the sterile waiting room, filling Juliette with relief and dread.

Grandville stood and picked Jolene up from Juliette's lap with gentle care, then said, "Sabrina, please keep us posted on how Franklin's doing. Please let me know if you need anything." He spoke with the calm authority of someone trying to hold it together for everyone else."I will, and Juliette, be sure to call me once you find out what's going on with Jolene," Sabrina directed, her eyes holding empathy.

"Will do," Juliette said, as she fought to stop the negative feelings that threatened to overwhelm her. She took a deep breath, as Grandville's words echoed in her mind: *Focus on your breath. It's going to be all right.*

She closed her eyes briefly, forcing herself to acknowledge Grandville's reassuring presence beside her. When she opened her eyes, he was patiently waiting for her. Giving her a gentle smile, he nodded toward the door as they headed towards the nurse who was patiently waiting. She held onto that calm feeling, desperately trying to anchor herself amidst the storm of fear raging in her mind.

Chapter 9

You Can't Get What You Want

('Til You Know What You Want)

Grandville sat in the office he shared with Franklin, peering out the picture window at the shimmering waters of Lake Erie. It was a beautiful, sunny day, and he tried to quiet his thoughts, which were all over the place. Franklin hadn't been in for more than a week, battling health issues, and Grandville wasn't sure when he would return.

Despite everything, Grandville was doing his best to stay positive despite the ups and downs of his world. Jolene, thank God, did not have COVID, but she did have pneumonia, which kept her bedridden and in need of constant attention. Juliette was spending every day at the hospital with their sick child and only coming home at night to rest, her face drained and weary from exhaustion. Franklin wasn't so lucky. He tested positive for COVID, and although he was sent home to recover, Sabrina kept Grandville updated—the news wasn't good. Franklin wasn't getting better, and Grandville could hear the worry in Sabrina's voice each time she informed him of his worsened condition.

Grandville sent up a silent prayer for both Jolene and Franklin. His gratitude extended to Greta, who was the glue holding everything together in their home. With Juliette staying at the hospital with Jolene daily and Grandville still going into the office to work, Greta was the only adult available to take care of their children. Greta was the reason their household continued to function; she took over every morning, cooking breakfast for the kids, and ensuring they were logged into virtual classes on time. Today, Grandville decided to surprise his family with French toast, pancakes and sausages and gourmet coffee—a sweet moment of normalcy, and a small effort to lift everyone's spirits. After Juliette left for the hospital and the kids settled down in front of their computers, he had a moment alone with his only sibling.

He found her sitting at the kitchen table, staring into a cup of coffee. The lines on her face betrayed a deep weariness, but when she looked up, she tried to smile.

"Hey, Sis, I just wanted to thank you for everything you've been doing to ensure that our household runs smoothly. Juliette and I wouldn't be able to manage without you," Grandville said, placing his hand over hers, trying to convey his sincerity.

"No problem, Grandville. I feel blessed to be here," Greta replied, but her eyes were dull, her smile fleeting. " It's because of your family that I have something worthwhile to fill my days with. Hell, I should be thanking you. It's because of you I have a family. And at this rate, it seems I will probably never get to have children of my own."

"That's not true, Greta," Grandville said, shaking his head. "First off, women are having healthy children later in life. And there are plenty of children right here in Cleveland who need a loving home. You're an amazing woman, Greta. You have so much love to give." He watched his womb mate press her lips into a thin line, her eyes looking away, as if she didn't believe him.

She sighed, her fingers tracing the rim of her coffee cup. After exhaling sharply, she placed a hand on her forehead. "I guess I should consider adoption since it sure doesn't look like I'll ever get married. What I can't figure out is why I can't trust the men I love not to cheat on me." Her voice cracked, and tears welled up, silently sliding down her cheeks.

"Listen, Greta, you're an awesome woman, and if someone cheats on you, that's on them, not you." He hesitated, then added, "I haven't told you this yet, but I met with Rayshawn the other day."

Greta's head snapped up, her eyes widening at the mention of her ex-husband's name. "You did?'

Grandville nodded. "It appears that Derek could have been set up."

"Set up?" Greta repeated, shaking her head as her eyebrows furrowed. "What do you mean, Grandville?"

"We don't actually know for a fact that Derek slept with that woman. And you're never going to know unless you talk to him. I think you need closure, and you're never going to get it by staying busy taking care of family."

"I know that," Greta whispered. "But Grandville, but I'm not ready. The embarrassment—having another woman claim my fiancé was the father of her unborn child at my wedding—it's too much to bear." More tears spilled down her cheeks.

"I know it feels that way, Greta. But you're not being fair. Derek deserves due process, and you never gave him a chance to explain himself. Just because Katilina said he was the father doesn't make it true. She's told Rayshawn that she has a grudge against you."

Greta frowned, narrowing her eyes. "A grudge? Against me? Why would some bitch I've never met care about me?"

"She's always wanted Rayshawn, but he never gave her more than sex," Grandville explained. "She wanted more, but his heart always belonged to you."

Greta's lips quivered, and she shook her head in frustration. "Okay, but what is this woman's connection to Derek? Did Rayshawn put her up to sleeping with Derek and ruining my wedding?"

"No. But according to Rayshawn, Katilina tricked him into coming to Cleveland and he swears he had no idea it was to crash your wedding."

"Once again, I don't understand what that has to do with Derek."

"Rayshawn said that Katilina was the entertainment at Derek's bachelor party arranged by the LA's front office team when he was visiting Los Angeles a few months before your wedding. Katilina knew Derek intimately long before he met you. When she found out he was marrying you, the same person who also has Rayshawn's heart, she snapped. Rayshawn thinks she could've drugged Derek that night… and he doesn't even remember."

Greta's mouth fell open, but no words came out at first. Her eyes searched his, a mixture of pain and confusion on her face. "So, you really think Derek might be innocent in all this?"

"I think it's possible. I think you owe it to yourself to find out, Greta. Otherwise, how can you ever move on?"

Greta swallowed hard, her fingers twisting together. She finally looked away, her shoulders sagging. "I'll think about it, okay? But I'm just not ready yet."

"Okay, I understand. And I'll support any decision you make, but, as your big brother, I'm telling you—talk to Derek. Invite him to the park for a walk, talk things out. And let me know when. I'll watch the kids." He expected to see her usual smirk at his big brother joke since he was only born a few minutes before her, but her face was clouded with doubt.

"What else was Rayshawn talking about?" Greta quickly changed the subject.

"What he always talks about; you. How much he loves you and how he's been working his 12-step program for sex addiction. According to him, he was only with Katilina that day to make amends for mistreating her in the past," Grandville explained.

Grandville could only hope that his sister would heed his advice. Suddenly, the office suite door creaked opened, slicing into the silence and jarring him from his thoughts. Grandville turned, half expecting Franklin, despite knowing better. Instead, it was George, Franklin's soon-to-be stepson, wearing a mask and standing timidly in the office reception area.

George slipped on a mask before emerging from his office and stepping into the main office area. "Hey George, I wasn't expecting you. What's going on?" Grandville asked.

George's hands were fidgeting at his sides. "I hope it's okay for me to be here. I… I understand if you don't want me around, you know, because of catching COVID," George stated quietly.

Grandville shook his head. "George, I'm not worried about that. We'll wear our masks to be safe."

They sat across from each other in the small conference room at the far end of the suite.

"George, it's great to see you. What brings you by?" Grandville asked.

George hesitated, his eyes lowering. "Well… I know Franklin hasn't been able to come in, but I was hoping you'd let me come in to help. I just moved back into Aunt Sabrina's condo. She hasn't sold it yet, so I haven't seen Franklin. I got tested—I'm negative. But I'm going stir crazy. I don't have a lot of friends, and they think it's too risky to hang out right now."

Grandville leaned back, nodding. He recognized that nervous energy, that sense of feeling lost. "Who is she?" Grandville asked, a knowing smile grazing his lips.

Giving a faint smile, George said, "Her name's Cora… she's not my girlfriend, but I wanna change that soon. Before this stupid virus, we were hanging out a lot. But she has asthma and her mom's tripping about her leaving the house. I'd be over with Aunt Sabrina, but with Franklin sick and my grandmother being there, I figured I'd stay out of the way. I need something to do to fill up my time. Can I help you out here? You don't even have to pay me."

"George," Grandville began, leaning forward, "you should be working on finishing your degree. I hear everything's online now."

George looked down, his fingers fiddling with the hem of his button down. "Yeah… but I was struggling before, when classes were on campus. I don't know if I can do it online."

Grandville watched George's brows furrow close together, knowing look. He often did the same thing when he thought there was no way forward. He frowned, his heart clenching at the sight of George's frustration. "George, with enough determination and the right support, you can do anything. How about this: You come help me out here, I'll pay you. But next semester, you start back working on your degree, alright? I'll help you study, and you can work around your school schedule. Deal?" He paused, a grin spreading across his face. "I'll even give you some tips for sealing the deal with Cora. But, you can't tell anyone you're coming here—my family's paranoid about COVID."

George's face broke into a smile, his eyes brightening. "Deal. Thanks, Mr. Stubbs. What's the first thing you want me to do?"

Grandville chuckled, wondering if it was the pay, getting out the house, or the tips for getting a girlfriend that sealed the deal for him. Handing George a pen and notepad, he said, "Alright, let's start by outlining your duties. Ready?"

George nodded, his handsome features brightening.

As they began, Grandville felt a flicker of hope. Maybe this unexpected chance to get to know his son better was exactly what they both needed—a chance to build something solid amidst the chaos, something that mattered. He looked at George, and for a moment, the world outside didn't feel quite so heavy.

Chapter 10

Devil is a Lie

Melinia walked through the grocery store, one hand pushing the car while the other tried to soothe her fussy infant son, Jesus. His carrier was securely nestled in the cart, but his angry cries echoed through the aisles, a high-pitched reminder of her exhaustion. She tried to calm him down, her words whispered and soft, but her mind was scattered, unfocused. Between Jesus's wails and Rafael pulling at her leg, begging for chips and sugary cereal, her patience was wearing thin. She wished she could have left them with her mother but she was older and suffered from diabetes. With her underlying condition, she couldn't risk exposing her mom.

She pushed down the worry bubbling inside her, forcing herself to focus on the task at hand—getting through the store and gathering what they needed. Ever since they entered the store, the feeling that she was being followed gnawed at her. Every few minutes, she glanced behind her, her eyes scanning the other shoppers. No one seemed out of place, but the prickling sensation at the back of her neck wouldn't go away.

Rafael tugged at her jeans again, his eyes wide. "Mommy, can I get potato chips? Please?"

She nodded absently, trying to push the nagging fear aside. "We'll get them before we leave, sweetie. Just stay close to Mommy, okay? "Ready to get out of there, she hurried to the baby aisle for formula and diapers. She stacked several cans of Similac infant formula in her cart, thankful for the WIC program that made it possible for her to provide for her kids. She was reaching for the last can when she felt it—the unmistakable sensation of eyes boring into her.

She turned her head, her heart skipping a beat. A man stood at the end of the aisle, his eyes fixed on her. He wore a mask, but as he slowly approached her, she recognized those steel grey eyes instantly. Dreadlocks framed his face, and she knew—it was the same man who'd shown up at her apartment a few days ago.

Panic shot through her. She turned the cart abruptly, trying to get away, but he stepped into her path, blocking her exit.

"Told you I'd see you again," he said, his voice low, almost mocking.

Melinia swallowed, her throat dry. She grabbed Rafael's hand and pulled him closer. "What do you want?" she demanded.

The man tilted his head, a sneer tugging at his lips. "I want what we all want." He reached into his pocket, flashing a small baggie. The sight of the white powder inside made her stomach drop, and her mouth filled with saliva.

She couldn't tear her eyes away from the baggie. Her mind flashed back to a time when that powder was her escape, when the numbness it provided was all she lived for. Her body betrayed her, craving the release it offered. She clenched her jaw, forcing herself to look away, her eyes darting to Jesus, who was now crying louder, his tiny fists flailing.

"I don't know what you're talking about," her voice trembled, and she silently cursed herself for displaying weakness. She reached for the cart, trying to push past him, but he didn't move.

"I want peace," he said, learning closer, his eyes darkening with intensity. "And I think you do too."

He waved the baggie slightly, his eyes flicking to Jesus. "Maybe you're gonna need it sooner than later."

Melinia closed her eyes and took a deep breath, the intensity of the craving hitting her like a freight train—the need to momentarily disappear, to float away from all of it—the exhaustion, the worry, the weight of her past. Just then, Jesus started wailing again, pulling her attention back to her children. She blinked, and the man was gone. Just like that—he'd vanished, as if he were nothing more than a ghost..

"Mommy, I want potato chips," Rafael cried, his little body jerking as he stamped on the ground.

She nodded, her throat tight. "Yeah, baby. Let's get your chips." She glanced around, her eyes scanning the aisles, but the man was nowhere to be seen.

Back at home, she worked on autopilot—putting away the groceries, making lunch for Rafael, feeding Jesus. Her hands moved, but her mind was still back in that aisle, replaying the man's sneer, the glint in his eyes. She hated how easily he'd rattled her, how quickly the craving had resurfaced.

Once the boys were down for their naps, she logged into her laptop that Zenobia and the Monarch program had purchased for her virtual session with Zenobia. She tried to push aside her anxiety, plastering on a smile as the screen flickered to life.

"Hello, Melinia. How are you today?" Zenobia's eyes were warm behind her glasses.

"I'm okay, Ms. Zenobia," Melinia said, her voice lacking conviction. "How are you?"

"I'm doing well, thank you. I'm sorry we have to meet virtually, but we can't have any clients in our building due to the Ohio Health Department's mandates," Zenobia stated.

"I understand," Melina nodded.

Zenobia adjusted her glasses, her eyes narrowing slightly as she studied Melinia's face. "You seem a little off today. Want to talk about it?"

Melinia hesitated, biting her lip. "I'm just… tired, I guess. The boys are a handful, and I'm not getting much sleep."

Zenobia nodded. "I understand. Lack of sleep can be a real trigger for cravings and I know your support group has been suspended so how have you been managing your sobriety without in-person support?"

Melinia sighed, her shoulders slumping. "I haven't used, but I'm not going to lie; sometimes I dream about being high, about how good it feels to be a million miles away. I hate it, but I can't help it. I thought by now the cravings would be gone.".

Zenobia's expression softened. "Cravings are normal, Melinia. Especially in times of heightened stress. The important thing is that you're not acting on them. You're fighting them, and that takes strength."

"I almost didn't," Melinia whispered, her voice barely audible. She looked away from the screen, a tear slipping down her cheek. "There was a man at the store today. He offered me drugs, and for a second… just for a second, I wanted to take it. I closed my eyes for a moment, and when I opened them, he completely disappeared."

Zenobia removed her glasses, her eyes sharp. "I need you to hear me. That was the enemy, Melinia. Testing you. And you passed. You walked away. That's something to be proud of. Remember, you have angels all around you and when you ask for help, God will send His Army to fight for you."

"Thanks. Yes, I know. And I'm managing my cravings right now, but I think the stress has a lot to do with my boys. I'm so busy caring for them that by the time I put them to bed, I'm exhausted. Also, Jesus is colicky and cries a lot. I miss being around my mom. When the kids cry, she always knew what to do."

"Call and ask her for tips," Zenobia advised. "She probably wants nothing more than to hear from you. You were missing for several years, and having you back is a blessing to your entire family. Don't deny them your company and your love. Let them support you."

Melinia wiped a tear from her face and looked away from the screen. "I want to, but I'm still embarrassed about getting myself into a position where I was giving my body away for drugs."

"Look, I'm going to be transparent for a minute here. I also have a history of giving my body away for drugs—on the worldwide web for everyone to see! During the first couple of years of my sobriety, I had regular cravings. Having them and managing them are always going to be a part of your journey. So is dealing with the judgment of others. But even if your family doesn't understand your choices, they still love you."

"Thanks, Ms. Zenobia. I'll try to remember that,"

They continued to talk and Zenobia helped her come up with a plan for the next time she felt tempted. By the end, Melinia felt a little lighter, as if some of the weight pressing down on her had lifted.

"I'll see you next week on Zoom at the same time. I'll send the link at the beginning of the week. You have a blessed day, Melinia."

Later that night, after Rafael and Jesus were fed, bathed, and asleep, Melinia sat on her couch, her thoughts drifting back to the man at the store. She felt her chest tighten, the anxiety creeping back in. He knew where she lived. He'd been to her apartment. What if he came back?

Her phone rang, pulling from her thoughts. She glanced at her screen—it was Julio.

"Hey, Julio."

"Hello, Chica," his familiar voice greeted her. "I was thinking about you, so I decided to give you a call. I'm going to be honest with you, you are always on my mind."

Melinia felt her cheeks flush as she said, "Julio, stop it. Tell me about your day."

"Melinia, I can hear something in your voice. I know something happened today."

Melinia almost gasped, but composed herself and said, "Julio, I have no idea what you're talking about."

"Yes, you do, and you'll confide in me when you're ready. I was also calling because I'm going to receive my paycheck, and I want to take you and the boys out to dinner," Julio said.

"Julio, you're so sweet, but I know your parents could use that money. I don't want you spending your money on me or the boys," Melinia said.

"I've already sent my parents money this month. Your relatives are generous with what they pay me. I'm rich here in the US, and the money I send home has been a godsend for my family. Let's take the kids to the park and then to the Waffle House. Big Joe showed me how to use the Uber app, and I can pick you and the boys up tomorrow around 4 p.m. I'm off, and I want to spend time with you."

Melinia hesitated, then nodded, even though he couldn't see it. "Okay. I'll agree to go on one condition."

"Alright, what is it?"

"It's not a date. I'm just not ready for that. I still have a lot of things I need to work through. Okay?"

"I understand, but I I'm here for you no matter what. I'm willing to wait for as long as it takes."

Melinia rolled her eyes and sighed.

"I'm not interested in anyone else but you, so I suggest that you and the boys be ready by four."

"Okay, Julio, we'll see you tomorrow." Melinia hung up with a smile on her face.

Maybe tomorrow would be a good day. Maybe, just for a little while, she could forget about the man with the grey eyes and focus on her boys—on the good things in her life. *Maybe,* she thought, as she closed her eyes and let out a breath, *she could still find a way to be happy.*

Chapter 11

Anxiety

Juliette was happy that Jolene was better and now at home. When Jolene was diagnosed with pneumonia, she was relieved that she didn't have COVID, but she was deeply afraid that she or Jolene would catch the virus while at the hospital. On the night Jolene was admitted, Juliette had felt an anxiety attack coming on, and the only thing that had soothed her nerves was Sabrina's presence.

After the doctors examined Jolene, they advised both her and Grandville that Jolene needed to stay in the hospital for a few days. The couple decided that Grandville would remain at home with Greta to take care of the other children, while Juliette stayed at the hospital to concentrate exclusively on Jolene.

Once Grandville left the hospital, Jolene fell asleep, leaving Juliette alone with her racing thoughts. To the outside world, she appeared calm and composed, but inside she was petrified. Jolene had a compromised immune system, and Juliette couldn't stop herself from thinking about what would happen if her daughter caught COVID. Media stories of its serious impact on healthy people who were falling ill and dying replayed in her mind, and even though she tried to push them away, they wouldn't budge. Juliette was wringing her hands, struggling to keep her breath steady when Sabrina walked in, her face partially hidden behind a mask, a large Starbucks cup in her hand.

"Hey girl, I brought you a chai tea," Sabrina said softly, her eyes warm above the mask. She handed Juliette the cup and pulled a second mask from her purse—it had a sparkly letter "J" on the side. "And this is also for you. Figured you could use a little glam in here, mama."

Juliette smiled, her chest loosening slightly. She took a cautious sip from the hot tea, the warmth instantly starting to calm her frayed nerves. "Thank you, Sabrina. You don't know how badly I needed this."

"Of course. I heard from the nurses that Jolene is doing okay. She's a fighter, just like her mom," Sabrina replied, winking as she sat down beside her.

Juliette's eyes filled with tears, and she looked away, blinking rapidly. "Yes, I know, but I'm still scared," she whispered. "I'm scared she'll catch it. I'm scared of what will happen if she does. I don't know what I'll do if I lose her."

Sabrina reached over, placing a comforting hand on Juliette's arm. "I know. But she's in good hands here. And you're doing everything you can for her. Just take it one breath at time, okay?"

Juliette nodded, squeezing Sabrina's hand. "One breath at a time. How's Franklin doing?"

Sabrina sighed, the pain evident in her features. "Girl, his doctors are still trying to figure it out. His issues appears to be respiratory, so it may be pneumonia. My mom and I were just tested for COVID, and luckily, we don't have it. I'm worried that if Franklin does have COVID, the hospital's practice and policy to keep only the sickest patients will cause them to send him home."

The Revelation

Three weeks later, just as Sabrina suspected, Franklin was diagnosed with COVID. As she had predicted, he was not admitted to the hospital and was instead told to go home and isolate. Despite receiving medications and getting plenty of rest, Franklin's condition seemed to worsen.

Juliette was sitting on her screened-in sun porch, feeling the weight of Sabrina's words as she ordered dinner to be delivered to Sabrina and her family. She knew that Sabrina was overwhelmed, and she wanted to help in any small way she could. She had finished placing her order when her phone rang.

"Hello, Juliette," Sabrina's voice came through the line, sounding strained.

"Hey," Juliette said, trying to sound upbeat although her instinct told her something was wrong. "You must have ESP because I was just about to call you. I ordered dinner for you and your family. It should arrive by 6:30."

"Oh, thank you so much," Sabrina said, her voice trembling slightly. "I was just trying to figure out dinner. It looks like you're the one with ESP. I honestly don't know how I would manage without friends like you."

Well, why don't I have winning lottery numbers then?" Juliette joked. "But really, you don't need to thank me. How are you holding up?"

There was a long pause on the other end. "Not great," Sabrina admitted. "Franklin has taken a turn for the worse and he's in the hospital.. I'm trying to stay positive, but it's so hard. I just… I don't know what I'll do if he doesn't make it."

Juliette closed her eyes, her heart aching for her friend. "I know you're scared. But we have to believe that he's going to pull through. He's strong, and he has you by his side, even if you can't be with him in the hospital. In fact, do you need me to come and stay with your mother so you can get up there?"

"I appreciate your offer, but the he's on the COVID floor and visitation is restricted. But I've been in touch with Franklin's doctor. He's talking about putting him on a ventilator. I'm terrified."

"My God!" Juliette gasped softly to herself, but focused on staying calm and strong for her friend. "Sabrina, I'm going to pray for Franklin and for you. Please don't hesitate to call or text us if you need anything."

"I most definitely will, Juliette," Sabrina said, her voice cracking. "And thanks for being so thoughtful. It means so much more than you know."

"Anytime. Always happy to help. Give my love to your family."

After they hung up, Juliette found Grandville in their bedroom, watching a Cleveland Indians game. She climbed into bed next to him, snuggling close. He turned, raising an eyebrow at her sudden appearance.

"Everything okay?" he asked, muting the TV. "I thought you were out enjoying the sunlight."

Juliette sighed, resting her head on his shoulder. "I just spoke to Sabrina. Franklin's not doing well. They might have to put him on a ventilator"

Grandville let out a long breath, his body tensing beside her. "Damn," he muttered. "I was really hoping he would get better. I'm not going to lie. I'm scared."

"Me too," Juliette whispered, "but Franklin is healthy, so I think he'll beat this."

"We'll take it one day at a time. That's all we can do. And we'll continue to be there for Sabrina, no matter what happens," Grandville said and Juliette detected a hint of uncertainty in his voice.

Juliette nodded, closing her eyes as she clung to him. She was unsure of what Grandville would do if he lost his best friend. She began to pray that Franklin would make it through, and that somehow, they would all come out of this stronger.

Chapter 12

Waffle House

Melinia sat on a blanket with Jesus and watched Julio and Rafael kick a soccer ball back and forth. They were at a park located right on Lake Erie, where Melinia gazed at the lush green grass and trees that were just beginning to bloom. She felt an emotion she hadn't experienced in years: peace.

"Melinia, do you see how good Rafael is at football?" Julio called out, his distinct Spanish accent adding emphasis. "He has outstanding footwork and incredible hand-eye coordination. I think he could excel and go far in in a youth football program."

"Boy, you're going to confuse Rafael. For the last time, in America it's called soccer," Melinia scolded playfully. "Football is an entirely different sport here in America, and it's probably one of this country's most beloved one. Remember, I taught you some of the game when we played that card game, Naked Bootleg, in the Bahamas right before we were rescued?"

"Yes, I remember," Julio said, a hint of nostalgia lacing his voice. He glanced at Rafael who was kicking the ball with fierce determination, and then turned back to Melinia with a smile. "But what's wrong with a little cultural exchange?"

She shook her head with a smile. "You're impossible."

"Now come on, let's take the kids over by the water," Julio suggested.

Melinia hesitated for a moment before standing up. She followed Julio, who had taken Rafael's hand as they walked toward the pier, while she trailed behind pushing Jesus in his stroller. The lake stretched out in front of them, shimmering blue vastness, calm and seemingly endless. The beauty of it all brought a sense of ease, but the sight of the water also filled her with a sense of dread, dredging up memories of the years she'd been held captive on the open seas by the Sandego Crew.

People were fishing and launching their boats, ready to spend the day enjoying all that Lake Erie had to offer. The water was calm and tranquil, and Melinia was enjoying the peaceful scene when she caught a glimpse of a man standing on the pier, staring at her. Something in his stance or the way his head was slightly tilted made her think of Rique, the leader of the Sandego Crew. Her heart hammered in her chest, and she froze, staring back at him.

She shut her eyes, then opened them again to look in the direction where the man had been standing, but he was gone. The knot in her stomach tightened.

"Melinia?" Julio's voice cut through her jumbled thoughts. He turned around, concerned by her expression. "What's wrong, Chica?"

"Nothing," she said, shaking her head. "It's really nice here by the water, but I think we need to get back and start packing up."

Frowning, Julio stepped closer. "What is it, Melinia?" he pressed, taking her hand. "What were you just looking at?"

Melinia hesitated, glancing back toward the pier, her eyes scanning the area where the man had just been standing. When she looked back at Julio, she saw the worry in his eyes. "I… I could have sworn I saw Rique," Melinia replied, her voice shaky.

Julio's eyes narrowed, and his grip on her hand tightened. "I don't think Rique would be stupid enough to come here to Cleveland. He knows the authorities are looking for him," he said, confidently, giving her hand a reassuring squeeze.

"If you believe that, then you are more naïve than I first thought," Melinia said forcing a smile. "Rique doesn't care about the authorities."

"Chica, I prefer to call it optimism," Julio said, as his smile reached his eyes.

She sighed, shaking her head. "Julio, optimism will get you killed out here. You're an excellent chess player, and I know you always think three moves ahead. But I think five moves ahead, and I know for a fact that Rique and the Sandego Crew will absolutely come to Cleveland to hunt me down like a dog and kill me because I took something from them that they want."

Julio frowned deeply, his eyes searching her face. "Listen, Melinia, you're irreplaceable to me, but not to Rique and the crew. If he's still out there, then he's already replaced you. I'm sure they have a new boat and are back to their usual ways. Now, come on, let's get out of here. There's a Waffle House right down the street with outdoor seating. Rafael, do you want some pizza?" he called over to the boy who was chucking rocks into the water.

"Yes!" Rafael shouted, running back to them with a wide grin. "I want pepperoni and pineapple, like the kind Aunt Romanita used to make. I miss her. When will we see her again, Mommy?"

A sadness flickered across Melinia's face. "I don't know, Rafael. We won't be able to see her for a while, but when we get home, you can write her a letter that we'll send to her."

"But I don't know how to write," Rafael frowned.

"That's why we're going to keep practicing. See how important it is," Melinia said as she returned a sleeping Jesus to his stroller.

Later, as they sat at the Waffle House, the smell of freshly baked waffles filling the air, Melinia turned to Julio, her face serious. "If we're going to potentially date in the future, there's something you need to know," she said quietly.

Julio's eyebrows shot up. "Okay, what is it?"

She paused to choose her words carefully, her gaze shifting to Rafael, who was busy coloring his menu with his crayons. "The Sandego Crew will never let me go, because I took something that was irreplaceable to them, and I wasn't referring to myself."

"Well then, what or who were you referring to?" Julio asked, putting more pizza on Rafael's plate.

She swallowed, her voice dropping to a whisper. "The kids. It's Rafael. Rique will come after me because of how close Romanita is to him. Rafael gave her a reason to get up every day when she was dealing with trauma and depression after what your brother did to her. Now that he's gone, she's probably not doing well. I guarantee Rique is not going to just let that go."

Julio looked down at Rafael, happily eating a slice of pizza. He sighed deeply, shaking his head. "Melinia, I'm embarrassed about what my brother did to Romanita," he said quietly. "But despite that, Rique and his crew had no right to misuse you and Mimi the way they did. I want you to know that I'm proud of you, and I admire your courage."

A frown tugged at Melinia's face as she stared at him with disbelief. "You're proud of me? I haven't done anything to be proud of."

Julio's eyes softened. "You survived, Chica. You got your sons out of danger."

"Don't forget that I had help," she said, her eyes meeting his. "I wouldn't have been able to do it without you, Julio."

Julio smiled, the warmth returning to his gaze. "Everything that happened was meant to happen. We're going to be okay despite everything we've been through. Now eat your waffles before they get cold."

Melinia took a bite, trying to savor the food, hoping that what Julio said was true. But she was also trying to shake the feeling that they were being watched.

Chapter 13

Never Understand Me

Grandville drove through the streets of Cleveland on his way to aA New Beginning with his sunroof open, his music blasting in an attempt to lift his spirits. The air was warm, and the sun's rays spilled through the open roof, but despite the brightness outside, Grandville's mood was clouded by worry. Franklin, his best friend and fraternity brother, had been in the hospital for two weeks, and the fear of losing him gnawed at him. The loud music was a desperate effort to drown out the anxiety that had settled in his chest like a heavy weight.

Grandville appreciated Juliette's support more than words could express. She had seemed to sense how deeply Franklin's illness was affecting him and had gently suggested that he check on the rooming house and ensure that Julio had enough food for the residents, knowing that he could still make a difference. He loved her all the more for her quiet understanding of his need for new scenery. Normally, Juliette handled the grocery shopping for both rooming houses, but the pandemic had upended everything. With Jolene's illness, it simply hadn't been possible. Julio had stepped in, spending his own money to ensure everyone was fed. Grandville's visit today was to reimburse Julio and see how things were running.

When he pulled up in front of the house, he took a moment to admire it. The lawn was manicured, and the blooming flowers framed the entrance, a small testament to care and stability of the environment. As he walked towards the rear of the house, he heard a familiar voice.

"Teach, it's awesome to see you!" Big Joe called out, using the nickname Grandville had earned while locked up at Oakhill.

"Aye, Joe. Great to see you too, man. How've you been?" Grandville smiled at him.

"I'm even better now that you're here because you owe me a chance to beat you at chess. Kane knows how to play, but he doesn't give me much of a challenge. Julio's a beast, but he's always busy. You, on the other hand, owe me a rematch. I've got the board set up on the deck, ready for a socially distanced beatdown," Joe said with a chuckle.

Grandville laughed. "Alright, alright. Let me check in with Julio before I spank you with the Ivory," Grandville said jokingly.

"Cool, I'll be here waiting," Big Joe said, sitting on an outdoor chair, is eyes bright with anticipation.

Putting on his mask, Grandville entered the kitchen through the back door, nearly colliding with Julio. The house was spotless, and the air smelled like bleach and pine, a testament to how meticulously clean he kept the kitchen. Grandville admired the younger man's dedication.

"Hola, Señor Stubbs. Cómo estás?" Julio greeted him, his voice warm. Hello Mr. Stubbs. How are you?

"Hey, Julio, I'm great, and I love how the place looks. You're doing a good job," Grandville complimented.

"Gracias, Señor Stubbs. We're blessed to live in this beautiful home. I'm preparing dinner--would you like to join us?"

"I'd love to, but Juliette's expecting me home for dinner. Thanks, though," Grandville paused. "But I'll definitely taste some before I go. Let me look around real quick."

Julio nodded, and Grandville moved through the spotless house. Everything was neat and orderly, and as he returned to the kitchen, he felt proud. "It all looks fantastic, Julio. And the lawn out front is beautiful."

"Thanks Señor Stubbs, but Joe took care of the lawn," Julio confessed modestly.

"Well, he's doing a stellar job. Do you have the receipts for the food you bought last week?" Grandville asked.

Julio reached in the cabinet and pulled out an envelope with several receipts.

Grandville took out three one-hundred-dollar bills and handed them to Julio.

"Señor Stubbs, I only spent two hundred," Julio said, trying to return one of the bills.

"Consider the rest a tip from Juliette and me. We really appreciate you stepping up and using your own money. "We're trying to get back on our shopping schedule, so hopefully we won't need you to go shopping again."

Julio's eyes softened. "Gracias, Señor Stubbs. I'm grateful to work here."

Grandville patted his shoulder. "No problem, Julio. Now, let me go humble Joe on the chessboard before I head out."

Big Joe was sitting patiently on the deck, the chessboard laid out before him. He looked up as Grandville approached. "Alright, Teach. We're all set up. And, because you are the guest, I'll even let you go first," he teased.

Grandville settled into the chair opposite Joe. "You know, Joe, Julio told me about all the work you've done on the lawn. It looks great, man."

Joe beamed. "Thanks, Teach. The city of Euclid gave out free flowers, and Kane helped me haul them back. It's good to have something constructive to do, especially since I haven't been able to find work with everything shut down. "

Grandville nodded thoughtfully, using his queen to take Joe's Knight. "I know it's difficult, but look at it this way—if we were still at Oakhill, this would all be so much worse. Hey, maybe landscaping is something you can pursue in the future."

Joe's eyes lit up with hope. "You think so? I'll talk to my employment counselor about it." He used his remaining knight to take Grandville's bishop, then looked at Grandville earnestly. "Teach, do you think you could give me something to read? Kane and I walked up to the library, and we both got cards. I want to keep learning, but there were so many books, we didn't know where to start."

Grandville smiled. "You'd love 'A Piece of Cake' by Cupcake Brown. It a powerful memoir—really inspiring."

Big Joe's grinned, his eyes widening with excitement. "Bet. Thanks, Teach"

"No problem. I'll even put together some discussion questions together for each of you—like a real book club," Grandville said.

"Thanks, Teach. I appreciate it. Thanks for allowing me to stay here. I've never been happier. I just worry about what I'll do when the money Oakhill's giving me for rent runs out."

"Don't stress about that. Juliette's resourceful. We'll cross that bridge if we come to it," Grandville reassured him. "How has it been attending your 12-step program online?"

Big Joe blinked, before a genuine smile crossed his face. "It's different, but I'm still working my steps. I'm grateful for the computer you all provided."

"Good. Keep it up, Joe. You've come a long way."

"You know it, Teach."

"Checkmate," Grandville said, moving his piece and smiling as Joe groaned.

"Damn, you got me again! I swear, one day I'm gonna beat you," Big Joe said, rubbing the top of his head.

Grandville sat back in the chair and laughed. Then he reached across the board to give Joe a fist bump. "Keep practicing, and you will."

Just then, Julio came out with a small plate of food. "Señor Stubbs, time for a taste."

Grandville took a bite and his eyes widened. "Oh my God, this is amazing. What is it?"

"Pica pollo, one of my specialties," Julio said, smiling brightly.

"It's fantastic, Julio. Thanks for sharing."

As Grandville stood, his eyes caught sight of someone walking up the driveway—Melinia, pushing her infant son in a stroller, Rafael's small hand clasped in hers. Julio's face lit up as he spotted her, his grin stretching ear to ear.

"Melinia! What a surprise," Julio said, hurrying over. "I wasn't expecting you, but it's great to see you."

"Julio, I'm dying of boredom. The boys had a doctor's appointment today, so I figured I'd surprise you," she said, her smile faltering when she noticed Grandville.

"Melinia, great to see you," Grandville called out, his voice warm. "Hey Rafael, come give your Uncle Grandville a high five!

Rafael grinned, skipping over to smack Grandville's extended hand.

Grandville looked back at Melinia, noting the sudden tension in her face. "Hey Melinia, can I holler at you for a minute?" he asked. "Julio, do me a favor and take Rafael inside for some of that tasty food you've prepared. Joe, give me a few minutes with Melinia. We need to discuss some family stuff real quick."

"No problem, Teach," Joe said, disappearing inside with Julio and Rafael.

Melina looked wary as she picked up her sleeping infant, following Grandville to the deck. She sat down, cradling Jesus close.

"You look well," Grandville said. "How are you and the kids doing?"

"We're doing well. Thanks for asking. How're Juliette and the kids?"

"Juliette and the kids are well, besides Jolene. She's been sick, but she's doing better now, thankfully. We're managing."

A tense silence settled between them and Melinia looked away, breaking the emotional gridlock.

Sensing her discomfort, Grandville leaned forward, and said, "Juliette mentioned that you needed me to speak to Rayshawn about Lovelle and the money. I want you to know that I talked to him."

Melinia raised an eyebrow and lifted her chin. "Did he say if Lovelle and his crew will leave me alone?"

"Well, Melinia, that depends," Grandville said, choosing his words carefully.

"On what?"

"On whether you're willing to give Lovelle the sex tape. They want all the copies of it."

Melinia's face tightened, and she rocked Jesus gently, her eyes filled with unease. "Did you tell Juliette about the tape?"

"No, and I won't. This stays between us," he assured her.

"Well, what guarantee do I have that Lovelle won't come after me or my kids once he has it?" Melinia asked with a definitive edge to her voice.

"According to Rayshawn, once you give him the tape, he'll set you up financially for ensuring the tape doesn't get out. I'll pay your debt to Lovelle, so once you give Rayshawn the tape, you shouldn't have any more problems with him."

Melinia nodded, biting her lip. "I sure hope you're right. I'll give it up if it means they'll leave us alone."

Grandville nodded, his expression softening. "I'll set it up with Rayshawn. You have my word."

"Thanks a lot, Grandville. I know I've been a pain, but I really appreciate what you and my cousin have done for me."

"Melinia, you're not a pain. Surviving your circumstances and having two healthy children during your journey is a blessing. We're so happy that you're home and your return has really helped Juliette because your absence was really hard on her."

Tears welled in her eyes, as she gazed at her son. "When I left, I never wanted to hurt anyone. I thought leaving was best, that I'd keep everyone safe by staying away."

Grandville nodded. "I get it. But you don't have to do this alone anymore. We're family. We're in this together."

Melinia nodded.

"Speaking of family," Grandville continued. "I have a question to ask you about Rafael."

The faint smile on Melinia's lips faded. She took in a deep breath, held it, then said, "What do you want to know about him?"

"Rayshawn shared with me that he had unprotected sex with you, and he seems to think there's a possibility that he could be Rafael's father. If I'm being honest with you, Rafael looks a lot like him. Plus, he's extremely tall for his age," Grandville explained.

She stiffened, and Jesus immediately sensed her tension. He began to fuss and wiggle in her arms. She bounced him lightly. "I don't know who Rafael's father is. I was out of it during the time he was conceived—doing any and everything I could to get high, including sleeping with a lot of people. I'm not going to lie—there's a possibility that Rayshawn is Rafael's father."

Grandville nodded as he rubbed his chin. "Okay, Melinia. I appreciate you keeping it real with me. I'm going to ask that you keep the info about you and Rayshawn confidential. You know my sister and Rayshawn were once married, and if that gets out, it might cause a lot of problems in our family."

"I know. That's why I never told anyone. I honestly want to forget about that part of my life. As far as I'm concerned, I'm both Rafael's mother and father," Melinia said, anger tingeing her shaky voice.

"Kids need their fathers just as much as their mothers," Grandville pointed out. "I'll talk to Rayshawn about getting a paternity test. If he's Rafael's father, he'll take care of him."

"Thank you, Grandville," Melinia said just as Julio emerged from the house.

"Hey, so sorry to bother you guys, but Melina, is it okay for me to give Rafael some of the pica pollo I prepared for dinner?"

"Sure, and I'd like some too, if you have enough to spare," Melinia said.

"Of course. I always make enough to feed a small army," Julio laughed. "I'll prepare a plate for you," he said, heading back into the house.

Grandville handed his phone to Melinia and said, "Put your number in here. I'll reach out once I've spoken to Rayshawn."

She nodded, quickly entering her information. "Thanks again, Grandville. Please give my love to Juliette."

"I will. And take care of those boys," Grandville said, standing up and heading toward his car.

He thought about what Melinia had said and resolved to call Rayshawn first thing in the morning. There was a lot they needed to discuss.

Chapter 14

Lights Out

Juliette smiled at her friend on the screen of her phone. She and Samantha hadn't had time to catch up since Greta's wedding fiasco. Life had been chaotic, and their conversations had been reduced to rushed texts or the occasional quick call. Samantha, as Cuyahoga County's top prosecutor, didn't have the luxury of working from home and was tasked with ensuring that her team could work remotely.

"Girl, it's been hell trying to get this system up and running," Samantha said, her expression both frustrated and exhausted

"Why's that?" Juliette asked, idly scrolling through her Facebook timeline as they chatted.

"Because half the legal community is all for virtual hearings, while the other half is adamantly against it," Samantha explained. "Judges think it's harder to determine credibility over a screen versus in person, and I get that. But with this pandemic, virtual is the safest way to go. Surprisingly, more people are showing up for court now—they don't have to take time off work, pay for parking, or deal with the hassle of traveling downtown."

Juliette nodded. "Honestly, I think virtual hearings are a blessing, Sam. All my involuntary commitment hearings have been by Zoom, and it's been a lifesaver. I've been so anxious since the pandemic. I'm worried to death about

Jolene or one of the other children getting it. I'm also nervous about Grandville catching it because Franklin has it, and he's still sick."

Samantha's face softened. "Oh my God, Julie, that's horrible. Considering they share an office, it's a blessing Grandville hasn't caught it. How's Sabrina holding up?"

"She's managing, but barely," Juliette said with a sigh. "Her mother's living with her now. She was in a behavioral health nursing home, but Sabrina was afraid her mother would catch COVID there, especially after Franklin got sick. She's balancing so much right now."

"Do they know where Franklin picked up the virus?" Samantha asked.

"Sabrina thinks it was from the administrator at her mom's facility. Apparently, the woman's mother lived there and passed away from COVID, and Franklin had been meeting with her a lot to arrange for Sabrina's mother to be released."

Samantha shook her head. "That's heartbreaking. Please let me know if there's anything I can do to for them or you. How's Greta?"

"She's okay, I guess. She's been such a huge help with the kids, but … I'm really worried about her. She's been stuck, Sam."

"What do you mean, 'stuck?" Samantha questioned.

"She hasn't left the house much since the wedding. She refuses to speak to Derek. He finally stopped calling because she wouldn't take his calls. It's like she's depressed."

Samantha's tone grew sharp. "Honestly, I don't blame her. What Derek did was unforgivable. As her sorority sisters and her girls, we need to do something to cheer her up."

Juliette perked up. "What do you have in mind?"

"A small outdoor get-together. We can stay socially distanced, and it would be great to see you all in person again. Let's do this for Greta."

"That's a fabulous idea," Juliette agreed. "I'll reserve a pavilion at Euclid Creek and we can coordinate the details with the others."

"Perfect, Julie," Samantha said with an excited grin. "We'll surprise Greta with a get-together in her honor. We'll bring party hats, champagne, and food. Let's celebrate her and remind her that she's still got a lot to look forward to."

"I love it. I'll figure out a date and let you know. Sabrina probably can't come with everything going on, but I'm sure Maria would appreciate the break. That newborn phase is no joke."

"I wouldn't know and thank God I never will," Samantha said, giggling like a little schoolgirl.

"Never say never, Sam."

"Oh, I'm saying it," Samantha teased. "I'll leave the kids to y'all."

"Whatever. So how's Jared holding up during all this?" Juliette smirked.

"He's doing great. He's been working from home, and I've basically moved in with him. It's been … nice," Samantha gushed.

Juliette's eyebrows shot up. "Oh, is that right? Look at you, Sam!"

"Girl, shut up," Samantha laughed.

"No, seriously, that's wonderful. I see a ring in your future. Not a ring pop—a carat," Juliette teased.

"Whatever. We're just having fun right now," Samantha said, rolling her eyes, but her smile gave her away.

Before Juliette could tease her any further, her landline rang. "Hold on Sam," she said, grabbing the receiver. "Hello?"

"Juliette," Sabrina's voice cracked with emotion on the other end, "Franklin's taken a turn for the worse!"

Juliette's heart dropped. "Oh no. Sabrina, I'm so sorry. What happened?"

"I had to rush him to the hospital. His breathing's gotten so bad, they're putting him on a ventilator. I was hoping that Grandville could call him … while he can still talk."

Juliette swallowed the lump forming in her throat. "Of course. He's not home right now, but I'll get in touch with him. Should he call Franklin's cell, or do you have the hospital room number?"

"He has his cell phone, but I'll text you the room number as soon as I get it."

"Okay. Sabrina, hang in there, and please call or text me if you need anything."

"Thank you, Juliette," Sabrina's voice wavered before the line went dead.

Juliette sat still for a moment, gripping the phone tightly. She closed her eyes and whispered a prayer, asking God to spare Franklin's life and that, no matter what happened, Grandville would survive it.

When she picked up her cell phone again, Samantha's face was worried. "Julie, I heard your end," Samantha said. "Call Grandville and let me know if there's anything I can do to help."

Juliette nodded. "I will. Thanks, Sam."

As she ended the call and dialed her husband's number, Juliette realized just how fragile everything felt in her life. This virus was stealing lives, upending families, and testing the limits of faith and resilience. She clung to hope as tightly as she could, praying it would be enough.

Chapter 15

Sad Girlz Luv Money

Melinia sat on her couch, her fingers tracing the fabric as her mind replayed the conversation with Grandville. The weight of her choices lingered, intertwining relief with dread. The ordeal with Lovelle was behind her, yet the lingering shadow of that dark chapter seemed impossible to escape. The tape she made with Rayshawn and Lovelle had once been her desperate attempt to gain leverage, a safety net during a time when her control was fleeting. She knew she owed him money for drugs he had provided, but she assumed that the drugs she used just before their threesome were free. Lovelle later informed her that she owed him for the drugs as well as past debts.

The phone call that started it all was still fresh in her memory. She'd been spiraling, trying to figure out how to get her next fix when Lovelle's number flashed on her throwaway cell phone.

"Hey Melinia, when will you be back in Akron to put something on your debt?" His voice had an edge that immediately made her tense.

"What debt?" she'd snapped. "I thought my performance last week canceled it out."

"Bitch, you must be crazy. I have a thousand hoes who'd line up to kick it with me and my cousin. And since you wanna act fly, now you owe me for the shit you shot last week."

Her rage had been instant, explosive. "You know what, Lovelle? Fuck you! I'm not paying you shit. And if you try me, I'll sell the tape I made with you and your famous cousin to TMZ. Now, I suggest you leave me the fuck alone."

Lovelle was silent for a moment before he spoke again, venom lacing his voice. "Bitch you're as good as dead." Then the line went silent.

That marked the beginning of her hell. After that phone call, Melinia believed she was being followed. Determined to break free from drugs and all the problems they caused her, she checked into rehab. After completing the program, she moved into A Better Tomorrow. But soon after, someone began slipping threatening letters under her door. Lovelle had found her. Fearful that he would act on his promise, she decided it was time to get the hell out of dodge.

Mimi, a friend she'd met at the Collins Rehab facility, had been released before Melinia. They later attended the same Narcotics Anonymous meetings. Afterward, the two would make plans to obtain their favorite blend of heroin, China White. Mimi suggested that they leave with the Sandego Crew for a fresh start and access to China White.

Back in the present, Melinia sighed, pulling herself from the spiral of memories. She never wanted her favorite cousin Juliette to know that she had slept with Rayshawn and had stooped low enough tape it. She had no intention of blackmailing Rayshawn, but she could use the money to put her and her sons in a better position.

She glanced toward the kitchen where Rafael engrossed in a computer game. Jesus stirred in his crib, almost ready for his feeding. As she prepared his bottle, Rafael's innocent voice penetrated her thoughts.

"Mommy, is it true that everyone has a daddy?"

Melinia froze, the bottle trembling in her hands. "What made you ask me that?"

"Elmo said it on the Sesame Street game," he replied with wide eyes full of curiosity.

"Well, yes, everyone has a mommy and a daddy, baby," she said carefully.

"Then where's my daddy? Why don't I ever get to see him?"

Melinia's heart clenched. "Sometimes parents can't be around, sweetie. It's not always because they don't want to be."

"So my daddy can't be here with us?" Rafael asked, his voice tinged with hope.

"That's right," she said softly. "We'll talk more about that later, okay? You're brother's awake. Do you want to help me feed him?"

"Yes, mommy!" Rafael's excitement brought a smile to her face.

Later that evening, after bathing the boys and putting them to bed, Melinia lay awake, haunted by Rafael's question. She knew the day would come when she'd have to tell him the truth, or at least a version of it.

The ringing phone startled her, breaking the heavy silence.

"Hello," she answered cautiously.

All she heard was breathing. Her chest tightened as she quickly disconnected the call and blocked the number. It wasn't the first time she'd received these calls. The heavy breathing, the silence —it was a reminder that even though she'd escaped Lovelle and then the Sandego Crew, she wasn't entirely free.

The phone rang again, this time the caller was private. Hesitantly, she answered. "Hello."

"Hey, cuz. Did I catch you at a bad time?" Juliette's familiar voice brought a wave of relief.

"No, not at all," Melinia replied, her shoulders relaxing slightly. "Your number came up as private. I've been screening my calls lately."

"Girl, I'm sorry about that. The twins were playing with my phone and they must've changed the settings to private," Juliette laughed softly.

"No problem, Jules."

"Melinia, what's wrong?"

"Nothing. Why do you think something's wrong?

"You may have been gone for a long time, but I still know you like the back of my hand. You're my favorite cousin, and I can hear the anxiety in your voice."

Melinia could no longer hold back her tears.

"Hey … Melinia, it's going to be okay," Juliette soothed. "Whatever it is, I'm here for you."

"Jules, I'm scared," Melinia sobbed, "for me, my children, and our safety. I'm worried about our future, or if they'll even be one for us."

Juliette's tone was soothing and steady. "Listen to me. You're safe now. Whatever you're going through, we'll get through it together. You have your boys, and you have us. You're not alone."

Melinia sniffled and took a deep, shaky breath. "Rafael asked about his father today. I don't know what to tell him. Soon I won't be able to avoid the question. And what if telling him the truth makes everything worse?"

"Cuz, I don't mean any disrespect, but do you really know who Rafael's father is?" Juliette asked gently.

Melinia began to cry again, but through her tears, she said, "When I got pregnant with Rafael, I was out of control. But I have a pretty good idea."

"Okay, do you know where he is? And does he know there's a possibility that he's Rafael's father?"

"I know where he is, but I haven't spoken to him since the one time that we were intimate."

"Well, Melinia, I think you should contact him and ask him to submit to a DNA test. Rafael deserves to have a relationship with his father. His father can be a positive influence in his life. Don't keep them apart."

"Thanks, Jules, for the advice," Melinia said, wiping her tears, "but I know you didn't call to counsel me on my problems. What's going on? Is everything okay with Grandville and the kids?"

"Yes, the kids are good, though they're going stir-crazy being stuck in the house so much, particularly Jabari. I was calling because Grandville's best friend has COVID and is really sick. He's being placed on a ventilator. Please pray for him. Prayer changes things."

"I'm so sorry to hear that about Franklin. I promise to pray for him, but I'm sure God doesn't want to hear my prayers after all the dirt I've done," Melinia said.

"God answers prayers no matter what you've done. Melinia, you're not alone. You have God who loves you along with a host of family members who care about you. We're always praying for you. When you were missing, we prayed daily for your safe return. I can testify firsthand that God hears us. We're so proud of how you've gotten yourself and your boys out of captivity. Remember that I'm always here to help or be a listening ear."

"Thanks, Juliette," Melinia said, a hint of joy returning to her voice. "Your words haven't fallen on deaf ears."

After they hung up, Melinia was lying in her bed, with Juliette's words echoing in her ears. Maybe she was right. Maybe she needed to face the past, not just for herself, but for her sons.

As she drifted off to sleep, one decision became clear: when the time was right, she would approach the man she believed to be Rafael's father and ask him to take a DNA test. She just prayed it wouldn't shatter the fragile peace she was trying so hard to rebuild.

Chapter 16

KARMA

Grandville drove towards the hospital as though he were a professional race car driver. His hands gripped the wheel tightly, and his breathing was shallow. The call from Juliette had him reeling; his best friend, fraternity brother, and business partner was fighting for his life.

He took a deep breath and dialed Sabrina's number. The phone barely rang before a frantic voice answered.

"Grandville?"

"Hey, Sabrina, it's me. Juliette told me what's going on. What's Franklin's condition?"

"Grandville, thank God you called. I need you here—now. Franklin's refusing the ventilator. He says he needs to talk to you first."

Grandville's stomach dropped. "What? Why?"

"I'm not in his room right now. There are no visitors on the COVID floor, but some of my friends at the hospital have gotten me in to see him because I'm a doctor. He says it's urgent that he speaks to you. They're worried he'll lose consciousness soon. I've arranged for the nurses to wheel him near a window so you two can talk." Sabrina's voice cracked. "Please hurry."

"I'm on my way. Text me the building and room number," Grandville said, slamming his foot on the gas.

Fifteen minutes later, he skidded into the hospital parking lot, attributing the tightness in his chest as nerves. Pulling on a mask, he ran through the parking lot to find Sabrina. He spotted her standing in front of the building.

"Sabrina!" Grandville called as he sprinted over. "I got here as fast as I could."

She turned, her mask unable to hide the strain on her face. "He's right there." She pointed toward a second-story window. "The nurse is positioning him now. I'll give you two privacy. Thanks again, Grandville." She brushed his arm briefly before leaving.

Grandville stared at the window and Franklin appeared moments later. Even from the ground level, Grandville was stunned by his friend's appearance. He was slumped in the wheelchair, pale and gaunt, his chest heaving with labored breaths. His eyes, once vibrant, seemed dulled by exhaustion.

"Frat," Grandville's voice cracked with emotion as tears welled in his eyes, "what's this I'm hearing about you refusing medical care? I need you, man! Your friendship and counsel mean everything to me. Tell me what's on your mind so you can get on this ventilator."

Franklin lifted a trembling hand to the window, pressing his palm against it. He slowly shook his head. "Frat … " His voice was weak, each word a struggle. "It's too late for me."

"No, it's not Grandville said firmly. "You're gonna get through this. Let them help you. Please."

Franklin's thin frame quivered with effort when he said, "Karma's real. It's time to collect." He broke into an uncontrollable fit of coughing.

"Karma? What the hell are you talking about, Frankie?"

Franklin's chest shuddered as he tried to steady his breathing. "I need you to take care of some business for me. I set up a trust leaving my half of our business, my house, and all the money in my personal accounts to you. I planned to include Sabrina closer to our wedding, but now, I don't think I'll get the chance." He paused as another coughing fit assailed him. When it finally ceased, Franklin resumed speaking, albeit with labored breath. "Please provide Sabrina with a monthly allowance. She won't accept it from you, so you'll need to be clever about it."

"You can do all that yourself, once you're better. You're not dying today, Franklin," Grandville said, tears stinging his eyes.

Franklin's voice dropped and Grandville strained to make out his next words. "I'm not gonna make it, frat. There's something I need your forgiveness for."

"Forgiveness for what?"

Franklin hesitated, his gaze dropping. "I love you, bro. Please forgive me and Juliette."

Grandville froze, the words hitting him like a blow to the chest. "What are you talking about?"

Before Franklin could respond, another coughing fit overtook him. He began gasping for air. Grandville saw the panic in his widened eyes as he clutched at his heaving chest. Then Franklin collapsed, falling out of sight.

"Frankie!" Grandville screamed. His heart raced as a group of nurses rushed into the room the help his attending nurse. He fumbled for his phone and redialed Sabrina. She answered on the first ring.

"Hey Grandville. Are y'all done talking?"

"Sabrina! Franklin collapsed! Get to him now!"

Sabrina shrieked before the line went dead.

Grandville stayed rooted to the spot, his body trembling as he whispered desperate prayers between ragged breaths.

Time stood still as he attempted to process Franklin's message about karma and forgiveness. Sabrina's voice soon interrupted his thoughts. "Grandville, come on, get up," she said. Her face was lined with worry, but her voice still held a sliver of hope. "They got him on the ventilator. You may have just saved his life by coming here."

"Oh, thank God," Grandville sighed in relief. He shook his head and tears streamed down his face.

They shared a tight embrace and Grandville released all the tension and anxiety onto her. Sabrina pulled away, offering him a reassuring smile. "Go home, Grandville. You've done all you can for now. I'll keep you updated, okay?"

"Thanks, Sabrina," Grandville murmured.

Sitting in his car, Grandville attempted to decipher Franklin's cryptic message while ghostly voices competed with his thoughts. He decided to go into his office to gather himself before going home, as he didn't want to concern Juliette or his children. It had been quite a while since he'd experienced symptoms associated with his mental illness, but extreme stress triggered the voices sometimes. He was afraid and didn't want to lose control. But the thought of losing his best friend was terrifying.

When Grandville unlocked his office, his mind wa s a blur. The office was dark except for the light streaming in through the windows. Why had Franklin asked him to forgive him and Juliette? What if Franklin died before he could get the answer?

He jumped when a familiar voice interrupted his thoughts.

"Grandville, I was wondering when you would get here," George said, sitting in the shadows.

"George? Why are you here in the dark? I just came from seeing Franklin and he's not doing well. You can take the rest of the week off, paid."

Grandville turned on the lights and when his eyes adjusted, he noticed that George's face was streaked with tears, and a mask covered his mouth and nose.

"George, there's little else we can do besides pray and hope that the medical staff can help Franklin. He's a strong dude. He'll pull through," Grandville placed a hand on his shoulder.

George sniffled and wiped his face clear of tears. "Cora's in the hospital. Her mother was afraid I'd give her COVID. But then I find out she let her go out with some other asshole who really did give it to her. I don't blame her mother for not wanting me around her daughter. I'm damaged."

"George, why would you say that? You're not damaged. And if Cora and her mother can't see that, then it's their loss."

"Really? Well, if that's true, why did you give me away?" George's lips twisted in a bitter smile.

The question knocked the breath out of Grandville. Before he could respond George raised a gun, pointing it at him.

Chapter 17

Believe

Juliette had got off the phone with Melinia. Hearing her favorite cousin cry broke her heart, but Juliette was prioritizing keeping her own mental health in check. Greta had left to run an errand and her children were outside playing. She realized that this was the first time in months that she was completely alone in her home, yet the stillness felt oppressive.

She sat on her loveseat out on the sun porch and enjoyed the view of their spacious backyard for a moment before she placed her head in her hands, trying to center herself. Her thoughts spun as fear gripped her. What if Franklin didn't make it? What would that do to Grandville? She began her deep breathing exercises, forcing herself to inhale and exhale slowly. The rhythm started to calm her, but her peace was soon disturbed when her name rang out from the other side of the porch door.

"Mom, why aren't you answering your phone? I've been trying to call you!" Jabari's irritation was evident in his voice.

Juliette looked up to see her son standing with a tall, light-skinned boy she didn't recognize. Despite the boy's mask, his freckles, green eyes, and almost blond hair stood out.

"Boy, have you lost your mind? We can't have company in the house. You're putting us all at risk," Juliette snapped, her voice sharp with anger.

"Mom, I tried to call you and you didn't answer, so don't blame me," Jabari shot back, almost earning him a slap on the face.

"Don't get smart with me! You and your friend need to leave this house before it gets ugly in here. What exactly do you think you're doing?"

"It's an emergency, Mom. Blake, tell her what you just told me outside," Jabari said, his tone pleading.

"No, I think I should just go home," Blake muttered, looking uneasy.

Jabari balled his fists and squared his shoulders. "Mom, you've always said I can come to you when something's wrong, but this is how you act when I do?"

Juliette closed her eyes and inhaled deeply. He's right. "Okay, you have a point, Jabari. What is it?"

Jabari turned to Blake, his tone gentler. "I swear, my mom is cool. Just tell her what you told me."

Blake hesitated, his voice quivering as he finally spoke. "It's my brother, Mrs. Stubbs. He said he's going to kill himself."

Juliette's eyes widened as her heart sank. "Oh my God. How old is he, and what's his name?"

"Ben, and he's eleven," Blake said, his tears threatening to spill.

"Alright. Is your mother aware of this?"

"Yes, Mrs. Stubbs. I told her, but she's busy working. It's my job to watch him when she's at work, but I can't be with him every minute of the day," Blake explained, his voice cracking.

Juliette clasped her hands and brought them up to her lips. "Hey, it's not your fault. You seem like a good big brother, Blake, and you did the right thing by telling Jabari. Where's your brother now?"

"He's at his dad's house, but he'll be back tomorrow. That's why I'm playing basketball with Jabari today."

"Where do you live?"

"A couple of blocks away. We moved here to Willoughby Hills right when the pandemic began," Blake said.

Juliette's voice softened. "Okay, I need to speak to your mother, and together we'll get your brother the help he needs. Can I give you my number to give to your mom?"

Blake hesitated. "I'm scared she'll get upset with me. She doesn't like me talking about our family business."

Juliette placed a comforting hand on his shoulder. She now realized that she needed to take the reins and contact the boys' mother herself. "Blake, I know you're scared, but imagine how your mother would feel if Ben followed through on his threats. Give me your mother's number, and I'll talk with her."

Blake nodded, but his eyes still held fear and worry as he recited his mother's name and number for Juliette.

"Okay, Jabari grab some cold drinks for you and Blake and head back outside. I'll be out as soon as I speak with Ms. Palmerston."

Jabari and Blake headed towards the kitchen, while Juliette gathered her thoughts. Four out of five suicides are preceded by threats. The pandemic had only worsened mental health struggles, and she knew the statistics were rising. She picked up the phone, attempting to steady her fingers as she dialed Bonita's number. After three rings, a voice answered.

"Hello."

"Hello, this is Juliette Stubbs, Jabari's mom. May I please speak to Bonita?"

"This is she. What's Blake done now?" Bonita asked, her tone sharp.

"Blake hasn't done anything wrong. In fact, he's friends with my son Jabari and he seems like a great kid," Juliette explained.

"That's nice. I only have a few minutes. I'm in the car on my way to my second job."

"I'm calling about your other son, Ben," Juliette said with caution.

"What? How do you even know Ben? Blake's not allowed to take him out of the house," Bonita demanded.

"I haven't met him, but Blake has confided in Jabari that Ben has made threats to harm himself. As a licensed mental health professional, I wanted to make sure Ben is getting the support he needs."

"That boy talks too damn much," Bonita hissed. "I told him not to discuss our business. Next thing you know, the white people will be at my door."

"I don't think Blake meant to share your family business. He's just scared for his brother. I feel like, as mothers of young black boys, we need to stick together. And because this is a delicate matter, as a mandated reporter, I need to ensure Ben's safety. I'm going to have to make a report to the Department of Children and Family Services unless you can assure me that Ben is receiving the assistance he needs. Otherwise, I can refer you to excellent children's therapists."

"Ms. Stubbs, I appreciate your concern, but Ben's fine. I'll take care of it," Bonita said curtly.

"Is Ben currently receiving professional help?"

"No disrespect, but that's none of your business," Bonita replied. "I said I'll take care of it. I really appreciate your concern, but I'm at work now and I have to go."

Juliette started to respond, but the line went dead. She sat back, staring at the phone, frustration and helplessness washing over her.

"Hey, Juliette. I need to talk to you," Greta's voice startled her.

Juliette turned to see Greta standing behind her. “I need to talk to you too. Sit down and take a load off.”

Greta hesitated before blurting out, “Juliette, I hope you meant what you said about mothers sticking together is true, because I’m going to need that.”

“I’m sorry, but I don’t get it,” Juliette said with a puzzled look.

“I’m pregnant. My wish is finally coming true—I’m going to be a mother.” Speechless, Juliette stared into her sister-in-law’s eyes, which overflowed with tears of joy.

Chapter 18

All Mine

Melinia gripped the one-year coin in her palm, the smooth metal felt warm from her grip. Her fellow group members had cheered her on for her one year of sobriety from heroin during the Narcotics Anonymous Zoom meeting, but now, in the quiet of her living room, doubt crept in like a shadow.

It was the first time she'd reached such a milestone, and though she was proud, she knew she could be tricked by the enemy into believing she could handle using again. She had seen too many people fall after believing they'd won. Her disease was cunning, and she couldn't let her guard down.

Her thoughts drifted to the hang-up calls that had become a daily torment. Each one left her feeling as if unseen eyes were watching, waiting. She hoped whoever was behind them would soon give up. She also found herself thinking of Mimi, her friend from rehab. Wherever Mimi was, Melinia prayed she was safe, no longer using drugs, and far from the hell they had once endured together. Her thoughts were interrupted by the ringing of her phone. She glanced at the screen and saw Julio's name.

"Hey Julio."

"Hello, Chica. I wanted to be one of the first to congratulate you on receiving your one-year coin. I'm proud of you. You're kicking addiction right in the behind and inspiring us all."

"Thanks, Julio. I'm taking the advice of my sponsor and Ms. Zenobia, my counselor. One day at a time."

"I need a favor," Julio said, his tone teasing.

"Okay, what is it?"

"Buzz me in. I'm outside your building."

Surprised, she ran to the window and saw him standing on the sidewalk, holding a box. She hit the buzzer and waited by the door.

When Julio stepped into her living room, he handed her the box with a grin. "Open it."

Inside was a small cake beautifully decorated with the word "Congratulations" piped in delicate frosting.

"Julio, thank you, but you didn't have to do this," Melinia chastised. "You should save your money for your family."

"I didn't spend much because I made it. The main ingredient is love."

Melinia laughed despite herself. "This cake looks fantastic, Julio. It looks like it was professionally made."

Smiling, Julio nodded in gratitude. "I followed a recipe from a show called Cake Boss. The question is, how does it taste?"

"I'm sure it's great," Melinia replied.

"Well, there's only one way to find out," Julio said as he headed toward the kitchen, returning with plates and forks. "Where's Rafael? He's not going to want to miss this."

"He's in his room on his iPad. Jesus is taking a nap."

Julio disappeared into Rafael's room and returned with the boy, whose face lit up at the sight of him. His arms were wrapped around him in a bear hug.

"Now, do us the honor of cutting your cake," Julio said.

"Julio, it's not my birthday. You can cut the cake," Melinia laughed.

Rafael tugged on Julio's shirt, capturing his attention. With large, bright eyes, he asked innocently. "Julio, are you my father?"

A gasp parted Melinia's lips as the weighty question hung over the room like a heavy fog. Before she could interject, Julio knelt in front of Rafael and gently ruffled his hair. "Rafael, I'm not your father, but I'd like to be —if your mother will have me. If she does, I promise to be the best father you and your little brother could ever have."

"Julio, what are you doing?" Melinia asked, her voice sharp.

"I'm telling Rafael the truth," Julio said, standing. "You wanted to wait a year after becoming sober before starting a relationship. Well, that's today. I love you and the boys, and I want us to be a family."

Rafael looked up between the two of them as the silence lingered for a few moments.

After staring at Julio, stunned, Melinia said, "I don't know what to say. I love you too, but I'm still have to work on myself. I'm also still processing everything that's happened."

"Why don't we get Jesus up and fed? I can help you get the boys down for bed so we can talk," Julio suggested calmly. Melinia was stunned by his nonchalant demeanor.

"Okay … but I'm not sure I have much more to say about it," Melinia said.

"That's okay. I can do all the talking," Julio grinned at her.

"Don't you have to get back to the rooming house to cook dinner?" Melinia asked, desperately trying to find a reason to avoid having the conversation about their relationship.

Julio shook his head. "Joe bought pizza and I have the evening off."

Melinia heard Jesus stirring, so she proceeded to warm the milk for his bottle. When she headed towards her bedroom, she heard Julio say, "Rafael and I are going to cook dinner," while opening her refrigerator.

While Melinia fed her infant son, she heard Julio and Rafael laughing and speaking in Spanish. She was amazed at how quickly her son was learning the language.

Jesus was a beautiful child and as she looked at him happily drinking from the bottle, she saw the same features as Remy, his biological father. After she burped and changed Jesus, she carried him into the living room and sat on the couch. The smell of garlic and onions wafted through the air, instantly making her hungry.

Before long Rafael came out to announce, "Mom, dinner is ready, and Julio said to bring the baby into the kitchen so we can eat."

When she walked into the kitchen she couldn't believe her eyes. On the set table was salmon croquettes, rice, and peas.

Melinia smiled as she placed Jesus in his high chair.

"Come on and have a seat, Chica. This is your day," Julio said, pulling out a chair for her.

Julio said grace before they dug in. The food was delicious, and Melinia enjoyed watching Rafael make faces at his little brother while eating. Jesus burst into adorable baby chuckles, kicking his chubby little legs. Since she'd missed most of Rafael's infancy, she savored every precious moment of Jesus' early months.

Julio ate quietly, and when he finished, he looked at Melinia and said, "It's moments like this that make life worth living. Melinia, I need you and your sons because you are a part of me. I promise to be a good husband and provide for you and your sons. Please consider my offer. Be all mine."

"I love you, Julio, and I don't doubt that you'll be an excellent partner and father figure for my sons. But I don't know if I'll ever be ready for a relationship. I need to get the boys their baths and get them down to bed."

Julio jumped up, and started running water in the sink. "Go ahead and get the boys ready for bed. I've got the dishes."

After putting the boys down, she sat on the couch with Julio, who had turned on the television.

"Julio, thanks so much for surprising me with my cake and for making dinner," Melinia said.

"You're very welcome. I'm proud of you and I believe you are the woman for me. No matter how long it takes, I'll wait. Take your time," Julio said kissing her cheek.

Later that night, after Julio left, Melinia lay in bed, her mind racing. Although she genuinely cared for him, she realized she wouldn't be able to accept Julio's advances until she got over Remy. She hated herself for loving Remy and knew that even though her body had been freed, her heart and mind were trapped in captivity. She vowed to do whatever it took to break the emotional chains keeping her bound to a man she knew was no good for her.

As tears slid down her cheeks, she realized that she couldn't let her past dictate her future. For her sons, for herself, and maybe even for Julio, she needed to find a way to truly let go.

Chapter 19

Save Me From Myself

Grandville stared at the gun George had pointed at him, swallowing hard as the gravity of the situation sank in. For just a brief moment, he doubted the reality of what was happening, but the cold steel in George's trembling hand brought him right back into focus. The voices in his head surged, competing with the fear tightening his chest. Grandville pushed down his fears and willed himself to focus on George.

"Son, you need to put that gun down," Grandville said, raising his hands slowly. His voice was calm, but inside, panic churned. "Whatever's bothering you, we can talk about it."

"We'll talk," George said, his voice tense and uneven, "but not here. Turn off your phone and put it on the desk along with your car keys. Do it now!"

Grandville hesitated but complied, turning off his phone and setting it, along with his keys, on his desk. "Where are we going?"

"Don't worry about it. Just start walking," George said, motioning with the gun.

Grandville slowly headed towards the door, careful not to do anything that would set George off. George was following close behind. His heart hammered in his chest, and he fought to maintain composure. When they reached the building's rear exit, George gestured for Grandville to lock the office door. "Don't want anyone breaking in while we're gone," he said, his tone laced with irony.

Grandville locked the door and walked out to the back parking lot, which was dimly lit with no security cameras. George's older red Honda Civic sat nearby. He clicked the remote to unlock it and motioned for Grandville to get in the driver's seat. George slid into the backseat, keeping the gun trained on him.

"You're driving," George commanded, "and you better not even think about pulling anything. I have nothing to lose."

Grandville started the car, and as he adjusted the seat, he suddenly thought about his beloved Juliette. Would he ever see her or his children again? The voices in his mind threatened to overtake him, and he struggled to stay calm and not lose control.

"C'mon, George. You don't have to do any of this," Grandville pleaded. "We can talk about whatever has you this upset."

"That's exactly what we're about to do. We're going to talk, and you're going to tell

me everything I need to know. Or I'm going to put a bullet right between your eyes, then kill myself. What reason do I have to be here?"

"Son, you have every reason to be here. Your future is bright, but you're destroying

it by behaving this way. You don't have to hold a gun on me to get me to talk to you. We can have a civil conversation. "

"Look, I don't care about your problems. All I care about is the truth. And, this is the second time you referred to me as son. You haven't earned that right, so stop calling me that," George growled. "Now just shut up."

Grandville maneuvered the downtown Cleveland streets with his thoughts all over the place. He knew this day would come, but he never envisioned the revelation would occur this way.

George's words brought him back to reality. "Take a left, we're getting on I-77 South headed towards Akron."

"Where are we going?" Grandville asked.

"The only thing you need to worry about is following my directions so you can make it back to your wife and real kids."

"George, Juliette's expecting me home. If I don't call, she's going to know something's wrong," Grandville said as he looked at George through the rear-view mirror.

"I don't care. We're going to do it my way. Now, this is my last time telling you to shut up and drive," George directed as he kept the gun aimed at Grandville.

As he pulled onto I-77 South, Grandville realized that apart from the day when he accidentally took his daughter Jessica's life, this was by far one of the worst days he'd ever experienced. His best friend was lying in the hospital dying, and he was being held at gunpoint by the son that he only recently found out about. As he drove, he prayed for God to help him explain the unexplainable to his oldest son. He prayed that they would make it through to the other side and that he would still have his wife, his family and his life.

"Take I-480 East," George directed.

The drive stretched in silence, tension filling the car like a thick fog. Soon, he was pulling in front of a condominium unit with an attached garage. The garage door immediately opened and George motioned for him to pull in..

"Park and get out," George commanded.

Grandville obeyed and George pressed the hard steel of the gun against his back. The garage door closed behind them, sealing them inside. Leading them into the condo, Grandville noticed the elegant décor—beige walls, carpeting, and sleek black furniture. They walked into a bedroom at the back of the unit.

"Pick up the handcuffs and put them on," George demanded, waving the gun towards the nightstand.

Grandville hesitated. "George, this isn't necessary. Why do you feel the need to handcuff me?"

"I got a little freak in me," George deadpanned. "That's not your concern! Just do what the hell I told you to do, or I'll kill you where you stand and bury you where no one will ever find you." George threatened, his voice laced with cold venom.

Reluctantly, Grandville secured the cuffs around his wrists.

"Now open the closet," George instructed, waving his gun hurriedly.

Grandville obeyed, pulling open the door to reveal a walk-in closet converted into a small office. Foam padding lined the walls, and a desk and chair occupied the center. A small couch sat against the back wall, and a faint disinfectant smell lingered in the air.

"Get in," George ordered, motioning with the gun again.

"George, this is extreme. You don't have to hold me hostage to get the answers you want," Grandville said.

"Extreme times call for extreme measures," George said. "Sit down. Get comfortable. You're going to be here for a while."

George locked the closet door, leaving Grandville alone in the padded room. The muffled sound of his footsteps faded, leaving only the pounding of Grandville's heart and the whispered cacophony of voices in his head.

Grandville leaned back against the chair, closing his eyes and drawing in deep breaths. He didn't know how long he'd be trapped or how this would end, but one thing was clear—he needed to survive, not just for himself but for Juliette, for his family, and for the chance to make things right with George.

Silently, he prayed for strength, for wisdom, and for a way out of the nightmare unfolding around him.

Chapter 20

Gotta Move On

Juliette blinked, convinced she must have misheard. "Wait, did you say you're pregnant?"

"You heard me right. I'm six weeks along," Greta beamed with a twinkle in the hazel eyes she shared with her twin brother.

Juliette tilted her head, trying to process the unexpected news. "But … I thought you and Derek weren't even speaking."

"We're not." Greta's grin widened.

"Okay, so who's your baby daddy?" Juliette asked jokingly.

Greta sat on the couch, took a deep breath, and began explaining. "Sis, you and Grandville have been so good to me. Letting me stay here has been a godsend. If I'd been alone during this pandemic, I don't know what I would've done."

"You don't have to thank us. Having you here has been a blessing for us too. The kids adore you, and you've been such a huge help," Juliette said.

"Being here with you all has made me realize just how much I want kids of my own. So, I decided to stop waiting for the perfect time or the perfect partner. I'm doing this on my own."

Juliette's brow furrowed. "I'm sorry, I'm still confused, Greta. How are you pregnant? Did you … meet someone?"

"Nope," Greta said, shaking her head with a big smile. "I used IVF."

"IVF?" Juliette's voice trailed off, her mind racing.

Greta nodded. "When Rayshawn and I were married, we weren't ready for kids, but I didn't want my biological clock to run out. So we went through fertility treatments and froze eight embryos. When we got divorced, my attorney made sure the embryos were awarded to me. they've been stored in California all these years. So, I've finally decided to use one."

"Do you plan to tell Rayshawn?" Juliette asked.

"No. Legally the child is mine. The divorce agreement severed his rights to any potential children."

Juliette's expression softened. "I'm trying to understand, Greta. I support your choice, but morally, don't you think your child deserves to know their father?"

Greta's smile slipped. "Grandville and I grew up without a father, and we turned out okay,"

"Everyone has a father," Juliette countered gently. "Sis, I'm here for you, but you just need to be prepared for the day when your child asks about their father. At some point, you might need to tell Rayshawn."

Greta sighed. "I'll cross that bridge when I get there. Right now, my goal is to bring this baby into the world. I'm past forty, Juliette. My window's closing fast."

"Fair enough," Juliette stood and gave her sister-in-law a big hug. "You know you're welcome to stay here as long as you need. And I'll throw you the best baby shower ever."

"Thank you. That means so much," Greta said, her voice trembling with emotion. "But let's keep this between us for now. I don't want to share the news until I'm at least sixteen weeks."

"Of course. Have you told Grandville yet?"

"Not yet, but I'd like to. Where is he, by the way?"

Juliette glanced at her watched. A frown crept onto her face. " He went to see Franklin. Sabrina called and said Franklin needed to go on a ventilator but was refusing until he spoke to Grandville."

"Oh no, I hope Franklin pulls through," Greta said, covering her heart with

her hand. "That's so serious. I can't believe they'd let Grandville see him, given all the COVID restrictions."

"They didn't." Juliette said. "Sabrina arranged for Grandville to speak to him through the window. I'm worried about how this will affect Grandville if Franklin doesn't make it. I've asked everyone to pray for Franklin."

"That's good. When do you think Grandville will be home?"

"I'm not sure." Juliette reached for her phone. "I'll call and find out." The call went directly to voicemail.

"He didn't pick up?" Greta asked, catching Juliette's expression.

"Straight to voicemail." Juliette sighed, her face tinged with worry.

"Maybe he's at the hospital with Franklin. Sabrina may have been able to pull some strings since she works there," Greta said.

Juliette nodded, forcing a smile. "Yes, that could be it. I'll try again later."

Greta stood. "I'll start dinner."

Juliette reached out to stop her. "Hold up, little mama. You need to rest. I'll handle dinner."

Greta laughed. "I'm pregnant, not an invalid. Let me do my part while I still can."

Before Juliette could respond, she was off to the kitchen. Then the home phone rang. She answered, hoping it was Grandville returning her call.

"Hello," Juliette said.

"Ms. Stubbs? This is Bonita. We spoke earlier about my son Ben."

"Yes, is everything okay?"

Bonita's voice cracked No. But I called to thank you. After we spoke, I contacted Ben's father and asked him to check on him. He found him unresponsive in his room. He … he'd taken a bottle of aspirin. If you hadn't reached out to me, my son might not be alive."

Juliette was trapped in shock for a moment as Bonita began to cry. "Oh, Bonita, I'm so sorry. How is he now?"

"He's in the hospital and will be transferred to the psychiatric ward once he's stable."

"I'm so glad he's okay. But, Bonita, do you know how to get the support you need through all of this? There are support groups that really help. I've personally been through National Alliance on Mental Illness' Family to Family program and can personally attest to how it's helped me."

"I'll look into it. Thanks, Juliette," Bonita said.

"Bonita, you're a great mom. You saved your son. He's still here with us."

"Yes, and I'm so grateful," Bonita said when Juliette's cell phone rang. Juliette looked and saw it was Sabrina.

"Bonita, thanks for updating me on Ben's status. Please don't hesitate to call if you need me. But I have to take this incoming call," Juliette said.

"Okay, and thanks again," Bonita said before hanging up.

"Hey, Sabrina," Juliette answered her cell.

"Hey, Juliette. I'm trying to reach Grandville, but his phone is going directly to voicemail."

"He's not here. I thought he might still be at the hospital."

"He left here hours ago."

Juliette's chest tightened. She sensed something was wrong, given Sabrina's no-nonsense

tone. "Is Franklin okay, Sabrina?"

The silence stretched unbearably before Juliette heard muted sobs on Sabrina's end. "Franklin ... he's in a coma."

Juliette closed her eyes, her world spinning. She whispered a prayer for him and braced herself for the storm that might come if Grandville couldn't handle the weight of it all.

Chapter 21

The Way

Melinia scrubbed the countertops vigorously, trying to push away the disturbing dream she had the night before. In it, she was surrounded by piles of China White, the air thick with the promise of a fix. She saw herself trembling and desperate, plunging the needle into her vein, resulting in a relapse. The sensation felt so real that she woke up drenched in sweat, the phantom pinch of the needle still vivid on her skin.

Shaken, she called Ms. Zenobia. The phone rang five times, and just when Melinia thought it would go to voicemail, a gravelly, yet comforting voice said, "Hello."

"Hi, Ms. Zenobia. Do you have a few minutes?" Melinia asked, her voice immediately betraying her anxiety.

"Of course. How are you on this beautiful morning?" Ms. Zenobia's tone was warm and steadying.

Melinia exhaled. "Honestly, I'm not doing the best today. Last night, I had a really disturbing dream."

"Alright, tell me about it," Zenobia encouraged her.

"I dreamt that I was in a room full of heroin. I couldn't stop myself—I relapsed. It felt so real, like I was actually using again."

"Ah, a relapse dream," Zenobia said knowingly. "It's not uncommon. I've had a few myself, even after years of sobriety."

"Really? Well, how do you deal with them?"

"First, you have to remember it's just a dream," Zenobia explained. "Relapse dreams are part of the healing and recovery process. They don't mean you've failed; they can actually be a sign that you're becoming stable and stronger. Your brain is still processing some of your old fears or anxieties. The key to working through these dreams is to identify the source of your anxiety, as it often contributes to them."

Melinia sighed in relief. "That makes a lot of sense. Thank you, Ms. Zenobia."

"Sure. That's what I'm here for. So, you just celebrated your first year of sobriety.

How are you feeling about it?"

"I'm scared. I've never reached this level of sobriety before. If I relapse, it'll all be for nothing. And then there's my boys … I can't do anything to risk losing them."

"It's good you're being honest about your fears, Melinia," Zenobia said. "But remember,

it was just a dream, not a prediction. You haven't relapsed. Focus on today. Pray, meditate, and use your support system. That's what we're here for. Now, I have got a feeling that you're experiencing anxiety for another reason. Do you feel comfortable sharing that with me?"

Melinia hesitated before confirming her suspicion. "Yes, it's about Julio, the guy who helped me escape captivity."

"Yes, you brought him up in a previous session."

"He wants to be in a romantic relationship with me," Melinia confessed. "He even baked a cake to celebrate my first year of sobriety. He's so adamant about wanting us to be a family."

"How do you feel about him?" Ms. Zenobia probed gently.

Melinia shook her head. She'd been trying to avoid this question because she was afraid of

what would happen if she forced herself to answer it honestly. "I don't know. He's my best friend, the only person in my life who understands what I've been through. But …" She paused, struggling to find her next words. "Although he knows a lot about my past, he doesn't know *everything* about me. If he did, I don't know if he'd feel the same way."

"You mean your past, before the Sandego Crew?"

"Yes," she whispered. "The things I did to get my fix … aren't easy to talk about. How could he love me if he knew the whole truth?"

"He might surprise you. Real love isn't conditional. But you're deflecting, Melinia," Ms. Zenobia chastised. A slight pause of silence filled the line as Melinia's heart swelled with anxiety for the inevitable question she knew she would be forced to answer. "How do you feel about him?"

Tears pricked her eyes. "I… I don't know how I feel. I'm confused."

Zenobia's voice softened. "That's understandable. Maybe you should ask Julio to attend a Nar-Anon meeting."

"Narcotics Anonymous or Alcoholics Anonymous?"

"No, it's actually a separate group for people whose lives were impacted by a loved one's addiction. It could help Julio to support you in your recovery without impeding your progress."

"I'll share the information with him," Melinia said cautiously. "But he's so busy managing my cousin's rooming house… I'm not sure he'd have time."

"If he truly cares for you, he'll make time," Zenobia said. "Give him the chance to decide for himself."

Before Melinia could respond, her phone beeped with an incoming call. She glanced at the screen. It was a private number.

"Zenobia, I've got another call coming in. Can I call you back if I need to?"

"Of course. Take care of yourself."

Switching to the incoming call, Melinia's voice was cautious. "Hello?"

"Ms. Melinia Gatlin?" a man's deep voice inquired.

"Who's calling?"

"This is Zach Jordan. I represent Mr. Rayshawn Robinson."

"Yes, this is Melinia. What's this about?"

"Mr. Robinson would like to meet with you."

Melinia swallowed hard, then found her voice. "Why?"

"Mr. Robinson will be in Cleveland tomorrow for a private event. He was hoping you could join him for lunch."

"Sure. That should work."

"Great. Also, Mr. Robinson would like you to bring your sons. He's very eager to meet them," Mr. Jordan said.

"I can do that."

"Good. I'll follow up later today with the time and location."

"Alright," she managed to say before hanging up.

Her hands shook as she set the phone down. She was scared, excited, and a little conflicted as she realized that tomorrow might bring the closure she'd been looking for.

Chapter 22

No Lie

Grandville stared at the soundproof walls that imprisoned him, his wrists aching from the cuffs. The discomfort tethered him to reality, a cruel reminder that this nightmare was no delusion. He racked his brain, searching for a way out, but every plan seemed impossible under George's watchful, volatile presence.

He had no idea how long he had been in the closet, but his exhaustion and rising panic caused him to close his eyes. He began deep breathing, and soon the voices competing for control of

his mind ceased. He hated that George was so tormented that he felt it necessary to go

to such extremes, and Grandville worried that George might do something stupid, like

hurt him or even himself.

Suddenly, the closet door opened, and George entered with a tray of food.

"I brought you some food," George said, his voice a mix of bitterness and forced calm. "If you're smart, you'll eat. Don't make me regret being nice."

Grandville sat up straighter, eyeing the tray warily. "How am I supposed to eat in handcuffs?"

George smirked, his eyes narrowing. "Don't worry. I'll feed you—like you should've fed me when I was a baby."

"Fair enough," Grandville said, his tone even. "But you first. Prove it's not poisoned."

George obliged, scooping a bit onto a spoon and eating it theatrically. "Delicious. See? No poison. Your turn" George took a separate spoon and dipped it into the food. Grandville hesitated, then leaned forward to receive it. The first taste surprised him. The rich, savory flavors spread across his tongue, and for a moment, he forgot the dire circumstances. He had barely eaten all day.

Grandville chewed the meat, realizing it was beef stew—even better than Juliette's, who was a pretty damn good cook.

"Damn," he said, swallowing. "This is on point. Where'd you get it?"

"I made it," George said, beaming with pride.

"You're lying. This is the best beef stew I've had except for my mother's. Restaurant quality."

George shrugged. "Believe what you want. I was planning to share it with Cora. But that won't be happening, not now, thanks to her mother."

"Why not take it into the hospital? The nurses can make sure she gets it," Grandville suggested, carefully probing for a connection.

George's face hardened. "Corrine wouldn't let that happen. That woman hates me."

"I doubt that. She's just protective of her daughter," Grandville replied, angling for calm. "You should try. If you don't, you'll never know. But let me get some more of the stew."

George complied and fed him another spoonful. Grandville savored the taste as he slowly chewed while George stared at him. His silence filled the room, and the flavors of the delicious stew were now muted by the change in his mood.

"You know," George said between clenched teeth, "the very first time I met you, I was amazed by how much we looked alike. I even joked to myself that we were related. But

never in a million years would I have guessed that you were my biological father. Or that I'd find out the way I did."

Grandville exhaled slowly, his chest tightening. "George, I didn't —"

"Now, " George continued as if Grandville never said a word, "you can get an over-the-counter home DNA test and easily learn who your relatives are, even the ones who gave you away."

Grandville sighed, realizing that what he said next would mean everything.

"George, when I first met you, I had no idea you were my son. I found out recently."

George's eyes narrowed, but Grandville detected a hint of sadness. "And you just kept it to yourself? What, were you ashamed of me?"

"Never," Grandville said firmly. "I'm proud to call you my boy. I didn't tell you because I didn't know how. I was trying to figure out the right approach."

George looked away, his expression conflicted, the hardness cracking to reveal something raw underneath. "Well, you'd better find the words," he muttered. "Because before you leave here, I want the truth. All of it."

Grandville nodded, his appetite vanishing as the heavy silence stretched between them. His mind churned with memories, pain, and regrets, along with the weight of the secret he wasn't sure he could share.

"Yeah," he finally said, his voice hoarse, "I know. That's what I was afraid of."

Chapter 23

Wrecked

Juliette paced her bedroom floor, clutching her phone as though it could somehow summon Grandville home. Her anxiety wrapped around her chest like a vice, squeezing tighter with each unanswered call. She was doing everything in her power to stave off a panic attack. Grandville never went AWOL like this. He always let her know where he was, even when he needed space.

She didn't want to upset the kids or Greta, so she did her best to act normally, but

inside, she was unraveling. Sabrina's news about Franklin collapsing haunted her, and her mind cycled through worst-case scenarios. What had Franklin told Grandville? Could it have been about the secret Juliette had buried deep, the one she prayed would never come to light?

Her frantic thoughts were interrupted by a faint knock at her door.

"Mommy?" Jolene's small voice called from the other side. Juliette opened the door to find Jolene standing there, her dark curls messy, her big watery eyes looking up at her.

"Hey sweetie, what's wrong?" Juliette asked.

"My head hurts," Jolene whined, leaning into her mother's arms.

Juliette swept her up and carried her to the bed. "Let's get your temperature, baby." After retrieving the thermometer from the attached bathroom, she tucked it under Jolene's tongue. After a few moments, the reading flashed. She had a slight fever. Juliette grabbed the Children's Tylenol, a folic acid supplement, and a bottle of water from her mini fridge.

"Here you go. Open wide," Juliette said, placing the pills in Jolene's mouth.

Jolene wrinkled her nose but swallowed them with a big gulp of water. "Mommy, why do I always have to take these nasty pills every day?"

"You need them to stay strong, baby. The folic acid is a vitamin that helps with cell division. Since you have sickle cell disease, there's a defect in your red blood cells. The vitamin helps

your body produce folate."

"What's folate, Mommy?

"It's a nutrient that helps to increase your body's ability to treat anemia," Juliette said, softly stroking her hair as she laid against her chest.

There was a brief period of silence, which Juliette appreciated. She normally encouraged questions from her curious little angel, but the stress of Grandville's absence still weighed on her.

"Mommy, does that mean that I am going to die?" Jolene asked, lying stock still.

"We're all going to leave this world one day, honey. But you're going to be here

with us for a long time."

Jolene seemed satisfied with that answer, snuggling into Juliette's side.

Juliette kissing her cheek and gave her a big hug. "Now, let's get you and Jenae to bed You need your rest to feel better."

After tucking the twins in, Juliette returned to her room, the silence of the house amplifying her worries. She tried calling his cell again, but it went straight to voicemail without ringing. She left a fifth voicemail message and sent him another text.

She decided to go sit on the sun porch, gripping her phone like a lifeline. Greta had gone to bed, and the boys were playing Nintendo Switch in their rooms. The Valium she had taken did little to calm her anxiety and guilt. She let her tears fall freely.

Had Grandville needed some space after learning that his best friend and business partner was at risk of dying? Or could Franklin have told Grandville about the one and only time he and Juliette had been intimate with one another? Either way, the information would affect Grandville's mental health … or possibly their marriage.

She rested her head in her hands, rocking back and forth, and praying. When she finally looked up, she jumped and gasped. She had no idea how long Jabari had been standing on the sun porch, staring down at her.

"Boy! Don't you sneak up on me like that," she scolded, trying to catch her breath.

"Sorry, Mom," Jabari said, his voice soft. "Why are you crying?"

Juliette quickly wiped her face. "I'm fine. Just worried about Franklin. Why aren't you in bed?"

Jabari hesitated. "I just wanted to thank you."

"Thank me? For what?"

"For helping Blake. He told me you called his mother and that helped save his little brother's life. He said that his mother thanked him for being brave and telling us about Ben. She said that you and I are heroes."

Juliette smiled weakly. " Blake seems like a nice young man. Is he your best friend?"

"Yeah, he's cool. He's good at video games and basketball. You know that there aren't a lot of black kids in our neighborhood, so it feels good to have a friend who looks like me."

"I understand," Juliette said, grateful her son had found someone to connect with.

"Mom, where's Dad? He's never missed dinner with us since he got home from jail," Jabari asked, his voice laced with worry.

Juliette sighed. She couldn't lie to him. "I don't know," she admitted.

"He hasn't called?"

"No. I'm worried because this isn't like your dad," Juliette admitted, wringing hands.

"I'm worried, too, Mom. Dad would've called to tell us he wouldn't be home for dinner. Do you think he was in an accident or something? Maybe we should call the hospitals."

"That's a good idea, Jabari."

Together, they called every hospital in the area, but there was no sign of Grandville.

"Listen, Jabari you're almost grown, so I'm about to share some news with you. But I need you to promise to keep it to yourself," Juliette instructed.

"You got it. What's up, Mom?"

Juliette took a deep breath. "Your Aunt Greta is pregnant." Jabari's eyes enlarged immediately but she continued. "I don't want to worry her about your dad's whereabouts in her condition. So I need you to help me keep this under wraps until he comes home. Understood?"

Jabari nodded. "Man, I can't believe Aunt Greta's having a baby," Jabari exclaimed excitedly. "I'm about to be a big cousin."

"Yes, you are. But Greta doesn't want anyone to know except for us, until she's further along. So, I'm swearing you to secrecy, bud."

"I won't say anything, Mom, I promise. But how are we going to find Dad?"

"If he isn't home by tomorrow evening, I'll file a missing person's report. He has to be missing for at least seventy-two hours. Plus, since he's still on post-release, I don't want the authorities to believe he just left without permission. He could get in trouble. We don't know for sure that he's missing. He may just need some time alone because Franklin's so sick. He could even be at his office."

"You're right, Mom. But I'm the man of the house since Dad's not here. So, while he's gone, I'll protect you and our family."

"Thanks, Jabari. I'm going to your dad's office early tomorrow morning, before Greta wakes up.

I'll need you to get your sisters and your brother breakfast and watch them and the house until I return. You can tell Greta I went over to one of the rooming houses."

"Of course, Mom. However I can help."

Juliette pulled her tall teenage son into a hug. "I love and appreciate you, son."

"Love you too, Mom.," Jabari said, hugging her back. "Everything's going to be alright. You'll see."

Later, as Juliette lay alone in her bed, she tried her best to avoid thinking the worst. Her king wasn't in their castle for the first time in three years and she had no idea how to bring him home. As she lay in the half-empty bed, she imagined Grandville's strong arms holding her. Exhausted, she drifted off to sleep, vowing to do everything in her power to find him.

Chapter 24

Clear

Melinia adjusted Rafael's collar and marveled at how handsome he looked in his blue jean suit and Air Jordans. At just five years old, his height made him appear much older, and his sharp outfit added to the illusion. Jesus, napping peacefully in his stroller, looked angelic in his Osh Kosh B'Gosh romper. The sight of her boys made her beam with pride, but her surging nerves quickly overtook her.

Melinia didn't want Rayshawn to know exactly where she lived, so when Rayshawn's attorney arranged for a private car to pick them up, she requested to be picked up at Tower City Mall in downtown Cleveland. As they rode the bus downtown, an unsettling feeling that she was being watched crept over her. She scanned the other passengers, her eyes locking onto a familiar face—the mysterious man who had confronted her at her apartment and in the grocery store. Although his face was partially hidden behind a mask, she recognized his gray eyes. She gasped quietly as her stomach twisted.

The man stood, sauntered across the bus, and slid into the seat directly behind her, Jesus and a dozing Rafael.

"Looking good today, Melinia," he said smoothly.

Her body stiffened. "What do you want? Why are you following me?" she hissed, instinctively clutching Jesus's carrier closer.

The man grinned, his voice mocking. "Who said I'm following you? And it's not about what I want. It's about what *you* want. And guess what? I got it."

She whipped her head toward him, her voice low but firm. "Listen, I've made myself clear. There's nothing you have that I want, except for you to leave me the fuck alone. I don't know how you know my name, but when you see me, act like you don't."

His grin faded as he leaned forward, his hand gripping the back of Rafael's seat. "Watch your tone, junkie. I'm not somebody you wanna piss off. You feel me, Melinia?"

"I'm not afraid of you," she said, raising her voice just enough to draw the attention of nearby passengers. "Leave me and my children alone!"

The man leaned back, his grin returning as a handful of passengers looked their way. The bus continued motoring down Euclid Avenue, and Melinia returned her gaze out of the window, trying to ignore him.

"So now that you're no longer on the junk, you think you're a somebody, huh?" the man said. "Don't act brand new. I've seen your videos and it wasn't too long ago that you were sucking random dicks for a hit. All of you junkie hoes are the same. It won't take long before you're begging for a hit of this good shit. I'll be here when you come crawling back and don't think I'll forget about how you talked to me."

Her breathing quickened and she glanced down at Rafael who stirred, but didn't wake. "Hell will freeze over before I ask you for anything. Now, for the last time, stay the fuck away from me before I call the police," Melinia growled.

"Aye, ma'am. You good over there?" A robust man with a graying beard asked from a few seats over.

"Mind your business, O.G.," the man barked across the aisle. "This is a public space, and I'm not bothering anybody."

"No, he's bothering me, sir. I've asked him multiple times to stop," Melinia said. Despite the bravado, Melinia was nervous because she hadn't told anyone where she was going. If she were to go missing again, her family wouldn't have a clue where to look, just like the last time. When the bus pulled into Public Square, she quickly gathered her belongings, woke up Rafael, and prepared to exit the bus. But when she glanced behind her, the man was gone.

Melinia ushered Rafael off the bus in front of the Terminal Tower and strapped Jesus into his stroller. They began walking toward the mall entrance when a large SUV with tinted windows pulled up beside them. The window rolled down, revealing Rayshawn sitting in the backseat.

"Hello, Ms. Gatlin," said a muscular man. "Mr. Robinson is waiting for you inside the vehicle." Another large man stepped out of the vehicle to assist her with the breaking down the stroller and stowing it in the trunk.

"Ms. Gatlin, you and your son can wear these," the man said as his gaze landed on Rafael. Melinia accepted the masks with a nod.

"Here, let me get the door for you," the man offered.

"Thanks. I'll keep the diaper bag with me," Melinia said as she helped Rafael climb into the vehicle. As she was getting in, Rayshawn said, "Hey, little guy. Hi, Melinia. Here, let me help."

Melinia passed him the baby carrier before climbing inside. The plush leather seats were so soft, her body sank into them, immediately relaxing her.

After buckling Rafael into his seat, she noticed that Rayshawn had already installed a car seat base in the SUV, effortlessly securing Jesus' carrier into place without disturbing his peaceful sleep.

"Ready? Let's go," he said, his tone casual, as if they were old friends.

The drive through downtown Cleveland was smooth. Rayshawn sat beside her, staring intently at Rafael, who was engrossed in his tablet. Finally, Rayshawn broke the silence.

"You've got some handsome sons, Melinia. They look well cared for."

She straightened in her seat. "Thanks. Despite everything I've been through, I've done my best to take care of them. I'm all they've got."

"I'd like to hear more about that over lunch," Rayshawn said, his tone gentle before turning his attention to Rafael. "Hey, little man, do you like basketball?"

Rafael looked up from his screen, locking his bright eyes with Rayshawn. "Yes! Julio showed me how to kick the ball and I scored a goal!"

Rayshawn chuckled. "Okay, my guy. That's outstanding. It sounds like Julio was teaching you soccer. Basketball's a little different. It's like soccer, except you use your hands to put the ball in a hoop. After lunch, maybe I can show you how it's done."

Rafael nodded and beamed before returning to his tablet.

They pulled in front of a restaurant known for its game room. Melinia hesitated, surprised. "I thought the Governor closed all restaurants for dine-in service?" she asked.

Rayshawn smiled. "Yes, but private parties with under twenty people are allowed. I rented the whole place for us. Thought Rafael might like the games."

Inside, the restaurant was empty, except for two masked waiters wearing gloves and preparing a buffet of wings, burgers, fries, and salad. Melinia's stomach growled. She'd been so nervous about their meeting that she'd skipped breakfast. Since Jesus would be waking up soon, she pulled out his bottle. Meanwhile, Rafael was running around the restaurant, awestruck by all the colorful arcade games lining the walls.

"Rafael, come over and eat first. Then you can play," Melinia said.

Once she got Rafael settled with a plate, Melinia turned back to her own plate to snag
a few bites before Jesus woke up.

Rayshawn turned his attention to her. "Melinia, I appreciate you meeting with me. I wanted to apologize."

Melinia paused mid-bite by his directness. She swallowed and put her wing down. "I
believe I'm the one who owes you an apology, Rayshawn."

"Yes, I agree that taping me without my knowledge was wrong, but I can admit that I was also wrong for taking advantage of you. I knew you had a drug problem, and I exploited you. And I'm sorry for that. I'd like to buy the tape from you. All copies."

Her eyes softened. "Rayshawn, I don't have any intentions of blackmailing you. I made it to protect myself from your cousin and his friends. So, I'll just give it to you."

Rayshawn nodded. "Okay, I appreciate that. But I have something else I want to discuss with you, and it's very sensitive."

Melinia's stomach dropped and she braced herself for what he might say next. "I'm listening."

"I noticed how much Rafael looks like me," he began cautiously. "Is there a chance he's mine?"

Melinia lowered her eyes to the table as the question hung in the air for several moments. She met his gaze before saying, "Yes, there is a possibility, Rayshawn."

Rayshawn nodded, his expression unreadable. "Okay, well, I'd like to find out for sure. My attorney has a nondisclosure agreement for you to sign, and we can do the DNA test today."

"I'll sign your form if you'll sign mine," Melinia countered and pulled out a manila folder from the diaper bag. As she slid it across the table, Jesus began to stir and let out a loud cry.

Rayshawn smiled, his eyes softening as he watched her soothe the baby. "He's a handsome little fella. A future heartbreaker."

"Thank you. I've been blessed with two very good-looking boys."

"For sure."

"You can review the paperwork while I feed him," Melinia said, offering Jesus a bottle.

Rayshawn picked up the folder and began reading as Jesus quieted. After a few moments, he stared at her, speechless.

Chapter 25

In the Closet

Grandville sat in the closet, trying to think of a way out of his predicament. The locked door mocked each of his attempts at freedom, and his search for anything useful brought him nothing but frustration. His gaze fell on an empty bucket in the corner with a roll of toilet paper next to it. This wasn't a spur-of-the-moment act. George had meticulously planned his kidnapping. The realization hit him like a punch to the gut.

This wasn't just a bad dream or some chaotic misunderstanding. George had gone to great lengths to orchestrate his captivity, and that knowledge brought a suffocating dread.

Grandville was hesitant to reveal the truth about George's origin story for fear of the truth sending him spiraling deeper into madness. The air in the small space felt heavier with every passing second, and Grandville's thoughts took him back to his time in solitary confinement at Oakhill Psychiatric Prison. He had been imprisoned after the accident that claimed his oldest daughter's life, which triggered a complete mental breakdown. Those endless, isolating days clawed at the fragile edges of his sanity.

Now, he was locked away again, reliving the helplessness, disorientation, and gnawing fear of the unknown. But this time, it wasn't the guards or the prison system holding him in—

it was his own son.

He didn't know if it was day or night, but he did know that his beloved wife was worried sick about him, and he hated being away from her.

The closet door creaked open, snapping Grandville out of his reverie.

"Well, good morning," George greeted cheerfully, ignoring Grandville's grim reality. "I hope you got some good rest. I slept like a baby knowing I'm finally going to get the answers I've waited for my whole life. You have no idea what it's like not to know who you are."

Grandville glared at him, his wrists raw from the handcuffs. "George, I couldn't rest if I tried. My wife has no idea where I am, and I know she's worried sick."

George's expression darkened. "Man, I hope you know that I don't give a fuck about your wife or your punk-ass friend, Franklin."

Forcing himself to remain calm, Grandville replied, "Whatever problem you have, George, it's with me. Juliette and Franklin haven't done anything to deserve your disrespect."

"How do you know?" George shot back.

"Because I know them. And I know you don't get to blame them for something that has nothing to do with them."

George ignored his comment. "It's time you tell me about how you came to be my biological father."

"George, I need to use the bathroom," Grandville asserted.

George walked over and inspected the bucket. "Looks like you already went."

"I need to have a BM, and you should be ashamed of yourself for treating me like I'm an animal. I've already been locked up, and I don't appreciate you traumatizing me again like this. What have I done to deserve this treatment?"

"Let's start with giving me away like I was a piece of trash!" George yelled.

"I did no such thing," Grandville sniped through gritted teeth. "I didn't even know you existed until my mother told me about you on her deathbed. If I had known about you, I would have been a good father to you, despite my age, when you were born. I was a teenager. Younger than you."

"Okay, Pops, that's a start. Where's my mother and how can I find her?"

George's question hit him like a punch to the face. He closed his eyes to avoid his son's wide-eyed, glassy gaze. "George, I'm sorry, but your mother passed away years ago. Now, I really need to go and if you don't get me to a restroom soon, we're going to have a whole other set of issues."

George sneered. "It'll be your issue because you'll be sitting in your own shit. Maybe then you'll understand how your actions have made me feel for all these years."

Grandville had had just about enough of George's games. If it weren't for the restraints,

he would have knocked the kid's head clean off his shoulders by now.

"No," he snapped with a booming voice, "you'll have an issue because that might motivate me to keep my story to myself. Look at how you're acting. Immature and irrational. It makes me wonder if you're even capable of handling the truth."

"You'd better believe I deserve the truth," George shouted, stomping his foot as his fist slammed into the wall. "I'm the victim in this situation!"

"I don't disagree with you, George. And I'm sorry for what you went through. But this isn't the way to handle things. It solves nothing."

George lowered his head and sniffled as he swiped a tear from his face. "Look, I'm sorry for doing this shit to you. I'm in a bad place right now, so telling me the truth is your best shot."

"Listen, George I'm ready to tell you the truth, but be warned, the details are very ugly. There're some things that are very unsettling, especially in the headspace you're in. When I learned the whole truth, I suffered a nervous breakdown and accidentally ended my daughter's life. Are you aware that I was incarcerated in a mental health prison for that?"

"Yes, I'm aware," George replied in a bored voice. "So I guess the apple doesn't fall too far from the tree. I'm losing it right now just like you were."

"Well, you have no idea what your condition will be once you hear everything. I'm physically uncomfortable, and when I feel dehumanized, it makes me less talkative," Grandville said.

A pause of welcomed silence fell between them, which Grandville took as a sign that the gears inside George's stormy mind were moving towards a possible compromise. George finally spoke. "Listen, Grandville. I'm going to allow you to use the restroom, but know that I don't feel like I have anything to live for right now. So don't make me shoot you. You're going to leave the door open so I can watch you. Just like prison." George motioned with the gun for Grandville to stand.

The voices inside Grandville's head returned, indicating he was under extreme stress. He feared he was on the verge of becoming psychotic and the last thing he wanted was to lose control and hurt George.

George walked him out of the closet and into the bedroom before opening the door to an attached bathroom. Grandville noticed a table with white linen and two place settings against the bedroom wall.

George motioned towards the bathroom. "Go ahead. There's no way out. So, once you've used the bathroom, we can discuss breakfast."

Grandville walked into the bathroom, which was stripped bare, except for a bar of soap, a roll of toilet tissue, and a hand towel. Afterward, Grandville had a difficult time cleaning himself but he managed to get it done. He washed his hands and splashed cold water onto his face. He looked into the mirror and began deep breathing, grateful the voices had subsided. Grandville realized he had little choice other than to follow George's lead. He re-entered the bedroom where George was sitting at the table.

"Damn, man, I see you weren't playing about having to go," George said, fanning his nose as a scowl marred his face. "I need to light some incense to knock the funk out of the air." George said and motioned towards the closet door with the gun. "Head on back into the closet. I promise I'll be back in ten minutes to get you for breakfast."

Grandville returned to the closet and sat on the couch. George closed and locked the door After waiting for about an hour, Grandville heard the door open.

"Okay, come on. I know you must be starving, so I made you an awesome breakfast," George gushed.

When Grandville walked into the kitchen, he couldn't believe his eyes. The table was set, and there was a platter filled with waffles, bacon, eggs, coffee, and orange juice.

"Wow, do you feed all of your hostages this well?" Grandville chuckled.

"Ha-ha. Very funny. Sit down so we can eat."

Grandville sat on a folding chair and George pulled another one right next to him. That's when Grandville realized that George planned to feed him again.

"Come on, George. Why won't you take the handcuffs off me so I can enjoy the food that you've prepared?"

"That's not happening," George said. "I don't trust you."

"Well, that goes both ways. How do I know that once I tell you what you want to know, you won't harm me? I can't do anything about the past, but I can be a father to you. Trust is earned, and you haven't gotten far with me by treating me this way."

"I'm sorry you feel that way. Now, the food's getting cold, so let's eat," George said dismissively as he poured syrup on the waffles and cut into them. He took a bite and said, "Delicious. Now it's your turn."

He picked up a piece with the fork. "Open up."

Grandville obeyed. The waffle nearly melted in his mouth.

"Well, what do you think?"

"Did you make these?"

"Yes, I created the recipe."

Grandville nodded. "You're one hell of a cook. How'd you learn?"

"Self-taught."

"Do you enjoy it?"

"Yes, it's about the only thing that I'm good at," George said, offering Grandville another bite.

He accepted it and said, "George, you're probably good at a lot of things. I'm not sure why you're so down on yourself. You might want to consider going to culinary school. I'd love to help you with that. But your future is at risk if you don't make the right choice. You could face jail time on felony counts. I want to spend time with you, but not like this. It's only going to be a matter of time before my wife realizes that I'm missing, and against my will."

George set the fork down and placed his interlocked fingers on top of the table, tilting his head forward. Grandville studied his eyes to discern what the young man was thinking. He noted that whenever he mentioned Juliette, George's demeanor changed. "Can I ask you a question, Grandville?"

"Sure."

"Why are you so down for Juliette, when she hasn't been true to you? Was she the

reason you didn't want me?"

"George, I didn't meet Juliette until years after you were born and well before I knew about you," he explained. "You barely know her, so why would you say something like

that?"

"I'll tell you once you share what I want to know. Have some more food." George stuffed scrambled eggs into Grandville's mouth. "Listen, Grandville, I'm prepared to let you go, but only if you tell me why I was put up for adoption. I want the whole story.

Then I'll share a story of my own. But first, let's finish this meal and then talk man to

man."

"Okay, but I'll need your word that you'll release me as soon as we have our talk."

George placed his hand over his heart. "You have my word."

Chapter 26

Whiskey Whiskey

Juliette didn't get any sleep as she tossed and turned all night, her body restless and her mind surging with questions. She stared up at the ceiling. Where was Grandville? Why wasn't he home with her and the kids? She hadn't realized how much she relied on his steady presence in their household until he was gone. Now, her worry consumed her like a slow-burning fire.

She wanted to break down and cry but she remained strong, ignoring the nagging feeling that

something was very wrong, and praying that Grandville was safe.

Her thoughts went back to something Grandville had mentioned in passing—that Franklin kept a bottle of whiskey in his office. She wondered if Grandville had broken years of sobriety by going there and drinking until he passed out. Perhaps he was still there, trying to sleep it off.

The idea filled her dread and determination. She needed answers.

Sitting up, she decided she couldn't wait any longer. She threw on some clothes, grabbed her purse, and headed to the kitchen to make herself a strong cup of coffee. She needed energy for what lay ahead.

When the clock finally struck 8 a.m., she couldn't wait any longer to call Sabrina. The phone rang three times before her weary voice answered.

"Good morning, Sabrina. I hope I didn't wake you."

"It's morning, but I'm not sure what's so good about it," Sabrina replied, the sadness

palpable in her trembling, throaty voice.

Juliette's heart sank. She hated to hear her friend cry. Once Sabrina's sobs died down, she said, "Aww, Sabrina. I'm so sorry. I know you're going through it right now."

"It's okay, girl."

"You know what? I'm on my way to you right now. Are you at home?"

"Yes, and I'd love to see you, but since my mother and I have both been exposed to COVID, it's best if you don't come around until after our quarantine ends. I'd feel terrible if you or anyone in your family caught it from me."

"I totally understand," Juliette said.

"We've both tested negative, thank God. But we could be carriers. This is all so new, so I'm being overly cautious to avoid spreading it."

"Thanks for looking out for our safety, Sabrina. Has there been any change in Franklin's condition?"

"No, he is still in a coma and when my colleagues realized that Franklin was my

fiancé, they banned me from the hospital. So, I can't be with him at all," her voice broke, saddled with emotion. "He's very sick and according to the doctors, he has little to no chance of

making it. I don't want him to die all alone."

Juliette shook her head, her own problems momentarily forgotten. "Sabrina, we're going to stay positive and prayed up, okay?" Juliette said with conviction. "Franklin is going pull through. Let's pray right now."

Juliette launched into a heartfelt prayer, her words pouring into her friend like a soothing balm over both their anxieties. When she finished, her eyes were full of tears.

"Thanks, Julie. That prayer… it meant everything." Sabrina's voice held a flicker of hope.

"It's my absolute pleasure. You know I'd do anything for you."

"And I for you," Sabrina said.

"So, listen," Juliette let out a deep sigh. "Although I hate to bother you, I have a favor to ask. I really don't have anyone else to ask."

"Anything," Sabrina replied without hesitation.

"Grandville didn't come home after seeing Franklin at the hospital yesterday. His phone is off, and I don't know where he is. I'm hoping he went to the office, but I realized I don't have a key to get in."

"Wait —Grandville didn't come home? That's not like him!"

"I know. I thought maybe he went to the office … and maybe he drank some of Franklin's whiskey or something to cope. I just need to know he's okay."

"Of course! I'll leave Franklin's keys in our mailbox for you. Be sure to wipe them down before touching them. You can never be too cautious."

"I appreciate the caution. I'm on my way right now. And thank you for this."

"Promise you'll keep me posted?"

"I absolutely will. Please keep me posted about Franklin's condition."

"Will do. I'll wave from the window."

Juliette arrived at Franklin's beautiful mini mansion in the suburb of Solon, with its manicured lawn that rivaled his neighbors'. After pulling into the circular driveway, she stepped out and saw

Sabrina standing at his picture window, waving at Juliette before blowing her a kiss.

Juliette returned the gesture before returning to her car.

"Thank you," Juliette mouthed before hurrying back to the car.

The twenty-minute drive downtown felt endless. Her breath caught when she pulled into the parking lot and saw Grandville's car. Relief flooded her veins. He had to be inside. She was going to give him a piece of her mind for making her worry herself sick.

When she tried to open the office door, it was locked. After several knocks, went unanswered, she used the key. The inside of the office was dark. After she flipped on the lights, she walk through to Grandville's office. After a slight pause, her trembling hand turned the knob and she entered the room. The first thing she noticed was Grandville's car keys and cell phone sitting on the conference table. But there was no other sign of him.

She walked over to Franklin's office, checked their bathroom, and even the storage closet, quickly realizing that Grandville wasn't there.

"What's going on? Where the hell is my husband?" she muttered as her ringing phone startled her.

"Hello, Jabari," she answered.

"Mom, it's Jolene," he said frantically.

"What's wrong, sweetie?"

"She's sick. She has a temperature of 102. I think she needs to go to the hospital."

Juliette pressed her hand to her forehead, trying to stay calm. Could she have contracted COVID somehow? "Okay, listen to me carefully. Keep her in her room and away from everyone else, especially your Aunt Greta. Put on your mask and make sure she stays hydrated. I'll be home as soon as I can."

Grabbing Grandville's phone and keys, she locked the office and rushed back to her car. Tears blurred her vision as she sped toward home, her mind torn between her missing husband and her sick child.

Nothing was clear anymore. All she could do was pray that she could hold it all together until Grandville walked through their front door.

Chapter 27

I Found You

Melina was ecstatic because for once, everything in her life seemed to be looking up. She couldn't stop smiling as she replayed the events of the past week. Her sons were healthy, she was taking steps to secure their future, and she felt more hopeful than she had in years.

Juliette had taught her a lot about contracts when Melinia was seventeen years old and interned at the teen residential facility. Juliette had served as the agency's legal counsel and had reviewed their contracts. Melina had anticipated that Rayshawn and his attorneys would insist that she sign an NDA, so she insisted on her own agreement, which went far beyond a standard agreement. Rayshawn would not even be allowed to test for the possibility of being Rafael's father unless he signed her paperwork and agreed to her conditions. It was ironic how life worked, but she wasn't complaining.

Rayshawn reaction to her terms at their lunch meeting had been as expected: part disbelief and part indignation.

"Melinia, are you serious?" he'd asked her.

"As a heart attack," she'd replied calmly, dabbing Jesus's spit-up with practiced ease.

He squinted at her, the tight line of his jaw betraying his struggle to keep his cool. "I don't understand why. If Rafael is my son, why can't I acknowledge him? Why keep him from the perks of being my child?"

Melinia's voice had softened, but her resolve remained firm. "I hear you, Rayshawn. But it's my job to protect him. You may not understand my reasons now, but one day, you will."

His expression had shifted from anger to something more resigned as he leaned back in his chair, his gaze fixed on her. "You're asking me to give him the world without the recognition he deserves. I can't agree to that."

Melinia had leaned forward, her eyes boring into his. "It's not about denying Rafael anything. It's about his safety. I don't want him anywhere near your drug-dealing cousin Lovelle, or your world of fame and scrutiny. And I'm not ready to face Greta's wrath. She's been good to me and I betrayed her. Now, I'm not sorry for having Rafael. He and Jesus saved my life." She paused to study the look on Rayshawn's face, which softened a bit. "So," she continued, "if Rafael is yours, I'm willing to give you a role in his life, but on my terms."

"Your terms?" Rayshawn's voice had been heavy with skepticism.

"Yes. A living allowance while I finish school. Two-hundred-thousand-dollar annual contributions to an interest-bearing account every year held in trust for Rafael's future. No one will have access to it without the trustee's approval, including me. That way, you'll know I'm not touching his money. You can see him whenever you want, with twenty-four hours' notice. All I ask is that when Jesus gets older, that you'll consider allowing him to tag along with his brother. He can spend summers and winter breaks with you. But publicly, you're his godfather until he turns thirteen. After that, we'll tell him the truth."

"Thirteen?" Rayshawn's raised falsetto voice displayed his shock. "Why? That makes absolutely no sense to me."

"By the time he's thirteen, you'll no longer be in the league," Melinia explained.

"It seems like I'll be spending a lot of money without getting much in return. You don't even want anyone to know that he's mine," Rayshawn said, anger in his voice.

"That's not true, Ray. First, we don't even know that Rafael is your son, and unless you agree to my terms, you'll never know. Secondly, everything I'm doing is protecting you. I was a heroin addict, and you had unprotected sex with me. If people find about me, that won't help you with selling your image."

Rayshawn exhaled sharply and dropped his eyes to the table. He shifted in his seat, then raised his eyes slowly to catch Melinia's gaze. "Listen. I can't sign this without having my attorney review it first. I hope you understand."

"No problem."

That meeting with Rayshawn was as memorable for Rafael as it was for her. Rayshawn was true to his word and taught Rafael how to bounce a basketball and shoot baskets. Melinia had not heard from Rayshawn since their lunch meeting but expected to hear from him soon.

Her ringing phone brought her into the present. She looked down at her caller ID and realized it was her mother.

"Hey, Ma."

"Hello, dear daughter of mine. How are you?"

"I'm good, how about you?"

"Not so good," her mother's tone was flat.

Melinia's heart speed up. "What's wrong, Ma?"

"I miss you and my grandchildren. You were gone for so long, and as soon as I get you back, this stupid pandemic hits us. I've already missed seeing Rafael as a baby, and now I'm missing Jesus, too."

"I know, Ma. We miss you too," Melinia said softly. "But it's better to be safe than sorry."

They talked for a while, reminiscing and laughing until Melinia's phone buzzed again. Her line clicked and she saw that Julio was trying to reach her.

"Ma, can you hold on for a moment? Another call's coming in."

"A call more important than catching up with your Mama? Alright, go ahead and take it. Call me back when you can."

"I will," Melinia promised before clicking over. "Hey, what's up, Julio?"

"Hey, Melinia. Nothing much. What are you up to?"

"I was just on the phone with my mom. She's been missing me and the boys."

"Oh, I'm sure. Well, look, I have the afternoon off, and I was wondering if you'd like to take the boys to the kiddie water park. It's outside, safe, and is close to where you live. There's also a park connected to it. Your mom can come, too. We can have a picnic, too, if you want."

Melinia hesitated but ultimately agreed. Her mother was thrilled, and before long, Melinia had the boys dressed and ready to go. Julio arrived and they walked the three short blocks from her apartment building to the park in Euclid. Her t-shirt was damp with sweat by the time they made it there. Her mother pulled into the parking lot, just after they arrived. They all walked over to greet her.

"Ma, this was great timing," Melinia said as she kissed her mother's cheek. "I couldn't resist kissing you, but that's the only contact you're getting today. You remember Julio, don't you?"

"Of course. Hello, Julio," her mother said, extending her fist for a bump.

"Hello, Ms. Gatlin," Julio chuckled, bumping her back.

Melinia showed her license to the park attendant to prove her residency and Julio pulled out a crisp twenty-dollar bill to pay for their entrance.

The park was not very crowded, so they had their pick of spaces.

"Look, this spot is perfect," Julio said, gesturing toward a shady spot beneath a huge oak tree. He set the picnic basket down. "Melinia, I'll set everything up here while you guys take the boys to the sprinklers."

Melinia rubbed suntan lotion on Rafael and Jesus, slipped on their water shoes, and grabbed their beach towels. Her mother pushed Jesus in the stroller while she took Rafael's hand and headed toward the sprinklers. Soon, she and her sons were running through the refreshingly cold water. Her mother watched from the sidelines, laughing while cheering on Rafael and his wild antics. Jesus also enjoyed the water, his squeals of laughter melting Melinia's heart. After an hour, they all returned to Julio's picnic setup under the tree. Julio had spread out a huge blanket with food and drinks.

"Wow, when did you have time to prepare all of this?" Melinia asked.

"The manager over at A Better Tomorrow shared her chicken salad recipe. I also made a fresh fruit salad and potato salad. We have bottled water, papaya juice, and a juice box for Rafael. Sit down and let me serve you."

"You've done enough. It's your day off. I can make the plates," Melinia said, shooing him away.

"No, I just want you to relax. I also brought some extra towels so you can dry off," Julio said, handing Melinia a large beach towel. "Rafael, I saw you running around. I know you worked up an appetite!"

The group enjoyed the delicious food, laughing and talking. Melinia fed a tuckered out Jesus, who promptly fell asleep afterward. Julio reached into the basket and pulled out two bundles of roses. "I saw these flowers and thought of each of you. Beautiful flowers for two beautiful women."

"Thanks so much, Julio. Melinia, this one here is a keeper," her mother winked.

"I should be thanking you for creating such a beautiful daughter," Julio replied.

"Julio, stop it," Melinia said, her cheeks flushing.

"Julio, can you take me back to the sprinklers?" Rafael begged.

"Yes, if it's okay with your mother," Julio replied.

"That's fine. Ma, do you mind staying with the baby while I run to the bathroom?" Melinia asked.

"Of course, darling."

After relieving herself, she was washing her hands when she looked in the mirror and jumped. A man was standing behind her. She turned to face him, and once she recognized him, fear invade her body.

"What are you doing in here?" Melinia yelled.

"I told you I'd see you again," the man said.

"What the hell do you want?"

"Someone wants to see you."

"My debt's been paid in full, so let Lovelle know that if he continues to bother me, I'm contacting the police."

"It's not Lovelle, silly," the man said with a low laugh.

Melinia's eyebrows knitted above her narrowed eyes, "Then who?"

A menacing sneer corrupted his face. Then she heard a familiar female's voice from the stalls.

"It's me."

Melinia didn't trust her ears because she thought she recognized the voice. She turned on her heel, her breath catching in her throat as Mimi, her long-lost best friend, emerged from the last bathroom stall.

Chapter 28

Lose Control

Grandville leaned back in his folding chair with a full and satisfied belly. The breakfast George had prepared was truly delicious and he could easily envision George owning and operating a food truck that specialized in breakfast food, along with a top-tier restaurant.

"You know, George, those waffles were the best I've ever had. You're on the verge of greatness but you don't even see it," He said, hoping to shift the mood. "We can turn your waffle recipe into a huge moneymaker for you. I'd be willing to invest in you on three conditions."

George tilted his head, his lips curling into a half-smile. "Conditions? You're really in no position to make demands, big guy. But, go ahead. Humor me."

"First," Grandville said, leaning forward, "you'd have to finish your degree or change your major to hospitality management. Fundamentals are the building blocks of success."

"Okay, keep talking," George said, crossing his arms.

"Second, you absolutely must get some mental health treatment. I understand that you're upset, but your response to this situation is way over the top. I'm saying this as someone who's been where you are. I know how it feels to snap and spiral out of control. Going all these years without knowing you even existed contributed to my mental breakdown. I was upset that you were stolen from me. I love you, son, and I want better for you than what I've been through."

George's expression softened for a moment before his defensive mask snapped back into place. "I know there's more, so keep talking."

"Before I continue, I have a question."

"I'm listening."

"Did you have a good childhood?"

Grandville could tell that his question caught George off guard. He recovered with a nod, but his facial expression darkened. "It was okay. My adopted parents were nice but they died when I was young."

"How did they die?"

"A fire," George replied, blinking rapidly.

"George, I'm sorry that you had to endure that. If I could take away your pain, I would."

"You can. By telling me the truth. I'm never going to stop these feelings of emptiness and unworthiness until I know. I've always felt this way. I love my aunt and my grandmother, but not knowing my biological family or why I was put up for adoption has always haunted me. I know there's something wrong with me. That's why you didn't want me."

"That's not true, George. I'll tell you what you want to know. But, I need to give you my last condition. Afterward, you have to release me. No more games, George."

When George didn't meet his gaze, Grandville continued. "There's nothing wrong with you, except that you need to talk to someone about your feelings. I went through the same thing, and it resulted in a tragedy I can never recover from. Don't repeat my mistakes. I promise that when we walk out of here, I'll do everything I can to ensure your success."

George sighed and nodded thoughtfully. Grandville took it as an agreement with his conditions, particularly the final one. "Okay, let's start with my mother. What was her name?"

"Her name was Gina."

"Gina and Grandville. I guess that explains why my name begins with a G," George laughed, which brought a smile to Grandville's lips. "Did you meet in high school and start dating? Give me the details."

"I knew Gina my whole life. I always loved her, but when I reached a certain age, she began to take liberties with my body that were inappropriate," Grandville explained, fighting through the anger and resentment that haunted him for most of his adult life.

"What does that mean?"

Grandville took a deep breath, then closed his eyes. "Gina was seven years older than me," he began, not fully believing that he was finally telling his son the story of his origin. "When I was ten, she started taking advantage of me sexually. I was afraid to tell anyone, so it went on for years. Once my mother found out, she put a stop to it. What my mother didn't tell me was that Gina had gotten pregnant. It wasn't until many years after you were born that I even knew you existed. My mother told me about you right before she passed away. She was afraid that you would find me one day, so she wanted me to hear about you directly from her. Then you found me."

"So, how did your mother know my biological mother was pregnant with me, but you didn't?"

"I wasn't around her when she was showing. My mother and Gina decided to put you up for adoption without telling me about you. My mother signed away my parental rights and planned to never tell me about you. But she changed her mind. Some of my mother's last words were about you."

"Okay, well where's my mother's biological family, and how do I get in touch with them?"

Grandville swallowed hard and took a deep breath. "George, this is where the story takes a turn. First, I want to warn you that the details are tough, and you can't flip out once you hear them."

"I think it's a little late for that, *Pops.* I mean, you're in a full-fledge hostage situation."

Grandville sighed, taking a moment to select the right words. "Me, my twin sister, and my mother were the only family Gina had left. Your mother was my first cousin."

The room seemed to tilt, the air charged with the weight of Grandville's confession. George rose sharply to his feet and his fists clenched at his sides. "Man, what?"

Grandville instinctively flinched at his sharp tone.

"George, I'm so sorry," Grandville said quietly.

"So, you're telling me I'm the product of … of abuse? That my mother was your cousin? This is …" he trailed off, his voice cracking.

"Trust me, I know it's a lot to process," Grandville continued, his voice trembling with long-buried pain. "But if I'd known about you, I would've stepped up. But the reality is, neither she nor I were able to take care of you. My mother was caring for all of us and we were barely surviving. I had to accept that my mother did what she felt was best in the situation. She wanted you to experience the life she knew we couldn't provide. After I found out about you, I had no way to attempt to locate you. I was so distraught that I became psychotic, which led to the accidental death of my daughter, Jessica."

"That's how you ended up at Oakhill," George muttered more to himself than to Grandville. He began pacing the floor. "So, what happened to my grandparents? Why did my biological mother live with you and your family?"

"They died."

"I gathered that. What I want to know is how?"

"Her mother had a psychotic break, killed my uncle, came over to my house, and killed herself right in front of us, including me and Gina. I didn't want to share those heartbreaking details with you. You don't need the weight of the past on your shoulders."

"You don't know what I need!" George exploded, glaring at him from the corner of the kitchen.

"Son, I know you're on edge, but I want you to be the exception to our family history, not the rule."

"Well, what the fuck does that shit mean?"

"When my aunt Genevieve was growing up, she was taught never to talk about her mental health issues. I was taught the same. It was our family's creed and it had a lot to do with being more afraid of the authorities than acting in our best interest. I now know that it's human to need help and inhumane to deny anyone assistance. I thought asking for help meant that you're weak. I don't want you to do something you'll regret out of desperation. There's little else I can say about the situation."

"One last question," George said after a long pause of silence.

Grandville slumped back in his chair. "I'll answer it, George, and that's all. I'm not well, and I need to get home and take my meds."

"When I confronted you at the office, you didn't seem surprised that I was your long-lost son. How did you know, for how long, and why didn't you tell me?"

"You know that's not one question; it's three," Grandville said with a chuckle, hoping to ease the tension. He realized that he still had to tackle the hardest questions of all. He hoped his response wouldn't make George angry enough to do something they would both regret.

Chapter 29

Fever

Juliette broke every speed limit on her way to the hospital. When she saw Jolene, she knew immediately that her daughter was very ill. Her heart pounded with fear and guilt, but she was grateful for Jabari's quick thinking and calm, astute reaction, which likely saved Jolene's life.

Jolene was burning up with fever. Juliette prayed desperately that her daughter hadn't contracted COVID. Although children weren't a high-risk group, some had succumbed to complications, especially those with underlying conditions like Jolene's sickle cell.

The moment they arrived at the emergency room, the urgency of Jolene's condition alerted the staff.

"Let's get her to the back," one of the nurses instructed as two others placed Jolene onto a stretcher and through the swinging double doors. Juliette trailed behind, clutching her purse strap and trying not to panic.

Dr. Anderson, an African American pediatrician with salt-and-pepper hair, greeted them as he entered the room. He moved quickly but with a calm demeanor that momentarily reassured Juliette. After listening to Jolene's heart and lungs, he said, "Her breathing is labored. I believe she's experiencing acute chest syndrome, but we'll need a chest X-ray to confirm."

Juliette's stomach sank, but she hid her concern as she squeezed Jolene's hand. "Will she be okay?"

"She's in the best hands. We'll start her treatment immediately if the X-ray confirms my suspicion," he said.

As they prepped Jolene to be transferred to a private room, Juliette was beside herself with worry. But focused her energy on devising a plan of supporting Jolene while also trying to locate Grandville. She had to figure it all out because she didn't have the luxury of breaking down. She reached over and stroked Jolene's cheek as she sniffled.

Once Jolene was in her own room, her nurse, Rhonda, walked in. She was sweet and accommodating with great bedside manner.

"Ms. Stubbs, the radiology team will be here very soon to take Jolene down for her chest x-ray. You won't be able to accompany her, but I'll stay with her the whole time. I promise to take good care of her. We'll be gone for about an hour, so please use that time to rest. Is there anything I can get for you, like ginger ale or water?"

"No, I'm fine right now. Thanks so much, and I will try to take your advice."

When the radiology team arrived, Juliette kissed Jolene's forehead. "Be brave, sweetheart. Mommy's here, and you're going to be just fine."

"Bye. I love you, mommy," Jolene said, waving as they rolled her out of the room.

Juliette sank into the chair by the window and pulled out her cell phone. She dialed Samantha, praying her best friend could offer some guidance, or at least a momentary distraction. The phone rang just once before Samantha answered. " Juliette, you have perfect timing. I was just about to call you."

Juliette couldn't help smiling at the excitement in her friend's voice. "What's going on?"

"Jared proposed this morning!" Samantha squealed. "And the ring is stunning! Of course, I said yes. I want a huge wedding, and you're going to be my Matron of Honor, right?"

"Wow, congratulations, Sam." Juliette kept her voice down, but allowed her excitement to show in her voice. "I'm so happy for you both. Jared's a great guy, and you deserve all the happiness in the world."

"Thanks! Just think, if I hadn't listened to you, I would have never gotten to know Jared. I'm so glad I opened myself up so we could fall in love. He makes me so happy, and he accepts me for who I am."

"That he does," Juliette remarked. "I liked Jared the moment I met him, and I think he'll be a great husband."

"Why don't you come over and hang out for a while? It's a beautiful day, and we can social distance on the deck and share a bottle of wine. It'll be just like old times."

"Samantha …" Juliette hesitated. "I'd love to, but I'm in the middle of a crisis right now."

"What's going on?" Samantha's joyful tone turned serious in an instant.

As soon as Samantha asked the question. Juliette could no longer hold back her tears.

"Come on, Juliette, talk to me. Everything's gonna be alright. Start from the beginning." Samantha instructed.

"Jolene's in the hospital with a high fever, and the doctors think it's acute chest syndrome. It's a condition caused by the sickling of red blood cells in Jolene's lungs. It's very serious."

Samantha gasped. "Poor baby. I'll be praying for Jolene. I hope she gets better soon."

"Thanks, girl. And…" Juliette faltered, unsure how to explain the other half of her stress. "Grandville never came home last night."

"What?!" Samantha shouted.

"I went to his office this morning, and his car, keys and phone were there, but there were no other signs of him. His phone was turned off, Sam. I have no idea where he is. I don't know if the news about Franklin sent him completely over the edge. And I'm trying to hold it together for Jolene, but I feel like I'm unraveling," she said, her face falling into her hands. "I hate to mess up your day by dropping my problems on you, but you were the only person I could think of who might help me think outside the box. Jabari and I checked all the hospitals in Cleveland and the surrounding areas. And with his car parked at his office, I haven't been able to come up with anything."

"Oh, honey, I'm so sorry about all this," Samantha said softly. "Have you contacted the police?"

Juliette shook her head, although her friend couldn't see her. "Not yet. If they think he's had a setback, they might send him back to Oakhill."

Samantha paused, clearly weighing her next words. "I have a friend on the police force who owes me a favor. I'll ask him to pull the security footage from Grandville's office building and the surrounding businesses. If he got a ride share, or however he left that office, it'll show up on the cameras."

"Oh, thank you," Juliette whispered, her voice breaking.

"Of course. I'm here for you, Julie. No matter what."

"Samantha, you're a blessing to me. Congratulations again on your engagement. I promise that as soon as I get a handle on what's going on here, you and I will get together and celebrate."

Juliette ended the call just as the nurses returned with Jolene. She quickly hung up as the nurses transferred Jolene from the stretcher back into the hospital bed.

"Well, Ms. Stubbs, Jolene's blood work and chest X-ray indicate that she does have acute chest syndrome," Dr. Anderson reported, sitting on his stool.

"Remember, defective red blood cells caused by sickle cell disease cause the cells to die early. Since these red blood cells carry oxygen throughout the body, it appears that Jolene likely has an infection causing the sickled cells to block the path of oxygen to her lungs."

"Have you tested Jolene for COVID?" Juliette hesitantly asked.

"Yes, her results came back negative," Dr. Anderson reassured her.

"Well, does her admittance to the hospital increase her risk of exposure? Is there any way for us to treat her at home?" Juliette inquired.

"Unfortunately, no. Jolene will need to be on oxygen and receive IV medications and fluids. We're taking every precaution to ensure that COVID patients are only treated on designated floors. Here, in the Cancer wing, is the safest area in the hospital. Most visitors are restricted at this time, but you can stay with Jolene, given her age. But no visitors other than you."

"Okay, doctor. How long do you think she'll have to stay in the hospital?"

"It depends on how well she responds to treatment. If favorably, maybe three days. I also want to emphasize that you did the right thing by bringing your daughter here. For SCD patients, fever is sometimes the initial indication of infection or another complication," Dr. Anderson said as he stood up.

"Thank you, doctor. I'm hypersensitive to any changes in my daughter's health or condition, as I'm sure you understand."

"I most certainly do." He placed a hand on Juliette's shoulder, slightly calming her. "I've ordered Jolene's IV medications and oxygen. The staff will be here shortly to begin her IV and to provide you with paperwork before we can start her treatment. If you think of any questions, write them down and I'll try to answer them when I return to check on Jolene during my evening rounds."

"Thanks, I will."

Dr. Anderson smiled at Jolene before leaving the room.

Juliette felt overwhelmed while sitting next to her sleeping daughter. She needed to stay with Jolene, but she also had to go home to at least get her essential items. Once Jolene received her medications and oxygen two hours later, Juliette informed Rhonda that she was running home to gather a few things. The commute home from Cleveland General Hospital usually took about thirty minutes, but she made it home in just over twenty. She entered the house and went directly to her bedroom to pack her overnight bag. As she searched her walk-in closet for her white sundress, she was startled to find Greta standing in the middle of her room when she emerged.

"Hey, Sis. You scared me half to death. What's up?" Juliette asked.

"I think I should be asking you the very same question," Greta replied, her hands planted firmly on her hips.

"I'm not sure what you mean," Juliette said, a perplexed look on her face.

"I've been calling my brother since I woke up today, and his phone is going straight to voicemail. Jabari mentioned that you and Jolene ran an errand when I tried to reach you earlier. Now you're back, with no sign of Jolene or Grandville. What the hell is going on?"

Chapter 30

Good Good

Melinia froze as she stared at her best friend. "Mimi?" she whispered, her voice trembling. "Oh my God. I can't believe it's you."

Mimi opened her arms, and they hugged tightly, tears streaming down their faces.

"Melinia, you look awesome. I'm so glad I finally found you," Mimi replied.

Before Melinia could respond, the voice she dreaded intervened.

"I'm glad I found her too, because it's time for you both to pay up," the strange man said, stepping toward Mimi. "Time to pay up, ladies. I want what I saw on the sex tapes. Now strip so I can give y'all a hit of this good-good. Because one hit makes everything good."

"Get away from her! You must be drunk and high off your own supply if you think I'm going back to that life," Melinia shot back.

Mimi tugged at Melinia's arm, her voice pleading. "Come on, Melinia. He has the good stuff. Just one hit, and we can get this over with."

"No, Mimi!" Melinia cried. "You don't need this. Let me help you get clean!"

"I came through, and a deal is a deal. Now Melinia, you could have been my bottom, and you wouldn't have to share the good-good. It would have been all yours," Larry said.

"I've already told you I'm not about to destroy my sobriety for you or anyone else. Come on, let's go, Mimi," Melinia said as she grabbed Mimi's hand.

Mimi yanked back and said, "Melinia, after everything we've been through, you can do this for me. I'm about to be dope sick if I don't get a hit soon," she cried, tears streaming down her face.

"You bitches better get ready. I've fantasized about this threesome for days, and you're going to give me what I've been waiting for. Come on, we're going in here," Larry said, motioning the ladies into the handicap bathroom stall.

"I've told you several times that I'm not afraid of you. The only thing you're gonna be getting is out of my way. I'm out," Melinia said angrily.

In one swift motion, Larry pulled a gun out of his waistband and pointed it at Melinia. "Oh, you're not going anywhere."

Melinia masked her terror by saying evenly, "You can hold a gun on me, but you'll have to kill me before I have sex with you."

"I don't care if you don't want a hit. You're going to give me what I want, willingly or by force. But before we begin the festivities, I need to let my girl get ready," Larry said as he reached into his pocket, pulled out a vial, and passed it to Mimi.

"Thanks, Larry," Mimi said, opening her purse and retrieving her heroin kit. It contained a needle and syringe, a spoon, a shoestring to tie off her vein, and cotton balls to soak up the residue on the spoon. Mimi tied off her vein and prepared to shoot up, while Melinia took deep breaths to prevent herself from vomiting.

"Mimi, you don't have to do this. Let me help you," Melinia pleaded.

"Sis, you know how it is. I'll be sick if I don't. But I promise, once when we're done here, I'll consider getting clean."

"You sure you don't want a hit?" Larry asked Melinia. "I've got plenty."

Melinia ignored him as Mimi pulled her sundress over her head and off her body. She said, "Listen, I'll do all the heavy lifting. It'll be like old times." She got on her knees, unzipped Larry's pants, and lowered them down to his knees.

"Yeah, that's what I'm talking about. Come on over here, Melinia, get in here," Larry directed, pointing the gun at Melinia.

"Please, don't make me," Melinia whimpered with tears streaming her face.

"I told you there would come a time when you'd beg me," Larry said, grinning.

Reluctantly, Melinia got down on her knees, resigning herself to do the unthinkable. They all jumped when a loud banging noise sounded by the front door. While Larry was distracted, she unlocked the door and ran out of the stall. Julio, stood on the other side of the door, looking horrified. His eyes lowered to Larry's gun and his eyes darkened. In an instant, Julio lunged forward, punching Larry square in the face. Larry lost his balance and dropped the gun, sending it sliding across the bathroom floor. Nothing could be heard beyond Julio's punches, Larry's grunts, and Melinia scuffling across the floor to grab the weapon. Larry crumpled to the floor and Julio kicked Larry's erect penis. As he howled in pain, Julio tossed him out of the bathroom stall. Larry's pants swam around his ankles and he could barely get away as Julio continued to pummel him.

Melinia was impressed by how well Julio could fight. His smooth and calculated jabs and punches were lightning fast. But as Larry lay unconscious on the dirty bathroom floor, she was nervous that Julio would kill him.

"Julio, enough!" Melinia screamed. "Don't jeopardize your immigration status over scum like him!"

Julio seemed to snap out of his trance. He stared down at Larry, who was motionless. "You're right, Chica. Come on, let's get out of here."

Melinia tucked the gun into the waistband of her shorts and pulled her t-shirt over it. "Mimi's here."

Julio looked over at Mimi, blinking rapidly. "Chica, I'm so glad to see you. Hurry up get dressed. We have to get out of here before this lowlife wakes up," Julio said. Mimi's moves were deliberate and slow as she struggled to put her dress back on. Julio helped Mimi to her feet and escorted the ladies out of the bathroom.

They were headed toward the blanket when Mimi suddenly stopped dead in her tracks with a distant look in her eyes. "Uh … I forgot my purse. I'll be right back," she said before running back into the bathroom. Melinia tried to follow her, but Julio placed a hand on her arm.

With eyes as dark as coals, he murmured. "You're not stepping foot back in there, Melinia."

She nodded and waited on the walkway while Julio stood in the bathroom doorway, making sure Larry didn't stir. With his eyes trained on the bathroom, Julio said, "Jesus woke up crying and your mother picked him up, trying to calm him down. When Rafael and I returned from the sprinklers and you still weren't back, I knew something was wrong. I left Rafael with your mother and headed straight to the bathroom."

Melinia exhaled a shaky breath and closed her eyes. She was thankful that Julio had followed his instincts that afternoon, or she could've been long gone and launched right back into the human trafficking trade. Mimi emerged from the bathroom holding her purse and the three of them headed back to Melinia's family. Julio immediately began packing everything. Her mother was so busy spending quality time with her grandsons, she didn't realize anything was wrong.

"Girl, did you fall in? I was starting to worry that you had become sick from the heat. But my grandsons kept me so busy, I didn't have a chance to check on you," Mabel said as she tickled Jesus, who was laughing and squealing.

"I'm okay, Ma. I ran into an old friend and lost track of time. Ma, this is Mimi. Mimi, this is my mother, Mabel," Melinia introduced.

"Hello, Mimi."

"Hello, it's so good to meet you. Melinia has told me a lot about you," Mimi said.

"Ma, Mimi was with Julio and me when I was missing," Melinia explained.

"Let's go," Julio directed as he grabbed Rafael's hand and stalked toward the entrance of the park.

"Ma, I love you, but we need you to go home. I'll call you a little later this evening," Melinia instructed.

"Okay. Well, thanks for inviting me along, Melinia. I had a great time," Mabel stood, dusting off her capri pants. "And Julio, thanks again for these beautiful flowers. I'm going to display them on my dining room table,"

"You're welcome, Ms. Gatlin. I'm going to get Melinia and the boys home," Julio said.

After Mable drove off, Melinia turned to Mimi. "Come on, let's go to my apartment. We don't know if Larry is going to come after us."

"That's probably not a good idea to go to your apartment. Larry said he knows where you live," Mimi replied.

"You're right. We'll go to A New Beginning. He doesn't know about my spot," Julio suggested.

"Before we go, I need to check something," Mimi said.

"Mimi, we need to hurry," Melinia urged.

Mimi pulled out her iPhone and stared at the screen. After a few minutes, she mumbled, "I knew it."

"What? Girl, we are wasting valuable time," Melinia said.

"Melinia, we need to check your purse. According to my phone, an Air Tag Pro is detected," Mimi said.

"What?" Melinia asked.

"I'll explain in a second. Purse," Mimi demanded, holding out her hand.

Melinia handed her purse over. Mimi walked over to a picnic table and dumped the contents out on the tabletop.

"Girl, have you completely lost your mind? Dumping my stuff on this filthy table. Why?" Melinia asked.

Mimi sifted through Melinia's belongings. "To get to this," she said, pulling a small circular device from between two envelopes.

"What the hell is that? That's not mine!" Melinia shouted.

"It's an Air Tag Pro, a tracking device designed to work with iPhones. This is how Larry's been tracking your whereabouts. Come on, we need to get rid of this now. I have an idea."

Melinia, her kids, and Julio followed Mimi to an RTA bus that was getting ready to pull off. Mimi ran to the door, and the driver opened it, thinking she was about to board.

"Sir, I was on this bus earlier today. I think I left my bag under the seat. Can I check right quick before you pull off?" Mimi asked.

"Sure, but make it quick," the bus driver replied.

Mimi ran to the back of the bus and returned in less than a minute.

"It's not there, but thanks," Mimi said to the driver.

"No one turned a bag into me. Maybe someone will turn it in to RTA's lost-and-found. You should email them or try calling. But I need to go so I can be on time for my stops," the driver said.

"Thank you, sir," Mimi replied as she exited the bus.

The bus pulled away, and the three of them jogged down the street with the kids.

"I left the Air Tag Pro on the bus," Mimi said. "That should buy us some time. The question is, what's our next move?"

Chapter 31: Insanity

Grandville stared at George and weighed his words. "George, I swear to you, I only found out a few months ago that you were my son."

"So, you've known for months?" George shrieked. Blood vessels bulged in his neck and sprouted across his forehead. "Then why the hell didn't you say anything?"

Grandville exhaled deeply, steadying himself. "George, I wanted to wait until the right time to break the news."

"Well, when exactly did you think that would be?" George asked, his shaky voice dripping with sarcasm.

"After my sister's wedding. But then COVID happened, and we've all been dealing with that," Grandville admitted.

"Oh, I see. So, how did you even find out that I was your biological son?"

"I learned it from Juliette," Grandville replied, meeting George's intense gaze. "Sabrina asked her to help search for your biological parents. Juliette used to work in adoption and foster care, and her connections came in handy."

George's eyes narrowed. "So, you're telling me that this whole time, Aunt Sabrina knew I was your biological son?"

"No, not at all. Sabrina asked Juliette to stop looking before the results came back, but Juliette had already started. When she received the information, it hit her hard, George. She suffered her own mental health crisis because of it. She was hesitant to tell me for fear that the news would send me spiraling into delusion again."

"Who else knew?" George demanded, his voice hot enough to melt steel.

"Just Franklin. He and I decided that we'd determine the right time to tell both you and Sabrina."

George shook his head, his jaw tightening. "I knew Franklin had something to do with this. And Juliette? That doesn't surprise me either. Neither of them is worth a damn."

Grandville stiffened. "That's the second time you've insulted my best friend and my wife," he said through clenched teeth. "Neither of them has done anything but treat you with kindness, and I really won't tolerate disrespect."

"That's too damn bad," George said, stepping closer until his face was mere inches away from Grandville's. His voice dropped to a threatening whisper. "I don't give a fuck how you feel. I said what I said because they're the reason you kept my identity a secret. They convinced you to hide it from me."

"They didn't talk me into anything. That was solely my choice," Grandville countered. "I wasn't ready to tell you, George. I was afraid of how you would react."

George's lip curled into a sneer. "That doesn't change the fact that they're trash."

"What is your issue with them?"

George smirked, his eyes gleaming with malice. "I guess it's time I hold up my end of the deal. I promised that once you told me the truth, I'd share something that would enlighten you about your wife and so-called best friend."

Grandville's stomach churned as he took in George's sick look of satisfaction. "Okay," he said cautiously. "I'm listening."

"Since Aunt Sabrina moved out, I've been bored out of my mind. With everything closed, I've had nothing but time. So, I decided to tackle some chores I'd been putting off. While packing away some of my college books in the crawl space, I found Aunt Sabrina's journals."

"You read her journals, George," Grandville asked, unable to mask his disappointment. "That's an invasion of her privacy!"

George shrugged. "Maybe. But I'm I glad I did because I learned how Franklin and Juliette's relationship *really* began."

Grandville's brow furrowed. "What are you talking about?"

"Franklin came to Aunt Sabrina completely hysterical and practically suicidal because he'd done something so horrible he couldn't live with himself."

Grandville frowned. "That doesn't surprise me. Your aunt's an amazing woman. Franklin hit the jackpot when he met her," Grandville said. "She was also part of God's divine plan to ensure that you and I connected. I'm grateful to Franklin for bringing Sabrina to us because that's how you and I found each other."

"Yes, but there's more," George said, his tone growing more intense.

"Okay, George. Take a breath," Grandville urged.

"What I'm about to say is serious, so cut the kumbaya shit and listen. Because when you hear what that *slut* Juliette did with that *bastard* Franklin, you won't be so calm anymore."

Grandville saw red. He stood up, towering over George. "Son, I warned you about disrespecting my people," he growled. "You're already holding me hostage and I've had just about enough of this shit. Let me go before this gets real ugly, real quick."

"No," George hissed, standing to his feet, "you're going to listen, and *then* I'll decide if you're free to go."

The voices in Grandville's head started whispering again. *Take him out. He's unstable. End this now.* He shook his head, trying to drown them out.

"No," Grandville said firmly. "You're going to let me go now because I've heard enough of your nonsense."

"You think it's nonsense?" George screamed. "They fucked each other behind your back while you were living your worst nightmare!"

Grandville's blood boiled as the words sank in. "What?" he roared. "How dare you defile my wife's reputation like that!" Without thinking, he charged at George, slamming his forehead into his son's face with all his strength.

George stumbled back, stunned but quick to recover. Before he could react, Grandville delivered a swift front kick to George's chest, sending him crashing into the wall. A loud pop echoed through the room, followed by a searing pain in Grandville's side.

George stood frozen, staring at the gun in his hand, the blood in his face slowly draining. "You made me shoot you!" he sobbed. "Why couldn't you just listen?"

Grandville staggered, his vision dimming. The last thing he heard before his world went dark was George's anguished sobs.

Chapter 32

Lost

Juliette pondered Greta's question carefully, trying to figure out the best way to respond without alarming her. "Jolene is sick," she said softly. "She's been admitted to the hospital with acute chest syndrome. I came home to get some clothes, but I need to get back to the hospital as soon as possible."

Greta's brows furrowed in concern. "Oh no. So Grandville's at the hospital with her?"

Juliette hesitated. "I hope so," she said finally. "I sent him a text to let him know what's going on, but haven't heard back yet."

Greta pursed her lips and cast her gaze towards the ceiling, as if she were trying to piece everything together. Juliette could tell Greta wasn't entirely convinced, so she decided to provide more details—more than she was comfortable sharing.

"Listen, Greta," Juliette began, taking a deep breath. "I know you want to tell Grandville about the new addition to our family, but he's in a bad place right now because of Franklin's illness. I think we need to give him time and space to process everything. Franklin is his best friend, and the thought of losing him is hitting Grandville harder than we might realize. I'm worried for him."

Greta sighed sharply. “I figured Franklin’s situation would devastate Grandville,” she admitted. “But I didn’t even know Jolene was sick. Why didn’t Jabari let me know?”

Juliette shifted uneasily, debating whether to explain. “I know you told me not to tell anyone about the baby,” she said carefully, “but I mentioned to Jabari that you were expecting. I didn’t give him the details and asked him to keep it quiet. I didn’t want you to have any added stress right now.”

Greta frowned, but nodded slowly. “Okay, but I still don’t understand why he didn’t come and get me when Jolene got sick.”

“I told him not to. I didn’t want you worrying about anything other than taking care of yourself and the baby. You’ve been through so much already.”

Greta sighed and shook her head. “Juliette, I really appreciate everything you’re doing, but I don’t want to be treated like I’m fragile. I’m stronger than you think, and I want to help. I don’t want to just sit back and feel like I’m a burden.”

Juliette placed a comforting hand on Greta’s shoulder and gave her a small smile. “Greta, you couldn’t be a burden if you tried. We love you, and you’ve been a blessing to our family. We only want what’s best for you and the baby.”

“Okay,” Greta relented with a nod. “But is there anything I can do to help while you’re at the hospital?”

“Yes, actually.” Juliette exhaled in relief, grateful for Greta’s willingness to pitch in. “I’ll have to stay with Jolene overnight, and once Grandville realizes that she’s sick, he might stay too. Could you order the kids pizza for dinner? I’ll check in later to ensure everything’s okay. I’m not sure how long they’re going to keep Jolene, but I’ll keep you updated.”

“Do you want me to tell Grandville about Jolene if he comes home?” Greta asked.

"No," Juliette said quickly. "Just have him call me. I'll need to gauge his mood before delivering more bad news. I'll keep my phone on, so you can reach me at any time." She paused to look Greta in the eyes. "Now, I want you to try and rest. I promise I'll call you later."

Greta nodded, with a concerned expression. "Okay, but remember to take a few minutes for yourself, too."

"I'll try," Juliette promised with a weak smile as she left the house. To avoid upsetting her other kids with the news that Jolene had to be hospitalized she decided to call them at a later time. The last thing she needed was to elevate the anxiety she was already feeling.

Once in her car, Juliette started the engine and played a Robert Glasper album, letting the soothing music fill the air. She tried to take Greta's advice to clear her head, but her thoughts were jumbled, and her heart felt heavy.

She was lost in the music when her ringing phone echoed her car's speaker system. The name on the display made her heart race: *Samantha.*

"Hey, Samantha," Juliette answered quickly. "Please tell me your contact found Grandville."

"No, not exactly," Samantha replied hesitantly. "What my contact found only raised more questions."

"What do you mean?"

"Well, he pulled the surveillance footage from the front of their office building. It shows Grandville entering the building, but there's no footage of him leaving."

Juliette gasped. "What in the world can that mean? Is he still in the building somewhere?"

"That's one possibility," Samantha said. "But there are two scenarios to consider. Either Grandville left voluntarily and purposely avoided all the cameras, or someone took him against his will, and also managed to avoid the cameras."

"Oh my God," Juliette whispered. "Why would someone want to take my husband?"

"Juliette, I don't have a clue. Maybe it's about money. Or something else entirely. But ask yourself this: would Grandville just leave without telling you? From everything I know about him, that seems completely out of character."

"It is," Juliette admitted, her voice trembling. "He's never done anything like this before and I haven't received any ransom calls. What should I do?"

"I think you need to file a missing person's report," Samantha advised. "That way, the detectives can pull his financial records and track his movements through his credit or debit card transactions. If someone else has used them, we'll find out."

Juliette swiped a tear from her face, overwhelmed by the gravity of her situation. She couldn't believe what was happening, as though their family hadn't already been through enough.

"Okay, which station should I file the report with?"

"Downtown headquarters," Samantha advised. "My contact, Detective Baker, is expecting you. I'm on my way there now. As District Attorney, I'll make sure Grandville's case is prioritized."

"Thank you, Samantha," Juliette sobbed. "You're a true friend."

"Of course," Samantha said gently. "You're my bestie, and I love you. But pull yourself together, okay? If you're too upset, you won't be able to help Jolene or Grandville."

"I will," Juliette said, trying to steady her voice. "I'll meet you downtown. Let me call the hospital to check in on Jolene and let them know I'll be delayed."

Juliette pulled over to the side of the road and called Jolene's room. Rhonda, her nurse happened to be in the room and answered the phone. After Juliette informed her that she would be arriving a little later than planned, Rhonda passed the phone to Jolene.

"Mommy, when are you coming back?" Jolene whined. "I miss you and I don't wanna be here by myself."

"Aww. I know, ladybug. I promise I'll be back soon. Keep watching television and concentrate on feeling better," Juliette urged.

"Okay, Mom. Will Daddy be here soon?"

Jolene's question seared Juliette's heart like a hot knife, stealing her breath away. "I don't know," she finally sighed, not liking how the insincerity played through her voice. "Try to get back to sleep, and when you wake up, one of us will be there. Okay?"

"Okay, mommy," Juliette could picture her daughter's lips poked out in a pout, which broke her heart, releasing all the guilt pooled inside.

"All right. Give the phone back to the nurse, please."

After a moment, Rhonda said, "Ms. Stubbs, don't worry. Jolene is in good hands. We'll see you soon."

"Thanks so much, Rhonda," Juliette said before disconnecting the call.

Juliette arrived at the police headquarters and her heart pounded as she walked inside. Detective Baker waited for her in the lobby, his short fade and deep mahogany complexion contributed to his striking appearance.

He stood, extending a hand. "Ms. Stubbs?"

Juliette nodded, shaking his hand.

"I'm Detective Baker. Samantha just called and said she'll be here in shortly," he said. "Why don't we go to my office and get started."

"Thank you, detective. I'll do whatever it takes to help find my husband."

“I’m counting on that,” he said with a reassuring nod. “Now tell me everything about Grandville.”

Chapter 33

Lived and Learned

Melinia and Julio exchanged glances, trying to process everything Mimi had shared about her experiences since they left the Bahamas. The three of them had gone to A New Beginning. Julio moved around the kitchen preparing dinner while Rafael and Jesus lay sound asleep in Julio's room, exhausted from their long day at the water park. Meanwhile, the trio gathered around the table, trying to figure out their next move.

"I know why you guys left," Mimi said, her voice soft but firm. "Honestly, I can't even blame you. If I were in your shoes, I'd have left me too."

"Mimi, you know we love you. But I had to think about my kids," Melinia explained, apologetically. "It wasn't an easy decision. Julio didn't want to leave you behind. It was me who made the call."

Julio glanced over from the stove, seasoning the ground beef. "Chica, none of that matters anymore. What's important is you're here now," he said with a big smile. "But we need to figure out where you're going to sleep tonight."

"I can go back to the women's shelter," Mimi offered. "As long as I'm back by 7 PM, they won't turn me away."

Melinia shook her head. "Mimi, it breaks my heart that you're staying at a shelter."

"It's fine. I made my bed, and I'm fully prepared to lie in it."

"No," Melinia said, her hand gently landing on Mimi's arm. "Listen, we've all made mistakes. But we're human, and we all fall down sometimes. You have to learn to forgive yourself. I tell myself that every day. My counselor, Ms. Zenobia, has been a huge help in reminding me of that."

Mimi stared at her hands, her voice trembling. "I don't know if I can forgive myself. The things I've allowed to happen to my body ..." Mimi said, her words trailing off as tears filled her eyes. "I stay high because it's the only way I can forget. But maybe you're right. Maybe I need to try."

Julio turned off the burner and wiped his hands. "Mimi, you've taken the first step by being here and opening up. That's huge. But we need to figure out a way to keep you safe from Larry and help you move forward. Where's Rique and the other members of the Crew?"

"I don't know. They never returned to the Bahamas. After two months, I did what I had to do with whoever could help get me back to the US. I owe too many people money, so I couldn't go home to Detroit. So I came back to Cleveland. I missed you so much, I didn't know what to do," Mimi said, tears spilling over as she stared at Melinia.

"I missed you too, but I don't miss that life," Melinia stated passionately. "I love you like a sister, but I'm not going back to that lifestyle. I have kids, and I owe them so much more than that."

"Melinia, I understand. The last thing I'd ever want to do is screw up everything that you've worked so hard for. I want to find that kind of peace too. I just don't know how." Mimi said.

"I can help get you into a detox and recovery program if you'll let me. I could call Ms. Zenobia right now to get you in."

"What happened to Romanita and Roberto?" Julio asked.

Mimi took a deep breath and smiled. "Well, they were upset when you guys left. Romanita cried for days about Rafael, and Roberto was furious because Romanita was so heartbroken."

Romanita, the sister of Rique—the leader of the Sandego Crew—played a significant role in caring for Rafael while Melinia endured the horrors of being trafficked by the Crew. Tragically, Romanita's life was forever changed when she was sexually assaulted by Julio's brother, a notorious drug dealer in the Dominican Republic. The assault caused her to lose her unborn child, leaving her unable to have children. In an act of vengeance, Rique and the Crew murdered Julio's brother, both for the assault and for killing Romanita's fiancé. Roberto, a nurse and Romanita's personal security guard employed by the Sandego Crew, remained by her side through it all. Together, Romanita and Roberto helped deliver Rafael during a harrowing storm, cementing their connection to Melinia and her oldest son.

"I know how much Romanita loves Rafael, but I saw my chance to escape from the crew with my son, and I took it," Melinia said.

"She's okay now," Mimi said. "About a week after you guys left, some people from the village came by with a three-month-old baby girl. They were speaking in Spanish, and I couldn't understand anything they were saying. But they left without the baby. Roberto later explained that the baby's parents died during the hurricane and that she had no surviving family members. Romanita and Roberto agreed to raise the baby as their own. They're happy and believe that the Crew and their ship went down during the hurricane. There were at least twenty people on the island who died during the hurricane, and they believe that Rique, Remy, Raul, and the rest of the crew died along with them. I found a guy who had his own boat and he brought me to Miami. From there, I did what I needed to do to get to Cleveland."

"So, how did you hook up with Larry?" Melinia asked.

"He would always hang out outside the women's shelter. People said he had the best product next to China White, which he calls good. He claimed to have recognized me from our sex tapes and promised as much product as I wanted if I could get you to join us for a threesome. I had no idea how to locate you, so he asked for your name and said he would find you himself."

"So he knows where you're sleeping. You can't go back there," Melinia said.

"Melinia, you should ask Ms. Zenobia what to do," Julio suggested. "Maybe there's a program where Mimi can be placed for help. The guys are at work for the next few hours so you can sit at the table out on the deck while you talk to her. "

"Okay," Melinia said. "I'll get right on that."

Julio turned to Mimi and took her hands in his. "I missed you too, Mimi. We're the three musketeers, back together again. I'm making a celebration feast and need you to keep me company while I cook."

"What, you can cook?" Mimi jokingly questioned.

"Julio doesn't just cook; he creates. His food is delicious," Melinia said before walking outside while pulling up Zenobia's number on her phone. She picked up after three rings.

"Hello, Melinia. How are you?" she greeted.

"Hello Ms. Zenobia. I'm in a situation, and I really need to talk."

"Okay, what's going on?"

"Mimi, my best friend from when I was in captivity, is here," Melinia revealed.

"Is she clean?" Zenobia wasted no time asking.

"No, she's actively using, but says she wants to get clean. How do we get her into treatment?"

"Okay. Where's she staying?"

"She was at the women's shelter, but she needs somewhere else to stay," Melinia replied.

"She needs a drug assessment before we can put her on the waiting list for detox," Zenobia explained.

"Well, how long do you think that will take?" Melinia asked.

"I don't know, but your friend needs to understand that she can only go through detox once per calendar year."

"Why is it limited to once a year?"

"Unfortunately, some people used to come to detox just to escape bad drugs on the street," Zenobia explained. "As soon as the product improved, they'd leave detox and go right back to using, wasting taxpayer dollars in the process. Now the system is set up to make sure it's a serious commitment."

"That makes sense. What can we expect from the detox process?"

"During detox, she'll get medication to help with withdrawal symptoms. While heroin withdrawal isn't typically fatal, there can be severe complications. Kicking cold-turkey without the proper support is a very painful and difficult process."

"Weaning off it was hell. I can't imagine trying to kick it cold turkey," Melinia replied.

"Yes, that's why it's imperative that we get your friend into detox and then treatment as soon as possible," Zenobia said.

"Agreed. Thank you. I'll talk to Mimi and see what she wants to do."

"So, how has your recovery been going?" Zenobia asked.

"Well, the devil came for me today, but I remembered your words and fought back."

"Oh no. What happened?"

Melinia recounted the encounter with Larry, her voice shaking slightly as she described the terrifying moments in the water park bathroom.

When she finished, Zenobia's voice was filled with pride. "Melinia, I'm so proud of you. You were strong, and you stood your ground. That's a huge victory. But remember, this is just one battle. The war is far from over. The devil isn't done with you yet," Zenobia warned.

"Yes, I know," Melina said quietly. "And that's what scares me."

Chapter 34

Lose it All

Grandville felt as though he was floating. His body was weightless, suspended in a dark void. That's when he saw her—Jessica, his deceased oldest daughter, standing before him. He reached out to touch her, but his hands went right through her, as though she were made of air.

"Hi, Daddy," Jessica said, her voice echoing softly, like a sweet memory.

"Jessica, how are you here? If I'm talking to you, does that mean I'm … dead?" Grandville asked, his voice trembling.

"No, Daddy," Jessica said, a sad smile on her face. "You're not dead. Not yet."

"Then I must be dreaming," Grandville murmured. "Because you … you're gone. How else can I be speaking to you?"

Jessica shook her head gently. "Daddy, no one really dies. I'm always with you. I'm with Mommy, my brothers, and my sisters. Grandma is here with me, too. But God told me to come and tell you: it's not your time. You have to go back."

"I don't want to leave you again," Grandville whispered, tears welling in his eyes. "I'm so sorry for hurting you, baby. Please, let me stay with you."

Jessica stepped closer, her face glowing with tenderness. "I know you didn't mean to hurt me, Daddy. And I'm happy here, with God. But you can't stay. You haven't fulfilled your purpose yet. God says you have more work to do. You need to have a forgiving spirit and unite our family. I love you, Daddy. I love Mommy and my brothers and sisters. And my little cousin. She's going to make Aunt Greta very happy."

Grandville frowned. "This has to be a dream. Greta doesn't have any kids."

Jessica's smile deepened. "Not yet, but she will. Now go back, Daddy," Jessica said, her voice growing more firm. She extended her right arm with her palm facing him. "Go back!"

Grandville's eyes snapped open and excruciating pain surged through his body. His entire side felt as though it were on fire. He yearned to return to Jessica, so he closed his eyes and tried to will himself back to that pain-free realm.

Grandville noticed he was once again lying on the couch, back in the closet where George had imprisoned him. He assumed that while he was unconscious, George had dragged his lifeless body back into his private hell.

"Oh, thank God you woke up. I was so scared," George sobbed, kneeling over him with tears streaming down his face.

Grandville licked his dry lips, then in a weak voice asked, "What happened?"

"You attacked me, and I … I shot you," George stammered through his sobs. "I swear I didn't mean to."

Grandville's searched his son's face. "I know, George," he said. "But you have to get me help, or I'm going to die."

"Just hold on, Dad. My friend Ayana's on her way to help you," George pleaded.

Grandville became so preoccupied with George calling him "Dad" for the first time, he temporarily forgot his pain. It sounded natural, as if he'd been calling him that his entire life.

The sound of the doorbell startled them both. The pain returned jolting Grandville back to reality.

"It's okay, Dad. That's Ayana," George said before rushing out of the closet.

A few minutes later, George returned with a beautiful, thick and curvy girl. Even in his current state, the woman's external beauty wasn't lost on Grandville. Her smooth skin was a rich, dark complexion, and she had a round face, almond-shaped eyes, and long dreadlocks.

"Did you bring your medical bag?" George asked her.

"Yes, I have it right here," Ayana's eyes darted around the dim closet. "But George, what the hell is going on?"

"I … I was showing him my gun, and it accidentally went off." George's words were rushed. "You have to help him."

Ayana took a slow step backward. "Boy, I thought you wanted to play doctor and get it in on some freaky-type stuff. That's the only reason I came. Didn't you say you didn't even know your dad?"

"It's complicated, Ayana. I'll explain it all to you later. Right now, he needs your help."

Ayana's expression darkened. "*My* help? Are you out of your fucking mind calling me over here? Why didn't you call an ambulance? Naw, I'm out of here."

She turned on her heel and was headed toward the bedroom door when George pulled out a gun from his waistband. He cleared his throat and when she turned, she saw it was casually pointed at her.

George's face hardened. "You're not going anywhere, Ayana. Now help my father, or you're going to need help too."

Ayana groaned, pressing her palms to her temples. "I sure know how to pick 'em," Ayana mumbled. With a resigned sigh, she knelt beside Grandville.

She opened her bag and pulled on a pair of gloves. She cut off Grandville's shirt off to get a closer look at his gunshot wound on his abdomen. "There's no way for me to know if his liver, bladder, or kidneys are damaged. He needs an MRI, ASAP. He could bleed out if we don't act fast."

"Ayana, do something!" George barked.

"There's only so much I can do," Ayana snapped back. Turning to Grandville, she said, "This is going to hurt, so I'm sorry in advance." She poured antiseptic on the wound, causing Grandville to scream and writhe in pain. "I told you it would hurt," she muttered as she packed it the wound with gauze.

"Are you a doctor?" Grandville asked weakly. "If so, you need to work on your bedside manner."

"No," Ayana replied, her tone sharp. "But I'm a third-year medical student. I met your loser son at Cleveland College and he hasn't done much for me since. I've had a crush on him since the day we met, so, here I am, like a fool, putting everything I've worked for at risk because you're going to die if we don't get you to a hospital."

"Son," Grandville said, his voice strained. "Please listen to her. We can fix this if you do the right thing and get me help. If you don't get me to a hospital, you'll regret it for the rest of your life. Learn from my mistakes and save yourself, son."

Ignoring his father, George turned his attention back to Ayana. "I'm not trying to take advantage of you. I didn't realize you were interested in me in that way. I asked you to come because I genuinely needed you to help my dad, and I've always considered you to be a friend I can count on."

Ayana frowned, removing her gloves. "Well, if you would have told me, I would've insisted you call 9-1-1."

"I need time to think," George muttered.

"Yeah, because we have all the time in the world." Ayana rolled her eyes.

"If I call an ambulance, what will you tell them?" George asked her.

Ayana pressed her palms to her eyes and groaned. "Damnit, George! I'll tell them whatever the fuck you want me to. I know you're a good dude, George. If you care about your dad at all, you'll call for help. Prove me right."

Grandville nodded in agreement just as his world began to blur as his vision faded. The last thing he heard before everything went black was Ayana's voice pleading, "Don't let your old man die!"

Chapter 35

Where You At

Juliette sat in silence, her eyes fixed on Jolene as she slept peacefully with the monitors beeping softly around her. The weight of the day's events was almost paralyzing. Hours of meetings with Samantha and Detective Baker had yielded little progress on finding Grandville. Despite all their efforts, they were no closer to locating him. There had been no activity on his credit and debit cards and no activity on his accounts since his disappearance. He'd issued an All-Points Bulletin and the police tech unit planned to search Grandville's phone for clues on his whereabouts.

Detective Baker's last words replayed in her mind: *"Ms. Stubbs, we've done all we can today. You and your support system might want to put out flyers and reach out to the local news to help get the word out about your husband's disappearance. The more people who know, the better."*

Even Samantha, her ever-confident and resourceful best friend, seemed shaken by their lack of progress. Samantha's words had been meant to reassure Juliette, but they felt hollow against the backdrop of fear swirling in her mind.

"Julie, did you know that even though African Americans represent over thirteen percent of the population, forty percent of missing persons are people of color?" Samantha had said, her tone more matter-of-fact than comforting.

Juliette had nodded absentmindedly, too exhausted and consumed by worry to care about statistics. *What do numbers matter when my husband is out there missing?* The question echoed in her mind as she tried to focus on the present.

She took a deep breath, attempting to stave off the rising panic that had been her constant companion for the past forty-eight hours. With Grandville missing and Jolene suffering in the hospital, she felt like she was one wrong move away from falling apart.

She reached into her purse and retrieved her Valium. The medication tasted chalky as she swallowed it with a gulp of water. She began her breathing exercises to control her symptoms when her phone began to ring. It was her therapist.

"Hello, Emily," Juliette answered, her voice barely above a whisper.

"Hello, Juliette. I hope I'm not disturbing you, but something told me to check on you," Emily said warmly.

Juliette's composure cracked as a flood of tears spilled out. "I'm not doing so well, Emily."

"Hey, it's okay," Emily reassured her, her tone calm and steady. "Where are you right now?"

"I'm at the hospital with Jolene," Juliette detailed Jolene's diagnosis and the events leading up to her hospitalization.

"Oh, dear. I pray that Jolene feels better soon. Let's connect properly. Do you happen to have your laptop with you?" Emily asked.

"Yes, but I doubt that I'll get any work done tonight," she sighed, the thought of productivity feeling laughable.

"Are you in a private place where we can speak for a few minutes?" Emily suggested.

"Yes, Jolene has a private room, so I'm going to set up my hotspot and put my ai r pods in."

"Okay, I'll send a Zoom link and we can hop on in a couple of minutes," Emily replied.

After they each signed on, Emily's kind eyes shone as she continued, "So, I know you're experiencing a difficult time, but we're going to figure it out. Let's start with some breathing exercises."

Afterward, Juliette felt more relaxed.

"Now, are you ready share what's been going on?" Emily asked.

The floodgates opened, and Juliette quietly recounted everything: Grandville's disappearance, Franklin's condition, and her own fears about the secrets she'd kept from her husband. Emily listened without interruption and took a few notes, her expression empathetic and understanding. Just as Juliette was finishing, one of the nurses came into the room to check Jolene's vitals. Noticing that Juliette was on a Zoom call, she documented the numbers and quickly exited the room.

"Juliette, you've been carrying a lot," Emily said after a few moments of silence. "I hope you realize how strong you are for holding it together through all of this. But I'm also worried about you. You can't keep pouring from an empty cup."

"I know," Juliette whispered, glancing down at her hands.

"Try focusing on what's within your control," Emily continued. "For example, you can't control Grandville's actions or Jolene's health, but you can control how you respond. Start by creating an emotional wellness plan. Write down some actionable self-care practices for when things don't go as planned. That way, you'll have a roadmap to follow when things feel overwhelming."

Juliette nodded, feeling a flicker of hope. "Thanks, Emily. I'll try, but I won't lie, I'm feeling scared that Franklin might have revealed the truth about us being together," Juliette said. "What if Grandville learned the truth, and isn't missing? What if he left?"

"Initially, you had your reasons for not telling Grandville about what happened with Franklin. But it may be time to create a plan for when or if he learns the truth. Better yet, for telling Grandville the whole truth yourself. Less than a year ago you were hospitalized for mental health issues. Given your situation, you may be at risk of suffering a setback," Emily warned.

Juliette nodded. "That's why I believe God put it in your heart to contact me. Talking to you has made me feel a whole lot better."

"I'm so glad I could help. We should schedule another virtual session next week."

"I agree."

"I know you're nervous about Jolene being in the hospital. If you or your family members contract COVID, you'll deal with it. But anxiously worrying about what could happen isn't good for you. Here's an assignment for our next session. Prepare an emotional wellness plan outlining what happens if you or a family member gets COVID," Emily suggested.

"Well, I'm not really sure what steps I would take," Juliette replied.

"That's the point, Julie. Spend some time researching a plan of action. Also, remember to practice your mindfulness and deep breathing exercises. If you're not mentally stable, you won't be able to show up for your family. They depend on your strength and resilience. Got it?"

"Got it."

They scheduled their next appointment before ending the meeting. Before long, her phone rang again. This time it was Maria.

"Hey Maria, how's my beautiful goddaughter?" Juliette asked.

"Hey! She's doing well."

That's when Juliette realized she wasn't speaking to Maria but to her husband Montell, who was Franklin's best friend at Oakhill.

"Hey Montell, how are you?" Juliette asked.

"I'm blessed. I've been trying to catch up with Grandville. He didn't show up for our weekly chess game. Rayshawn's also been reaching out, but his phone is going straight to voicemail. Is he with you now?"

Juliette's heart sank. She quickly explained the situation, her voice heavy with worry.

"Damn," Montell muttered. "Grandville would never just disappear like that."

"Right," Juliette sighed into the phone while massaging her temples. She was emotionally exhausted from retelling the recent, stressful events of their lives.

"Well, you're not in this alone, Juliette. What do you need from me?" Montell asked.

"Please just pray that Grandville comes home safe."

"Done."

As she ended the call, Juliette eased back into the chair. Although she felt only a slight reprieve from her stress, she still felt a sliver of hope penetrating the dark cloud that had loomed over her all week.

Chapter 36

Best for Me

After hanging up with Zenobia, Melinia found Julio and Mimi in the kitchen, laughing and talking. Julio was teaching Mimi how to sauté mushrooms.

"What are y'all up to?" Melinia asked, entering the kitchen.

"Preparing dinner," Julio said, smiling. "We're almost done with the prep. Then I'll work my magic."

Melinia clasped her hands together in front of her face, smiling. "I can't wait! But honestly, I'm still stuffed after that huge lunch we had."

"Don't worry. I'll pack up your plate and you can eat when you're ready," Julio said. "Why don't you take Mimi out on the deck while the boys are still napping. I'll make some lemonade, and I'll bring out a pitcher."

The two women lounged comfortably on the patio, the warm afternoon sun embracing them.

"So, I spoke to my counselor, and we have a plan," Melinia said. "We'll get you into detox, and then you'll transition to rehab. After that, I'll reach out to my cousin about placing you at her female rooming house, A Better Tomorrow. She has funding programs that cover room and board, so you won't have to worry about Larry or finding a place to stay. You can just focus on your recovery."

Mimi smiled faintly, but there was a flicker of doubt in her eyes. "I don't know, Mel. What if I fail?"

"You won't. I won't let you. I have big plans in the works, Mimi, and I need you to be part of them. I want to start a nonprofit to help women who've survived human trafficking, just like us. We know the humiliation and shame firsthand, so we can help others in ways no one else can."

"I'm not sure if I'm ready to share my story yet," Mimi admitted, her voice soft.

"You don't have to right now, maybe not ever. What matters is that you start with the first step: admitting you're powerless over heroin and committing to the process. I love you, Mimi, like a sister, but I've changed. I'm not the same woman I was back then. I can't risk my sobriety or my boys' safety."

Mimi nodded, tears welling up in her eyes. "I get it. I'm not asking for anything except the chance to try. I just need to know you're here for me."

"I am. Always. But Mimi, you have to meet me halfway. No one can do the work except you," Melinia replied, her voice firm and full of love.

Julio emerged onto the deck with a pitcher of lemonade and two glasses filled with ice. "I know you both must be parched. It's hot today." Just then, Joe came out to join them.

"Julio, I see we have company." His broad smile brightened as he glanced at Mimi.

"Aye, Joe. Yes, you remember Melinia. And this is Mimi, a dear friend we've just reconnected with. They'll be joining us for dinner."

Joe shook Mimi's hand. "Nice to meet you, Mimi. How are you ladies doing today?"

"We're good. How are you?" Melinia responded.

"I'm great. I got off a little early from my landscaping job today," Joe replied. "Do either of you play chess?"

"I do." Mimi nodded.

"So, why did I always get stuck playing Rique on La Barca?" Melinia teased.

"What's La Barca?" Joe asked.

"It was the name of the ship where Melinia and I worked," Mimi explained quickly.

"Well, if you're up for it, I'd love to play a game with you." Joe asked with a smile.

"Sure, I'd like that," Mimi said, a hint of enthusiasm in her voice.

"Great! Let me get my chess set. I'll be right back," Joe said as he went inside.

Melinia said to Mimi. "After dinner, we need to decide our next move. Larry isn't going to give up easily."

"Hell, we should be planning our next two moves," Mimi added with a scoff.

Joe returned, setting up an ornate chessboard on the table.

"This is a pretty nice set," Melinia complimented.

"Yes, it's my favorite. It was a gift from Grandville," Joe shared.

Mimi and Joe started the game and Melinia excused herself to go check on the boys, who were sleeping in Julio's room. Their small bodies were curled up peacefully. On her way back to the kitchen, she saw Julio stirring something in a large bowl.

"Need any help?" she offered.

"No, I've got it under control," he replied. "But I've been thinking—it might be a good idea for you, Mimi, and the boys to stay here tonight … to give us time to regroup. You and the boys can stay in my room and I'll sleep on the couch."

"Julio, are you trying to get me into your bed?" She teased, unable to restrain her laugh.

"Yes. I can't stand the thought of Larry showing up at your place. At least if you're here, I can protect you."

Melinia smirked. Her little joke clearly went way over Julio's head, which she blamed on the language barrier. "You're hopeless."

Julio ignored her teasing and continued. "Seriously. I was so scared when I saw that man hurting you. If I hadn't found you in time …"

Melinia placed a hand on his arm. "Julio, I was terrified too. Everything happened so fast. Larry's been following me for weeks. I thought he was working with a drug dealer I owe money or something."

"What! Why didn't you tell me?" Julio demanded.

"I didn't want to worry you. At least I still have his gun and can use it for protection for when I'm alone with the boys."

"Well, we can change that whenever you're ready," Julio said suggestively.

"Whatever, Julio. One of these days, I'm going to say yes," Melinia teased.

"I'm counting on it, but back to the gun. You can't have it around the boys. And it could have bodies on it. If you're caught with it, you can be charged for who knows what," Julio explained. "I'll take care of it. Now I have to get back to making dinner," Julio explained as he opened the refrigerator and pulled out a jar of mayonnaise.

"Okay, if you say so. I don't know how to use a firearm, anyway," Melinia shrugged. After a few moments of thoughtful silence, she was ready to change the subject. "So, what's for dinner?"

"Pernil and macaroni salad. The meat has been in the crockpot since this morning."

"I have no idea what pernil is, but it sure smells delicious," Melinia said.

"It's a popular Dominican dish made with pork shoulder, lime juice, oranges, and seasoning. You're going to love it, I promise," Julio said, smiling confidently.

Later that evening, everyone enjoyed dinner on the deck. The pernil sandwiches were a hit, their savory flavors earning praise from everyone. Mimi proved to be a formidable chess opponent, but Big Joe ultimately claimed victory.

"This was a good game," Mimi said with a smile. "But next time, I'm coming for you."

"Bring it on," Joe teased.

After dinner, Mimi helped bathe the boys and tuck them into bed. Julio made a pallet on the floor for Mimi to sleep on as he prepared to sleep on the couch. After he fell asleep, the ladies got a chance to talk alone.

"I'm so glad I found you and Julio again," Mimi said.

"Yes, I thought about you often when we were apart. But Mimi," Melinia took her friends' hands in hers, "what's your plan if detox takes weeks to open up. I don't want any drugs around me and the boys. God has given me the gift of life and delivered me, so I plan to stay drug-free, sis."

"I get it, Melinia. I have methadone, and I'm going to use it to wean myself off," Mimi said. "I'm just praying it works."

"Do you think you can do it?" Melinia asked.

"I've asked God to deliver me from heroin like He did for you. I know He hears me and I hope He'll answer my prayers," Mimi said.

Melinia silently prayed for her friend, her heart heavy with hope and fear. "Me too, sis. Me too."

Chapter 37

Freedom

When Grandville's eyes fluttered opened, his vision was blurred, and his body was drenched in sweat. The unbearable heat in his abdomen made it feel like he'd woken up in hell. Every muscle screamed in pain, and when he attempted to pull the covers off his body, a sharp, searing ache tore through his side. It was heavily bandaged. He barely had time to process it before two faces came into focus. Anaya and George.

"You're one hell of a doctor," George exhaled in relief. "He's awake."

Ayana crossed her arms. "Yes, I can see that, but I'm not a doctor. And if I keep getting dragged further into this, I never *will* be."

"Relax. When this is over, I'll take the fall," George assured her. "I'll tell them I lured you here, forced you to help."

"Oh, you won't be taking the fall. That's just facts," Ayana shot back with a glare. "I didn't sign up for this mess."

Grandville lay weak and still, his breathing shallow. Ayana placed the back of her hand on Grandville's forehead, then stuck a thermometer into his mouth. "Just what I thought. He's burning up with fever."

"Then fix it," George snapped.

Ayana sighed heavily. "There isn't much I *can* do. I have some oral antibiotics, but a fever can mean an infection or poor circulation from blood loss. He's lost a lot and if he does have an infection, I have no idea where it is!"

"Give him the antibiotics and some pain meds," George ordered. "I see that big-ass bottle of Oxy sitting on top of your stethoscope."

"That's my emergency stash and I'm not supposed to have it. I took it from the room of a patient who had passed away," Ayana whined.

"Well, considering that this is an emergency," George said flatly. "use it."

Grandville listened, but his mind was elsewhere. Juliette. His heart ached for her. Was she okay? He pictured her sitting with their kids, worried sick, searching for answers. He hated knowing she was probably suffering—and that he wasn't there to fix it.

Grandville realized that with his fever and blood loss, his chances of survival were slim. He wanted his beloved to know how much he loved her, and the thought of not seeing her again brought tears to his eyes. He recalled the first time he laid eyes on her in that coffee shop and ached to see her again, to feel her caress and kiss once more.

He was jolted out of his thoughts by Ayana's words. "Here, take these pills. Hopefully, they'll reduce the pain."

Ayana shoved the pills between his lips and lifted a bottle of water to his mouth. The bitter, chalky taste lingered long after he swallowed.

"We need cold compresses to bring your dad's fever down," Ayana advised.

George hesitated, causing Ayana to roll her eyes. "Now, George. And bring ice."

With a warning glance, George stalked out of the room, locking the closet door behind him. As soon as he was gone, Grandville turned his head toward Ayana. His voice was weak, but firm.

"If I don't make it," he rasped, "I need you to deliver a message to my wife."

Ayana's brows lifted. "Why can't your demon-seed son deliver it himself?"

Grandville frowned at the venom in her voice. For a moment, she no longer looked beautiful. Just bitter. He felt his energy fading. "Please, tell my wife Juliette that I love her. And that I want her to forgive George for what he's done to me, just as I forgive her. I don't want her to hold on to that hate. She needs to ensure George gets the help he needs."

Ayana studied him for a while before nodding. "Okay, but you'll tell her yourself."

Before Grandville could respond, the door burst open. George walked in carrying ice and a few towels. "What were you two whispering about?"

"His pain," Ayana said smoothly, grabbing the ice. "Nothing else."

George eyed her but didn't push. "So, what now?"

"I want you to let us go. But since I know you won't do that, put a compress with ice on his wrists," she instructed.

George hesitated but did as she said, gently placing the compress on his clammy skin. Ayana placed another compress on his forehead.

"If his fever rises above 105, it will damage his organs. If it reaches 108, he can suffer brain damage," Anaya said.

"I'm really grateful to you, Ayana, for helping me through this," George said. "But I need you to do one last thing."

"What now?"

"Give me your phone."

Ayana stiffened. "Why?"

"Just unlock it and give it to me."

Ayana reached into her bra and obeyed his order.

"Send a text to Claire," George replied as he scrolled through her contact list. "She's your roommate, right?"

"She moved out last month."

"But she's still your best friend. Tell her you're spending the night with this guy, who you met online." He held up her screen, showing her a guy's picture. "He looks just like your type."

"Claire will never believe that," Ayana said while applying another compress to Grandville's head. "I'm not like that. She knows I only wanted to be with you, and I kept waiting for you to notice me. I don't know what I ever saw in you."

George hesitated. "So, you're not pulling game? You actually wanted me? A college dropout?"

Ayana scoffed. "Yeah. And I was an idiot for it."

George's grip on her phone tightened. "I don't get it. I don't have anything going for me." He gestured toward Grandville. "I didn't even know who I was. That's why I did all this. He owes me an explanation."

She exhaled sharply. "George, I know you're struggling. But *this*—" she gestured to the locked closet, to Grandville's feverish body, to herself "—isn't the way."

"Son," Grandville whispered. "Listen to her."

George glanced between them, emotions warring on his face. "Be quiet. Save your strength."

Grandville closed his eyes. Because he didn't have much of it left.

Chapter 38

Wake Up Alone

Juliette's restless sleep was disturbed by the shrill ringing of her phone. Still groggy, she picked it up without checking the caller ID.

"Hello?"

"Mommy," came Jenae's small, sweet voice on the other end. "When are you and Jolene coming home?"

Juliette's heart ached at the longing in her daughter's tone for her and her twin sister. "Jolene is really sick, sweetheart. I have to stay with her, but hopefully, she'll get better soon so we can both come home."

"Okay …" Janae whined softly.

Juliette glanced at her watch. "What are you doing up at six AM?"

"I couldn't sleep," she admitted. "I'm used to Jolene being in the room with me."

"I know, baby, but you need to rest," Juliette gently urged. "I don't want you getting sick too. Did Aunt Greta help you call me?"

"No, Mommy. I don't need any help. I just dialed your cell number. Aunt Greta made us learn both your numbers by heart."

Juliette smiled faintly, hearing Greta's distinct voice in the background.

"Little girl, who are you talking to and why are you up so early?"

"I couldn't sleep, and I missed my Mommy," Jenae replied.

"Okay, let me speak to her while you go and get back in bed. I'm going to make breakfast, and I'll come and get you as soon as it is ready."

"Okay, Auntie. Mommy, Aunt Greta wants to speak to you," Jenae said into the phone.

"Okay, sweetie, give her the phone. I love you, and will see you soon," Juliette said.

"I love you too, Mommy."

Greta came on the line sighing. " Hey Juliette. Sorry if she woke you guys. How's Jolene?"

"It's no problem. My baby can call anytime. Jolene's still not feeling well, but I'm hoping the treatment starts working soon. I'll know more when the doctor returns. Hopefully, he'll tell me when she might be able to come home. How are things going there?"

"Well, we were having an uneventful night until I received a call from Grandville's parole officer. He asked all kinds of questions about him."

Juliette froze. "What kind of questions?"

"When I last saw him. If he'd called or texted from a different phone number in the past seventy-two hours. Juliette … is Grandville in trouble?"

Juliette realized she couldn't keep lying to her sister-in-law, so she took a deep breath and said, "Greta, I love you like a sister. But your pregnancy is why I haven't been completely honest."

"Juliette, please don't treat me like this. Whatever's going on with my brother, I can handle it. I might even be able to help."

Juliette sighed. "I know you're strong, and you've been an enormous help. I didn't want to add to your stress. Which is why I didn't tell you that Grandville is missing," Juliette said, her voice breaking.

"What do you mean he's missing?" Greta's voice was edgy.

Juliette explained everything—the hospital visit, Grandville's disappearance, and the lack of leads. "Greta, I just don't know what to think."

A heavy silence followed, and Juliette waited nervously for Greta's response.

Then, as if the details had suddenly sunk in, Greta let out a sharp gasp. "Wait. What?" Her voice pitched higher, laced with disbelief. "Grandville's been missing, and you didn't tell me?"

Juliette swallowed. "Greta, I—"

"No!" Greta's voice cracked, and Juliette could hear her footsteps pacing. "How long has he been missing?"

"Since he left the hospital after visiting Franklin."

Greta let out a string of curse words, her breaths coming in sharp gasps. "Are you—Juliette, how could you not *tell* me? That's my brother! My *twin*!"

Regret washed over Juliette as she squeezed her eyes shut. "It was for your protection, Greta."

"My protection?" Greta practically shrieked. "Who gave you the right to decide what I should and should not know? This isn't a random person—we're talking about *Grandville*! And I'm just finding out now?"

"Greta—"

"No, Juliette," Greta snapped. "You don't get to decide for me. I felt something was off, but I ignored it because I completely trusted you."

Juliette flinched. Not at her tone, but at the hurt in her voice.

After a shaky breath, and another, Greta whispered, "I just can't believe this."

"Greta, I—"

Greta cut her off, her tone suddenly ice-cold. "Tell me everything. *Now*."

“I don’t know where Grandville is, but I’m working on locating him. I’ve involved the police and Samantha’s arranging a press conference to get the word out. There’s very little we can do right now except wait and pray.”

“My brother would never just leave without telling you or me. He’s still upset about the time he was forced to spend away from his family when he was in Oakhill. He would never just leave,” Greta said. “Promise you’ll keep me updated on any information that might indicate where Grandville might be.”

Juliette nodded emphatically, even though her sister-in-law couldn’t see her. “Yes, I promise.”

“ I’m going start breakfast for the kids. Then I’ll reach out to my contacts and see what else we can do to try to find him.”

When they hung up the phone, Juliette rubbed her forehead trying to ease the growing tension behind her eyes. The pressure of the exhaustion of the past few days coupled with Greta coming down on her in a hormonal rage crushed her head and chest like an unrelenting vice.

She desperately needed coffee.

After checking on Jolene one more time, she slipped out of the room and followed the signs to the hospital cafeteria. The hallways were eerily quiet in the early morning hours, the only sound she heard was the occasional shuffle of nurses and the soft hum of overhead lights.

Inside the cafeteria, the smell of burnt coffee and disinfectant filled the air. She poured herself a large cup, added sugar and cream, then headed toward the register. As she reached for her wallet, a quiet sob caught her attention.

She turned her head and spotted a woman seated alone at a nearby table. Her shoulders were hunched and her hands covered her face.

Juliette hesitated, but something in her gut told her not to resist the opportunity to encourage another woman in need. She slowly approached her. "Hey," she said softly. "I don't know what happened, but it's going to be okay."

"I'm fine," the woman said as she lifted her head. Her red-rimmed eyes locked with Juliette's and widened in surprise as she said, "Wait, I recognize your voice."

Juliette frowned, studying the woman more closely. Her voice sounded familiar to her as well. Then it hit her.

"Is your name Bonita?" she asked with uncertainty.

"Yes." Bonita wiped her cheeks hastily. "Ms. Stubbs?"

"Please, call me Juliette," she took a seat across from her.

"What are you doing here," Bonita asked.

"My daughter's in the pediatric wing. She's been sick. What about Ben? How's he doing?"

Bonita's face crumpled. "Not good. He's also in the pediatric wing. He caught COVID while he was in the pediatric psychiatric ward," she said, wiping her face.

Juliette gasped, covering her mouth with her hand. "Oh, Bonita …I'm so sorry."

She nodded. "Thanks. I can't believe this is happening. He's only eleven; just a kid. And I had no idea… no idea what he was going through until it was too late."

Juliette's stomach twisted. "What do you mean?"

"While he was in the psych ward, I found out Ben was being blackmailed by some damn adults!"

A chill ran down Juliette's spine. She immediately reached out and grabbed Bonita's shaky hands. Right now, she needed her, and whatever was going on with Ben was more important than her own exhaustion.

Chapter 39

As It Was

Melinia set the table while watching Julio make breakfast for the New Beginning household, silently wondering what her next move should be. She and her sons couldn't stay with Julio and the residents indefinitely. And then there was Mimi. She needed a safe place to go, away from the temptations that had nearly destroyed her. More concerning was the risk of Mimi's presence jeopardizing Joe and Kane, both of whom were part of the Oakhill Post-Release Program. If parole officers conducted a surprise visit and found Mimi in the house, they could be sent back since they were prohibited from associating with active drug users or felons. Melinia had to act quickly.

"You're deep in thought. What's wrong?" Julio asked, cracking eggs into a bowl.

"Do you have ESP? You always seem to know what I'm thinking," she replied.

"Not always," Julio said, sprinkling in cheese. "Right now, I have no clue, but I can tell that something's bothering you."

"Julio, we need to get Mimi out of this house. Her being here puts everyone at risk."

"I don't think Mimi being here is a problem," Julio said, whisking the eggs. "Besides, Rafael is going to love these cheese eggs."

Melinia frowned. "Julio, we have much bigger problems than breakfast. Kane and Joe can get sent back to Oakhill, and if that happens, Juliette could lose her funding. If that happens, you'll lose your job. And without a job, you'll be out of compliance with your visa. You could be sent back to the DR."

Julio's easy demeanor shifted. "Damn, Chica, I didn't think about all that." He set the whisk down. "What are we going to do? I don't want to abandon Mimi again. She needs us."

"I have an idea. Mimi, the boys, and I can go to a motel for a few days. I'll call Ms. Zenobia and ask if there's funding available to cover the cost."

Melinia's phone rang, startling them both. The caller ID displayed "Private Caller."

"This may be Juliette. I need to take this," She said, stepping onto the deck for privacy.

"Hello?"

"Ms. Gatlin, this is Zack Jordan."

Her posture straightened. "Hello, Mr. Jordan. How can I help you?"

"Mr. Robinson reviewed your proposal and agreed to your terms. I'm in Cleveland today and have arranged for a private doctor's office to conduct the DNA test. Can you and your son meet me this afternoon?"

"I would, but I have to work," Melina lied.

"Mr. Robinson is willing to compensate you for lost wages."

Melinia hesitated. "Has Rayshawn signed my agreement?"

"Yes, I notarized it myself. When we meet, I'll also notarize your signature of Mr. Robinson's documentation of your arrangements, including a non-disclosure agreement. Additionally, Mr. Robinson requests all copies of the tape. Once I receive them along with a sworn affidavit confirming there are no other copies, I'll provide a cashier's check. Shall I send a car service?"

Melinia exhaled, feeling an unexpected wave of relief. "Text me the time and the address. I'll meet you there."

After ending the call, she sent up silent prayer of gratitude. A text came through from Zack, stating their appointment was schedule for 3 PM. She had eight hours to pull everything together.

She needed fresh clothes for herself and Rafael, and there was no way she could risk returning to her apartment—not with Larry lurking.

As she walked back into the house, she collided with a solid wall of a human named Big Joe.

"Sorry, Joe," she said, looking up at him. "You okay?"

Joe eyes were casted downward. "I'm fine. I should have been watching where I was going."

Melinia studied his face. "You seem a little down. Are you okay?"

He sighed. "Yeah, I guess I am a little down. My job didn't need me for the second time this week. I'm saving up to buy a car and need the hours."

"Ah, that's too bad," she said. Then a thought suddenly came to her. "I have a legal way for you to make a hundred bucks for less than one hour of work. I just need you to promise that you won't tell anyone about my proposition."

Joe eyed her warily. "That usually means trouble."

"I said it's legal, Joe. I promise, I'd never ask you to do something wrong. I'm trying to be a better person just like you," Melinia said, joining him at the patio table.

Joe thought about it for a second, then nodded. "Okay, Melinia. I'm listening."

"I'm going to level with you. I have a creep who's after me. He knows where I live, and I need to get some clothes for me and my boys. Since he doesn't know what you look like, I was hoping you could grab them for me. I'll cover your Uber there and back."

"Okay, that doesn't sound like it would be a problem. And you're sure this guy isn't law enforcement?" Joe asked suspiciously.

"I swear. It's just a guy who's been threatening to hurt me. I'm taking my sons to a motel tonight, but we need clothes and more baby formula. Please, help me out, Joe," Melinia pleaded.

"Of course, Melinia."

"Wonderful. Let's plan for after breakfast," Melinia said as she went back into the house. Julio was putting the finishing touches on breakfast, which consisted of waffles, eggs, and bacon.

"Let me help you with the food," she offered.

"I got this, but you can go wake Mimi and the kids so they can eat," Julio directed.

"Sure. Julio, I need to ask a favor," Melinia said.

"Anything for you, Chica."

"I need to borrow two hundred dollars. I'll get it back to you tomorrow."

Julio set down his spatula and studied her for a long moment.

"But if you don't have it, I understand," she said.

"Okay. As long as you can promise you won't spend it on drugs."

"I'd never do that," Melinia said, her voice tinged with hurt. "Not for myself, and not for Mimi."

"I believe you, Melinia. You wouldn't do anything like that to her." He retrieved the money from his wallet and handed it to her.

She smiled. "Thanks, Julio."

Melinia went to wake Mimi, who was sound asleep on the floor before waking up the boys. After changing and feeding Jesus, she made a list of items she needed from her apartment.

Melinia smiled because her plan was coming together without a hitch. Now, she just had to hope her luck lasted.

Chapter 40

Creepin

Grandville drifted in and out of consciousness, the agony in his body dulled only slightly the pills Ayana had given. But the ache in his body paled in comparison to the pain in his heart.

George. His own son had done this to him.

And then there was Juliette. Was it true? Had she and Franklin betrayed him? Franklin's last words haunted him: *Forgive her. It's my fault.* But what did he mean? Had he survived? Grandville had lost all concept of time. How long had George been holding him there? For all he knew, Franklin was dead.

The voices crept in, sinister and unrelenting.

Momma said don't trust anyone. You deserve this hurt. You lied to Juliette and she and Franklin lied to you.

"Shut up!" Grandville yelled, startling Ayana and George.

"What the hell?" George frowned. "We didn't say anything."

Grandville swung his restrained arms, attempting to fight the voices only he could hear.

"What are you doing?! Ayana, do something!" George barked.

Ayana pressed her hand to Grandville's forehead. "He is burning up again. He might be delusional. We need something stronger to hold his hands so he doesn't hurt himself."

George ran out of the closet, locking the door behind him.

"Tell them to shut up! They're lying about my mother," Grandville whispered to her.

"Hey, it's going to be okay. Try to relax," Ayana said soothingly.

You're worthless and a liar. Just wait until everyone learns he's the child of your dead half-sister/cousin. Grandville whimpered, too exhausted from the internal and physical pain, he could barely keep his eyes open.

He closed his eyes and attempted to drown out the noise by thinking about Juliette. Was Juliette having an affair with Franklin? How could she do that? Is that what Franklin meant about karma coming for him? He would have died for either of them. The questions swirled endlessly in his mind, along with the whispering voices.

He felt someone touching his hands and realized that George had returned with a piece of rope. He was tying his hands to the side of the small couch, leaving Grandville unable to move his handcuffed hands.

"Just relax. It's going to be okay," George said.

"No, it's not going to be okay," Grandville snapped. "Thanks to you, nothing will ever be the same."

George scoffed. "You act like I wanted this. I just needed you to listen, but no, you had to fight me. I never meant to hurt you."

Grandville let out a bitter laugh, immediately regretting it as pain shot through his abdomen. "You shot me, George. You don't get to play victim here."

Grandville closed his eyes, done with the conversation. George wasn't going to get him real medical help, so there wasn't anything else to say.

"It was an accident. And I got Ayana to come over and care for you, didn't I?" George said.

"For the last time, George, I am *not* a medical professional. I'm a student. And this will be the last time that I say it," Ayana snapped, applying ice to Grandville's forehead.

"Maybe I should just do it," George mumbled, beginning to pace across the floor.

Ayana narrowed her eyes and asked. "Do what?"

"Kill us all. Hell, I don't have a fucking thing to live for!"

"You selfish asshole," Ayana spat.

George asked, lifting his shirt to reveal the gun in his waistband. "You wanna rethink that?"

Ayana didn't flinch. "Nope. You've got a whole lot of nerve, threatening us when the real problem is that you're too much of a coward to face your own demons."

"Let me ask you a question, Ayana. Do you know who your biological parents are?"

"Yes, and that has nothing to do with you holding us hostage," she shot back. "You think not knowing gives you the right to ruin lives? Your father may have made some mistakes, but so have you, especially right now. Maybe try forgiveness instead of vengeance, because you'll need a lot of forgiveness after today."

George's eyes darkened. "He should be begging for my forgiveness."

Ayana scoffed. "God, you sound ridiculous. Look, I get it—you're angry, confused. But news flash: everyone's been hurt before. The difference is, most people don't resort to kidnapping and attempted murder."

George exhaled sharply. "You don't understand."

"You're right. I don't understand why you think destroying your life will fix anything." Ayana softened slightly. "You have a choice here, George. You don't have to go down this road."

George let out a dry chuckle. "You know, I never thought a woman like you would give me the time of day. I've been trying to date Cora, but her mom can see right through me. She knows I'm messed up."

"This is all over that chicken-head girl who's the president of the Black Student Union?" Ayana questioned.

"Yes, she's the president of the BSU. No, she's not a chicken head," George corrected her.

"Well, why didn't you call her today instead of me?"

"My sperm donor needed help and I knew you'd come through for me. In a different time and under different circumstances, you would have been the love of my life. I'm sorry that I dragged you into this mess."

"George, it isn't too late. We can be together right now. But that won't ever happen if you're locked up for murder. Only you can make this right," Ayana pleaded.

Grandville was barely listening to their conversation because he was busy praying that she'd be able to convince George to let them go. He was in so much pain that he was starting to lose touch with reality. The voices in his head blurred into white noise, his pain overshadowing everything. Then, he felt his body begin violently convulsing.

"Oh my God! Ayana, what's happening to him?" George yelled in panic.

He felt his body being turned on its side. "He's seizing! We're out of time," Ayana said. "We need to get him to the hospital—now!"

As Grandville's world slipped into darkness, the last thing he heard was Ayana shouting orders and George cursing under his breath. His fate was now resting in his son's hands....

Chapter 41

On Everything

Juliette half-watched *The Proud Family, Louder and Prouder* while Jolene who giggled at the antics of the animated family. She wished she could share in her daughter's amusement, but her mind was still trapped in the conversation she'd had with Bonita.

"After Ben was taken to the hospital, I went into his room, hoping to find a suicide note or some explanation for why he'd want to harm himself," Bonita had sobbed. *"That's when I discovered that he was being blackmailed."*

"How did you find out? Did he leave a letter?" Juliette had asked.

"No. So, I checked his computer. That's when I saw it," Bonita had said, breaking down completely, tears soaking through her mask.

"Bonita, take a breath," Juliette had soothed, reaching into her purse for a fresh mask. After doing a few breathing exercises together, Juliette continued. "I know this is overwhelming, but we'll get through it. Let's start over."

Bonita nodded, replacing her mask.

"Now, you were saying that you looked at Ben's computer. What did you find?"

"Ben received three hundred messages in the past three weeks from Russian cybercriminals.

They'd apparently tricked Ben into sending them incriminating pictures of himself," Bonita explained, shaking her head. "The police said they use artificial intelligence programs to pose as American kids. Once they get the images, they extort them for money." Bonita's hands trembled as she wiped her eyes. "Ben is only eleven, but he had saved up about two hundred and fifty dollars. He gave them everything he had, but they still wanted more."

"Oh my God."

"It gets worse." Bonita's voice cracked. "When he told them he didn't have more money, they threatened to post his pictures on his social media accounts. They said they'd also send them to his teachers, to me, and to his father. They told him he should just kill himself."

Juliette clutched her chest. "Bonita! That's horrific."

"He tried to explain that he was just a kid, and that he didn't have access to any more money, but they kept pressuring him. They sent over five hundred messages in one month, taunting him, urging him to take his own life. The only reason we found out in time is because he confided in Blake. And thank God Blake told your son, and you called me. We got to him just in time. Now, I'm just praying he survives COVID, too."

Juliette sighed heavily and closed her eyes. "Bonita, this is beyond heartbreaking, but Ben is strong. He's going to get through this."

"Thank you. I'm going to remove all social media from the boys' phones. I can't monitor everything they do and I can't worry myself to death about what they're doing or who they're talking to when I'm not around."

Juliette had shared about monitoring software she and Grandville used to track their children's online activity. *"Some parents think it's invasive, but I believe it's another tool to keep them safe."*

The conversation stayed with Juliette long after they'd parted ways. Now, as she absently stroked Jolene's hair, her phone buzzed on the hospital bedside table. Greta's name flashed on the screen. She hesitated before answering, still feeling the sting from their last conversation about Grandville. Exhaling, she picked up.

"Hello."

"Hey," Greta said, her tone neutral. "How's Jolene?"

"The same. I'm waiting for the doctor to check in." Juliette kept her voice even, unsure of where this conversation would go. "How are the kids?"

"They're fine." Greta paused. "Jabari helped me with taco night. You know how much he loves 'helping.'"

Juliette smiled despite herself. "I really miss them. I think I'll stop by later to see them and grab some fresh clothes."

There was another pause, this one heavier.

"Look, Juliette… I'm sorry," Greta sighed, "for how I reacted the other day. You were only trying to protect me, and I shouldn't have snapped at you."

Juliette closed her eyes. "I'm also sorry. I should've told you sooner. I just—" She stopped, rubbing her forehead. "I didn't want to complicate things so early in your pregnancy."

"I get it. But Grandville's my brother. So, keeping me in the dark only worsened the impact of the news."

"I can understand that."

Silence settled between them, but this time, it wasn't as tense.

"I forgive you," Greta said softly. "And I hope you'll forgive me, too."

Juliette let out a slow breath. "Of course, I do. You know I hate it when we have disagreements."

"Me too, Julie," Greta said. Then she cleared her throat. "Now, I need to tell you something important."

Juliette tensed. "What is it?"

"I organized a campaign to help find Grandville. We've scheduled ads on Facebook, Instagram, satellite radio—all of it."

Juliette's eyes widened. "Wait, what?"

"I couldn't just sit around waiting. I had to do something."

Juliette swallowed back the lump in her throat. "When did you—how?"

"Last night. Yvette Lawson—I don't know if you know her, she's a soror from the other chapter—introduced me to a talented voice actor named Patience Hampton. She's from Cleveland and her voice is like velvet, but strong. The kind that makes people stop and listen. I hired her to record the ads, and I paired it with pictures of Grandville."

Juliette pressed a hand to her chest. "Greta… that's amazing."

"I just sent it to your email. Watch it when you can."

"I will. But how much did all this cost? I can help."

"No, you won't." Greta's voice was firm. "You and Grandville have let me live with you rent-free for all this time. This is the least I can do."

Juliette swallowed hard, getting emotional. "I don't know what I'd do without you."

"Thank me when he's home," Greta said. "I also hired a private investigator."

Juliette sat up straighter. "Who?"

"Montell put me in touch with a retired cop-turned-PI named O'Leary. He and Montell are working together to follow any leads from the ads."

"Do you think a private investigator will find out more than the police?"

Greta hummed thoughtfully. "Maybe, maybe not. But I also put up a cash reward—ten grand."

Juliette's jaw dropped. "Greta! That's crazy! You—"

"Don't argue with me," Greta interrupted. "If money motivates someone to come forward, it'll be well worth it."

Juliette shook her head in disbelief. "I just can't believe you pulled all of this together so quickly."

"I don't play about my twin. We need to bring Grandville home."

Before Juliette could respond, the door swung open, and Jolene's medical team stepped in.

"Hey Greta, Jolene's doctors just walked in. I'll call you back later, okay?"

"Okay. Keep me posted."

As Juliette ended the call, she felt much lighter. The tension between her and her sister-in-law had lifted and been replaced with something far stronger—determination.

The two of them were much stronger as a team. And they would bring Grandville home. Together.

The nurses began examining Jolene while her doctor approached her.

"Good morning, Ms. Stubbs," the doctor said, offering her a kind, but serious smile. "I'm afraid we need to discuss a next step for Jolene."

Juliette's stomach clenched. "What is it?"

"I'm sorry to say that despite the blood transfusions, her sickled cells continue to compromise her oxygen levels."

"What does that mean?"

"It means that Jolene is getting sicker. We need to give her an exchange transfusion."

"I'm sorry, I don't know what that is."

"It's similar to dialysis. We'll slowly remove Jolene's blood, filter out the sickled cells, and replaced it with healthy donor blood."

Juliette swallowed. "Can you use mine?"

The doctor shook his head. "Unfortunately, no. You're a sickle cell carrier, which means your blood contains some abnormally shaped cells. We need to eliminate them, not add more."

"What are the potential risks?"

"Shock, blood clots, lung injuries, even cardiac complications. But in Jolene's case, the benefits far outweigh the risks."

Juliette glanced over at her daughter, who had dozed off in the midst of things. Her vision blurred with unshed tears. "I need a moment, doctor."

"Of course. Take your time."

As the medical team left the room, Jolene watched her darling daughter resting peacefully, totally oblivious to the weight of the decision her mother had to make.

Chapter 42

When I Was Young

Melinia paced the floor, bouncing Jesus in her arms. It was almost one o'clock, and Joe still hadn't returned from her apartment. Anxiety gnawed at her.

"Girl, sit down before you walk a hole in the floor," Mimi teased.

Melinia sighed and sank onto the couch beside her.

"Thank you. All that pacing was driving me crazy. Let's find something to watch," Mimi suggested, reaching for the remote.

"No, I can't focus on anything right now."

"What's wrong? Why are you so antsy?" Mimi asked.

Melinia exhaled sharply. "Maybe it's the fact that I can't go home. Or maybe it's because I have a stalker."

Mimi's face fell. "I'm sorry, Melinia. I never meant to bring Larry into your life. When he said he'd find you for me, I thought he was just talking shit. I never thought he'd actually do it." She sniffed. "But I can't lie, I'm glad he did."

"I'm glad too," Melinia admitted, eying her. "How are you feeling? Any withdrawals?"

Mimi shook her head. "I took a methadone pill this morning, and so far, I'm okay."

"Good. I'm praying that Ms. Zenobia finds a detox placement before you run out."

Mimi nodded, then nudged her. "Now tell me what you're really waiting on."

"Joe. I sent him to my apartment to grab a few things."

Mimi groaned. "I wish I'd known. Most of my clothes are still in a locker at the Greyhound station and the rest are at the shelter. If I don't pick them up, you'll see some random skank walking around in my outfit."

Melinia laughed. "You can just wash the clothes you have on. I have a meeting, and if everything goes well, I'll buy you some new clothes."

Mimi studied her. "What type of meeting?"

"I'll tell you more later. I need you and Julio to watch Jesus. He'll be going down for his nap soon." She pressed a hand to Mimi's arm. "While we're gone, enjoy a long, relaxing bath. When we were being held by Rique and the crew, that was what I missed the most. Immersing yourself in water cleanses more than your body—it helps restore your soul."

Mimi's eyes glistened. "When are you coming back? You're not leaving me again, are you?"

A cautious smile spread across Melinia's face. "No, I'm not leaving you. I love you like a sister, and I want to help you. As long as you want the same for yourself, I'm not going anywhere."

"I get it. I promise, I'm committed to working on myself and I won't drag you down," Mimi replied.

Before Melinia could respond, the front door opened and Joe stepped inside with her duffel bag.

"Hey, Ms. Melinia. Sorry it took so long. When I got to your apartment building, it was surrounded by the police," Joe confided.

"What happened?" Melinia asked, handing Jesus to Mimi.

"They arrested some guy, but I don't know who. I may be a big dude, but I'm intimidated by the police. They see me as a threat before I even open my mouth and I wasn't trying to get caught up. So I waited until they left before going inside. It also took longer than I anticipated to gather everything on your list," Joe explained.

"Thanks, Joe, for everything," Melinia said and hugged him.

"It's no problem. You still want me to order an Uber for you?"

"Yes, please. Come out to the deck with me real quick," Melinia said as she walked out to the deck with Joe behind her. Melinia handed seven twenty-dollar bills to Joe.

"Thank you so much. Here's forty dollars on top of the one hundred. I promised to cover the Uber."

Joe stared at the money in his hands before responding. "Ms. Melinia, it shouldn't cost that much."

"Keep any leftover money as a tip. Here's the address of where I'm going. I need the Uber to be here at 2:30."

"Okay, I'll get the request in now and keep you posted on the estimated arrival time," Joe replied as he pulled out his cell phone. "Here you are."

Joe handed her the large duffle bag and she slung it over her shoulder, and headed toward Julio's room to get Rafael, who was watching TV. She heard Rafael and Julio laughing and talking in Spanish before she opened the door.

"Here she is," Julio said as Juliette entered the room.

"Yes, time to get dressed, buddy. We're going out."

"No nap today?"

She ruffled his hair. "No nap."

Rafael happily jumped up and followed Melinia into the bathroom for a bath. She looked through the duffle bag and saw that Joe had gotten everything on the list, including the old phone with the sex tape. She sighed and realized that she was almost there. She could feel it—her life was about to be forever changed and she would soon have the fresh start she so desperately needed.

Chapter 43

Calling All Angels

Grandville drifted in and out of consciousness. When he opened his eyes again, he realized he was on his side. His body ached in ways he didn't think possible.

George stirred from his chair, nudging Ayana awake. "Look. He's awake again."

Ayana walked over and pressed a hand to Grandville's forehead, sighing in relief. "His fever's down."

"Then why did he start convulsing?" George questioned.

"Probably a febrile seizure," Ayana explained. "It rarely occurs in adults. But it's hard to tell if it will happen again because I can't be sure what's wrong with him, because, again, I'm not a doctor."

"Just be quiet for a moment," George said.

Grandville peeked out of the corner of his eye and saw George sitting in a chair near him, eyes closed. He was so tired, but he was afraid that he would die in his sleep. Despite his efforts, he couldn't keep his eyes open. Soon, he was slipping into a deep dreamlike state.

He was standing in that very same field where he'd last seen his beautiful Jessica. In his mind's eye, he stood in the middle of the colorful flowers swaying in the wind. He longed to see his daughter again.

"Jessica, where are you? Please come and talk to me again!"

Franklin emerged from behind a tree, and walked over, standing directly in front of him.

"I know this has to be a dream," Grandville said.

"Hello, Grandville," Franklin replied.

"Hey, frat. Why are you in my dreams?" Grandville asked.

"I can't leave this earth without talking to you one more time," Franklin said. "I love you, brother, and I know you're going to miss me. But I'll always be with you."

"What are you saying? Are you telling me that you're dead?" Grandville asked.

"Not yet, but soon. I want you to know that I'll help God take care of Jessica until it's your time to join us."

"You can't die, man. You're my best friend. I need you," Grandville cried.

"Grandville, no one really dies if they're remembered. I hope you and your family will never forget me."

"I won't forget you, Frankie, but please tell me what you meant about me forgiving you and Juliette. George has taken me hostage and said you were intimate with Juliette. You're my best friend and my brother, so I know it can't be true. I lost my temper and rushed at him, and he shot me. Now, I'm dying."

"What George said is true, Grandville. I never set out to hurt you or Juliette. You're both family to me. I was broken. It only happened once. Juliette loves you, and I love you too. It wasn't an affair; what occurred was borne out of our mutual love for you. We were both so hurt and broken that we tried to make each other feel better, if only for a moment."

"I don't believe this," Grandville whispered.

"It was not her fault; it was all mine because she was vulnerable, and I took advantage of her. Juliette is a good woman who loves you with every fiber of her being, but she's human. Humans are flawed and make mistakes, and I made a big one. I should've been a better brother and friend to you. I'm slowly leaving this earthly world, and I've asked God to let me talk to you before I enter the pearly gates. Please tell my ride-or-die, Sabrina, that I really love her and wish we had more time to have a family together. Grandville, please help her deal with my death because she's going to need it. God said I could talk to you only if I delivered a message to you from Him."

"How do I wake up from this nightmare?" Grandville cried.

"God said that everything's going to be okay, but only if you find forgiveness within your heart for what you think George and Juliette did to you. I have to go, but don't ever forget that I'll always be with you. When you think about me, please remember the good times we had together and forget the rest." Franklin flashed a faint smile and then he was gone.

Grandville woke up with a start, tears clinging to his eyelashes. He knew he'd just had a dream, but it felt so real that his soul was shaken. When he looked up, Ayana was looking down at him. Through his pain, he found the strength to whisper, "How long have I been asleep?"

"I don't know. I dozed off myself, and George took my phone, so I have no idea what time it is," Ayana replied.

"I'm thirsty. Can you please get me some water?" he croaked.

"Sure," Ayana said, pulling a bottle of water from her bag and unscrewing the top. She slowly poured some into his mouth.

After swallowing, he said, "You've been so helpful, Ayana. I'm so sorry you're in this position."

"Not your fault," Ayana whispered. "Apparently, your son has a few screws loose. No wonder you didn't tell him he was your son."

“I can hear you,” George muttered.

“I don’t care,” Ayana shot back. “This is your mess.”

George clenched his jaw. “If my sperm donor had just told me the truth, none of us would be here.”

Ayana rolled her eyes. “You were adopted by a great family,” she said. “Your aunt loves you. And look at this condo that she lets you live in rent-free. My family has always been poor. I’m the oldest of six, and it’s my dream to be in a position to buy my mama a house. Thanks for compromising my dream with this nonsense.”

When George didn’t respond, she asked, “How do you think your aunt will feel when she finds out what you’ve done?”

George finally flinched, then looked away. “I’ve thought about my aunt, and she knows how much I love her, even though she’s going to marry that piece of shit, Franklin.”

“Enough,” Ayana snapped. “Let us go. Now.”

Grandville silently watched the exchange between George and Ayana, admiring her bravery.

George eyed her suspiciously. “If I let you go, what will you tell the police?”

“Like I said, whatever you want me to. I’ll stick to the story you told me when you lured me over here: you were showing your father the gun, and it accidentally went off. You can coach me from there,” Ayana said. George stood and began pacing. Then he stopped abruptly, exhaling through his nose. “Fine.”

“Good. Now give me my damn phone so I can call an ambulance.”

George smirked. “No, I’m keeping your phone for now. I need a little more time to figure out my story. I have to make sure there are no holes,” George said, sitting back down, his eyes dark. “Pun intended.”

Grandville barely heard him. He was slipping —falling into that space between life and death again, where voices whispered, and his body felt light.

Time was running out. And he wasn't sure if he had any left.

Chapter 44

Crossroads

Juliette marveled at the sheer number of calls she had received regarding Grandville's disappearance. The influx had become overwhelming, prompting her to let all calls go directly to voicemail. Her plan was to vet the messages, forwarding any credible tips to the private investigator working the case.

Greta's Facebook ad had been nothing short of compelling. The visuals were striking, but it was Patience's voice that truly set it apart. The voice actress had an arresting tone and her voice was filled with such rich emotion, it carried an urgent plea that would captivate any listener. *Lord, please let this be what brings him home,* Juliette prayed.

Juliette shifted her focus to Jolene, who lay quietly reading a book in her hospital bed. The decision had been made—her daughter would undergo the exchange transfusion. The hematology team was set to arrive any minute, and Juliette's nerves were on edge. She tried her best to conceal her jumping leg from Jolene as she smoothed her hair. Moments later, Jolene's hematologist, Dr. Ruda, walked into the room.

"Ms. Stubbs, the transport team will be here shortly," the older white doctor said.

"Thank you, Doctor. How long will the exchange transfusion take?"

"The process will take about five hours," the doctor said with a calm, Southern drawl.

"Can I stay with her?" Juliette inquired.

Dr. Ruda offered a gentle, but firm head shake. "I'm afraid not. Now would be a good time to go home and restore for a bit. Or you can stay here in her room. The cafeteria is open, if you'd like something to eat."

Juliette hesitated. She ached to see her other children, even for a few minutes. But if there was a complication, she couldn't be too far away.

"I'll stay here in case Jolene needs me," Juliette said.

Dr. Ruda gave a small nod. "Understood. I'll check back in once the procedure is done, but if you need me, have the nurse page me."

The transport team arrived a few moments later. A young Black male nurse prepped a syringe and inserted it into Jolene's IV.

Juliette asked, "What did you just give her?"

"A mild sedative to keep her calm and comfortable during the procedure," he responded.

Jolene barely stirred as Juliette kissed her forehead. "I love you, baby," she whispered.

"We'll keep you updated," the nurse said.

Juliette watch as they wheeled one of her most precious possessions away. The silence left in their wake was suffocating. Her hands trembled as she clutched the edges of Jolene's bed, suddenly feeling untethered. She had to remain strong because she was a queen, and her family depended on her to make moves that would sustain them while her king was absent. She fought to quell the anxiety churning in the pit of her stomach. To distract herself, she headed toward the family bathroom to beautify herself, grabbing the items she needed and placing them into her bag.

The hospital's private bathrooms thoroughly cleaned after each use, which provided her a little comfort. She stepped into the steaming shower, letting the water wash away the anxiety clinging to her.

By the time she emerged, she had put herself together … at least on the outside. She slipped into a flowing green sundress, twisted her box braids into a neat bun, and applied a bit of makeup. A fresh face didn't change her reality, but it made her feel less like she was falling apart.

She reached into her purse, intending to check her phone, only to realize she'd left it in her second bag in Jolene's room. *I'll grab it after I eat,* she thought, deciding to stop by the cafeteria. In the quiet cafeteria, she stood in line to pay for her sandwich and a large cup of coffee.

As she waited, a woman entered the room wearing a mask and PPE over her street clothing. Juliette noticed her posture was stiff and her movements seemed oddly familiar. Juliette's line was longer, so the woman reached her cashier first.

"One large coffee. Is that it?" the cashier asked.

"Yes," the woman replied.

"Three dollars."

"Wow, this place has really gone up," the woman uttered, handing over a five-dollar bill. That was when Juliette recognized the woman's voice.

"Sabrina?"

"Juliette! Hey, girl!" Sabrina exclaimed.

Juliette waited for the cashier to give her change, before they walked to a corner of the cafeteria and sat at an empty table.

"So, what are you doing here? I didn't think Franklin could have visitors," Juliette asked.

"I got word from my friends who work here in the hospital that Franklin's taken a turn for the worse."

Juliette gasped. "I'm so sorry, Sabrina!"

"I'm meeting some friends who are helping me disguise myself as hospital staff so I can get into his room. I can't let the love of my life die alone, Julie," Sabrina shook her head as her eyes filled with tears.

Juliette couldn't help herself. She reached out and pulled her friend into a hug.

Sabrina pulled back quickly, wiping her eyes. "I don't want to get you sick. I need to protect you and Jolene. Speaking of your baby, where is she?"

"Sabrina, she's really sick. She's having an exchange transfusion procedure done as we speak," she explained.

"I'll be praying for our little darling. Has there been any news on Grandville?" Sabrina inquired.

Juliette shook her head. "Nothing. It's like he vanished into thin air. I try not to let my mind go to dark places, but … it's so hard. Grandville has no idea how bad things have gotten with Jolene. I know he would be here if he could."

"You're right. He would." Sabrina placed a hand on her leg. "Is there anything I can do?"

"Just the same thing I'm doing for Franklin. Pray," Juliette whispered, knowing her friend was living one of the worst days of her life.

Tears welled in Sabrina's eyes. Before she could respond, two women approached.

"That's them," Sabrina said, standing up. "I'll call you once I know something."

Juliette watched as she walked away, praying her friend's antics didn't get her kicked out of the hospital. She picked up her sandwich and coffee, heading back to Jolene's room. But her appetite was gone, replaced by a deep, lingering sadness.

Halfway down the hall, the hospital's PA system crackled to life.

Juliette Stubbs, please report to the emergency room.

Her heart slammed against her ribs. She spun on her heel, her breath coming in short, panicked bursts. *Why would they call me to the ER? Jolene's in the OR. Oh God, what's happened?*

She forced her legs to move, following the posted signs leading to the emergency room. Each step felt heavier as dread relentlessly clawed at her.

When she reached the nurse's desk in ER, she said, "Hello, my name is Juliette Stubbs. I was just paged to report here. Where's my daughter? Did something go wrong with her procedure?" Juliette anxiously questioned.

"Your daughter?"

"Yes, my daughter, Jolene Stubbs," Juliette tried her hardest to remain calm. "She's having an exchange transfusion right at this moment. Was there a complication?"

The nurse frowned. "I'm sorry, ma'am, I don't have any information about your daughter. But the doctor needs to speak with you."

"About what?"

"He's currently with another patient. Please have a seat, and he'll be with you shortly." The nurse's gaze returned to her computer screen. Juliette stood there alone, anxious, and completely unprepared for whatever she was about to hear.

Chapter 45

Stick to the Plan

Melinia sat in the back of the Uber and looked around at the clean car. The Uber driver, an older man with salt-and-pepper hair, took great pride in his ride. The exterior was freshly washed, and the interior had been recently vacuumed.

Adjusting the hem of her white sundress, she glanced at Rafael, who looked dashing in his Oshkosh shorts and matching shirt, topped off with a fresh pair of Michael Jordan sneakers. Before leaving Julio and Mimi, she fed Jesus and put him down for his nap. Now, she was ready for the meeting with Rayshawn's attorney.

"Where are we going, Mommy?" Rafael asked, his small hands fiddling with the strap of his iPad case.

"You'll see soon," she said, giving him a reassuring smile. "Just play your game for now."

"You have a well-behaved young man there," the driver said. "How old is he?"

"Four."

"Wow! He's tall for his age. Thought he was closer to seven."

"Yeah, we get that a lot," she said absently, watching as they merged on I-90 headed toward downtown Cleveland. After about twenty minutes, they exited the highway and crossed the Lorain Bridge, which connected the east and west sides of Cleveland. They were nearing their destination. It was do or die time, and she silently prayed that she was right about Rayshawn being Rafael's father. She desperately wanted her son to know his dad, and if Rayshawn wasn't his father, she honestly had no idea where to turn next.

The car pulled up to an office building, and Melinia unbuckled Rafael's seatbelt. "Make sure you have everything, baby."

"I only have my iPad," Rafael said.

"Okay, give it to me. You can play with it later." He handed it over, and she slipped it into her large purse.

"I hope you'll take a minute to rate my driving," the driver requested.

"I definitely will. Thank you," Melinia said as she handing him a five-dollar tip.

Once inside the office building, They took the elevator to the fourth floor.

"Mommy, where are we going?" Rafael asked when they stepped off the elevator.

"To see a doctor, Rafael."

"No, I don't want a shot," Rafael whined.

"I promise you that you're not getting a shot today. I need you to be a big boy for me and follow the doctor's directions. I'll be with you, so don't worry."

As they reached Suite 418, the door swung open before she could knock. A tall Black man in a sharp suit stood in the doorway.

"Hello, Ms. Gatlin. Thank you for coming today. I'm Zack Jordan. It's a pleasure to meet you in person," he said, extending his hand. "Come in, have a seat. It's hot out—would either of you like a cold bottled water?"

"No, we have some in my purse, but thanks," Melinia replied.

Just as she was sitting, a familiar voice said, "Hey, Melinia and Rafael."

She turned to see Rayshawn walking toward them, smiling.

Melinia's eyes stretched wide and she forced a smile to mask her shock. "Hi. I wasn't expecting to see you."

"Of course, I wouldn't miss a chance to see my main man Rafael. I picked up a few toys for him," Rayshawn said.

"Toys?" Rafael's eyes lit up. "Can I go play, Mom? Please?"

"Yes, you can," Melinia said, rolling her eyes slightly at Rayshawn's play for affection.

"Come on, little guy," Rayshawn said, leading Rafael by the hand into an adjacent room with toys.

Zack cleared his throat. "Let's get down to business."

Melinia turned her attention back to the lawyer. "Sure. Where's my paperwork?"

He handed her a manila folder. She flipped through the pages, ensuring they were notarized, then nodded. "Looks good."

"Now let's discuss my client's conditions," Zack said. "The first document is a standard nondisclosure agreement. It states that you will not disclose any information about Mr. Robinson or your encounter with him. Speaking of which, did you bring the tape?"

"Yes." she hesitated for a moment before pulling the phone from her purse. "Everything is on this phone. I never made copies."

"Good," Zack said, taking the phone. "Please show me the file."

Suppressing a grimace, she pulled up the video and handed it over. Zack played a few seconds to verify before locking the screen.

"You can have the phone; I have a new one," Melinia said.

"Great. Inside the paperwork, you'll find two cashier's checks—one for your time today, the other as the payment for the footage. The doctor is currently with Rayshawn and Rafael, conducting the DNA test. The doctor will run a rapid test, and we will know in a matter of hours if Rayshawn is, in fact, Rafael's biological father. If he is, you'll receive a third cashier's check for two hundred thousand dollars."

Melinia's fingers tightened around the papers as she eyed the checks. One for $1,000 and another for $50,000.

"Now, one more condition, Ms. Gatlin."

She arched an eyebrow. "Yes?"

"I've prepared an addendum to your contract that must be signed before we can proceed. Given your previous status as a heroin user, Mr. Robinson wants to ensure that if he is found to be Rafael's father, you maintain your sobriety. You must agree not to engage in any drug activity or associate with active drug users to ensure Rafael remains in a stable environment."

Melinia looked at the attorney long and hard before she finally responded. "I've been sober for more than a year, and I live a substance-free life. I don't plan to relapse."

"Great, then you should have no problem signing this paperwork."

"What does the contract addendum say?" Melinia asked.

"It states that if Mr. Robinson is Rafael's biological father and if you relapse, you agree to allow Mr. Robinson to become Rafael's legal guardian. It also states that you agree not to have Rafael around active drug users."

Melinia read the agreement. The language was straightforward.

"I plan to help women who recovering from addiction and human trafficking," she said firmly. "Therefore, I insist that you add an exception that I won't be penalized for working with addicted women in a professional capacity."

"That shouldn't be a problem," the attorney said as he took the paper, handwrote the exception, and had Melinia initial his addition. Melinia signed the paperwork while the attorney watched. He then notarized the documents and made copies. She folded her copy of the contract and placed it in her purse.

"Now you may follow me," Zack said, leading her to a large exam room. Inside, a short Black man dressed in a white lab coat nodded and smiled at them. Melinia saw Rafael and Rayshawn in the corner, engrossed in a video game they were playing on the wall-mounted TV.

Rayshawn looked up across the room and acknowledged Melinia's presence with his eyes. His gaze shifted to the attorney, who nodded in response.

"Hey, Rafael, do you like this game?" She heard Rayshawn ask.

"Yes, I really like it," Rafael replied happily.

"You are my main man, so I'm going to give it to you. You can also pick five toys to take back you with you."

"Really?" Rafael questioned.

"Yes. Can you do one thing to help me out?" Rayshawn suggested.

"What's that?"

"Let Doctor Obuigi examine you. Your mother and I will be right here with you, and I promise that there are no shots involved," Rayshawn stated.

"Okay," Rafael replied, his innocent eyes looking up and searching for his mother.

Melinia nodded and smiled at him.

"Great, let's get you over here so the doctor can take a look at you." Rayshawn picked up Rafael and set him on the hospital bed.

The doctor began his examination by listening to Rafael's heart and lungs and checking his throat and ears. Then he swabbed Rafael's cheek before doing the same to Rayshawn.

"All done," the doctor announced, lifting Rafael off the bed.

"Can I play now?" Rafael asked eagerly.

"Go pick out your toys you want while I unplug the Switch," Rayshawn said.

"Yay!" Rafael exclaimed, running off.

Melania's phone rang and she saw it was Julio.

"I need to take this," Melinia said, walking toward the waiting room.

"Hello?"

"Melinia, we have an emergency. Get to Cleveland Hospital right now!" Julio's voice was tight with urgency.

Chills ran through her. She tried to keep her voice down. "What happened?"

"I can't explain right now. I'll meet you there!"

"Julio, just tell me if it's Je—"

But the line had gone dead.

Melinia gasped, trying to keep from crying.

Chapter 46

Father Time

Grandville awoke from to find George standing over him, his expression unreadable. His body ached, and his throat felt like sandpaper. He forced his dry lips apart.

"Why are you staring at me like that?" he croaked.

George exhaled heavily. "I've been thinking about how different my life would've been if you had raised me. Maybe I wouldn't feel so lost all the time." His voice wavered before he continued. "I want you to know that I'm letting you and Ayana go. We're taking you to the hospital."

Grandville closed his eyes, relief washing over him, but George wasn't done.

"For what it's worth, I'm sorry," George admitted. "I never wanted to hurt you—I just needed answers. To know who I am. I've always felt lost. But when I read my aunt's diary and learned what Franklin and Juliette behind your back while you were in prison, I lost it. They did you dirty at your lowest point, and you still defended them while denying me—your actual blood." His face twisted in anguish. "I lost control. I know I went overboard and lost my temper. I know I went too far. But my reasons don't matter anymore. After I drop you and Ayana off, I'm going to find a nice quiet place to end it all."

Grandville's gut twisted—not from pain, but due to George's words.

"George, listen to me," Grandville whispered. "Please … don't do anything stupid."

George shook his head. "Too late for that. Besides, I've made up my mind."

Exhausted, Grandville closed his eyes again. He had no strength left to fight. He just needed to hold on a little longer.

***

When he opened his eyes again, George was gone. Ayana came over to him and whispered, "Just hold on," while caressing his face. "This nightmare is almost over."

Grandville nodded weakly. He tried to speak, but his voice was strained. "Talk … to George. Make sure … he doesn't do something…irreversible."

Ayana nodded. "I will, but right now, you need to focus on surviving."

Grandville inhaled slowly, his chest burning. "If… if I don't make it," he whispered, "you'll tell Juliette I love her … despite everything?"

"I promise," Ayana said, her voice thick with emotion. "Now, just rest."

Grandville let his eyes close, but the voices in his head whispered relentlessly, their taunts a cruel reminder of his past. Too tired to fight them, he allowed himself to drift into unconsciousness.

***

Suddenly, he was outside his own body. He could see himself lying on a gurney in the emergency room, a flurry of doctors and nurses working feverishly to save him.

"He's barely got a pulse—get fluids and blood into him right now!" a surgeon shouted "We need to get him into surgery ASAP!"

Grandville watched as his body was rushed down a hallway to the OR, the overhead lights flickering above him.

A long beep that indicated his heart had stopped. "He's flatlining! We're losing him! Shoot him with epinephrine!" the surgeon yelled. Grandville then felt himself being transported through a tunnel and experienced a peace his soul had always yearned for. Then, a strange pull overtook him, and he was no longer in the hospital. Instead, he was sitting on the banks of Lake Erie, the soft lapping of the gentle waves calming his soul. He wasn't alone.

Franklin sat beside him, a fishing pole in hand. He looked at ease, dressed in the same worn Ohio State hoodie he always wore when they went fishing.

"Another dream," Grandville murmured.

Franklin turned to him, his face filled with warmth. "I needed to see you, frat."

A deep sense of dread settled in Grandville's chest. "Frankie … are you—"

"I need you to hear me," Franklin said, his voice quieter. "There's only one way to survive this. Let it go. Don't let anger destroy you, bruh." He motioned toward the water, where a bright light shimmered beneath the surface, calling him forward. Franklin set his fishing pole down and stood.

"No," Grandville whispered. "No, don't go."

Franklin met his gaze, his eyes heavy with emotion. "I just wish I had more time to make it all right."

The light in the water grew brighter, illuminating his body. Franklin turned to face it.

"Don't go," Grandville pleaded.

Franklin smiled sadly. "Goodbye, brother."

Before Grandville could respond, he was gone.

He blinked, then found himself in a reception hall bathed in a golden glow of chandeliers, their light flickering across the polished wooden floor. Laughter and the hum of conversation wove through the air like a familiar melody, but Grandville felt only the steady warmth of his mother's hands as they swayed together. The scent of her lavender perfume wrapped around him, grounding him in a moment that felt eternal, yet fleeting.

Her fingers gently curled into his shoulder as if she were holding onto time itself. The soft rustle of her evening gown brushed against his suit, the rhythmic sway of their dance in perfect harmony with the beat of his heart. Then, she pulled him close—closer than she ever had before—cradling his face between her hands like she used to when he was a boy. Her lips pressed against his cheek, warm and lingering, a mother's kiss that carried the weight of both love and farewell.

Her breath was soft against his ear as she whispered, "Grandville, it isn't your time yet, love. God said you must go back."

Her words echoed throughout the empty room. The music faded and the room dimmed. And just like that, the warmth of her embrace slipped away like morning mist, leaving behind the imprint of a love that would never let him go.

***

Grandville gasped awake, his eyes flying open. He was back in the hospital.

A doctor stood over him. "Mr. Stubbs, you gave us quite a scare."

His throat was raw, his body ached, the sweetest signs that he was still alive.

"You've been shot," the doctor continued. "You lost a lot of blood. We performed surgery to stop the bleeding, but you'll need another surgery to repair the damage. Is there someone we should call?"

Grandville swallowed, forcing out the words. "My wife … Juliette."

The doctor nodded. "Try to rest. If we can't reach her, do you give consent for the next surgery?"

Weakly, Grandville squeezed the doctor's hand.

As the doctor stepped away, a tall detective in a black suit entered the small space. His blond hair was neatly combed, and his brown eyes were sharp behind his mask.

"Mr. Stubbs, Detective Finnegan, Cleveland PD. I know you're in a lot of pain, but before they take you to surgery, I need to know who did this to you."

Grandville's lips barely moved. "My son … George."

The detective's eyebrows lifted. "Your son? Is his last name Stubbs?"

Grandville hesitated. "I'm not sure. But…it was… an accident." He paused to catch his breath and to gather more strength to continue talking. "He didn't …mean to hurt me. I'm … not pressing…charges."

"Mr. Stubbs, your wife and your family have been looking for you. We're glad that you've been found, but there will be many questions I have for you upon your recovery. Right now, I need to know where I can find George," Detective Finnegan pressed.

Before Grandville could respond to the detective's question, the surgeon reappeared with a team of doctors.

"We need to take him into surgery right now," the doctor said firmly. "You can question him later."

The detective stepped back and the medical team moved in. As they wheeled him toward the operating room, Grandville felt himself slipping away again.

"Mr. Stubbs, you're very lucky," the doctor said. "The bullet missed all major organs. However, it nicked an artery. We're going to attempt to repair the damage and then we'll treat your infection."

"Go ahead and take a deep breath," the doctor directed as the anesthesiologist placed a mask over his nose and mouth.

A deep breath. The world blurred again. As Grandville drifted under, he whispered one final thought. *Please…let this nightmare finally be over.*

Chapter 47

Been Like This

Juliette sat in the emergency room, gripping the armrests of her chair, trying to steady her breath. Her chest felt tight, her skin damp with sweat. She focused on the rise and fall of her breathing, but despite her efforts, she felt herself slipping into a full panic attack. Had something gone wrong with Jolene's transfusion? Was another one of her children hurt? Her mind spun in frantic circles, grasping for answers she didn't have.

She'd been waiting for what seemed like hours, terrified. Her phone was in her other bag, back in Jolene's room, and she was too afraid to leave the waiting room in case someone came looking for her. Every passing second felt heavier than the last.

Just as she was about to return to the reception desk and demand answers, a tall man approached her.

"Hello, my name is Detective Finnegan. Are you Mrs. Stubbs?'

"Yes, I am," Juliette said quickly. "Please—can you tell me what the hell is going on?"

"Did you report your husband, Grandville Stubbs, as a missing person?"

Juliette's breath hitched. "Yes! Did you find him?"

"We did," the detective confirmed. "He's here, at the hospital."

A sharp gasp ripped through her chest. Relief, confusion, and dread crashed into her all at once. "Oh my God, thank you, Jesus! Is he okay? What happened? Can I see him?" She barely recognized her own voice as the questions all spilled on top of one another.

Detective Finnegan's face fell. "Mrs. Stubbs, your husband was brought in with a gunshot wound. He's currently in surgery."

Juliette's body swayed. She reached blindly for something—anything—to hold onto, but grabbed air. *"Gunshot wound?"* she echoed in disbelief. "No, no, no—there must be some mistake. Who shot my husband? Why?" Her hands trembled as she pressed them against her mouth.

The detective placed a hand on her shoulder, but the contact only made her feel more unsteady. "Ma'am, I need you to try to stay calm. The doctors are doing everything they can."

Before Juliette could process what he'd said, the sound of hurried footsteps made her turn. Greta rushed into the waiting room, her face streaked with tears, her breath coming in short gasps. Once Greta spotted her, she hurried over.

"Juliette!" Greta's voice cracked. "What's going on? I've been calling you over and over. The hospital called and told me Grandville was here, but they wouldn't say why." She clutched Juliette's arms, her fingers digging in. "Please tell me my twin's okay!"

Juliette could barely form the words. "He's … he's been shot," she whispered, the weight of her own statement nearly knocking her over.

Greta's entire body stiffened. *"Shot?"* Her voice rose an octave, her hands flying to her face. "No, no—who would do this?"

Juliette valiantly fought to unscramble the words to explain what little she knew.

Thankfully, Detective Finnegan cleared his throat. "Ma'am, we don't have all the details yet. We do know that Mr. Stubbs was dropped off at the hospital, and the individual who brought him left before we arrived."

Greta turned on the detective, her grief shifting into fury. "Well, that's not good enough! Who shot my brother?"

Juliette watched the detective, silently warning him not to share his earlier request that she calm down, because if he dared say that to her sister-in-law while she was with child, he'd better count his days.

The detective took a measured breath. "Mr. Stubbs briefly regained consciousness before surgery. He told us his son, George, shot him by accident."

Juliette's mind reeled. "George?"

Greta blinked. "Who the hell is George?"

Juliette sighed. "Sabrina's nephew."

"The one who looks just like Grandville?" Greta asked

The detective frowned. "I need to clarify exactly who George is and how your husband knows him," Detective Finnegan said. "From what your husband told me, George is his son."

"That's … a little complicated," Juliette admitted. "We only found out recently. Grandville never knew he had a son until recently."

After studying her for a moment, the detective asked, "Do you know where I can find George?"

Juliette hesitated. "I'm not sure. I can try to get his address, but … Franklin, Grandville's best friend, is also in the hospital. His fiancée, Sabrina, is George's aunt. So I may not be able to reach her to find out because he's very ill."

Finnegan exhaled sharply. "I'm sorry to hear that, but my priority is finding George before he disappears. If you can get me his information, I'd appreciate it."

Juliette nodded. "Will do. Where was Grandville shot and how bad is it?"

"Yes, we need to know this information," Greta added.

"I'm sorry, but I don't have those details," the detective said. "But the doctor said it was a stomach wound. They'll need to assess the damage once he's out of surgery."

"Will he make it?" Greta clutched Juliette's hand and sobbed.

"I don't know," the detective sighed, shaking his head. He hesitated. "The fact that he was speaking is a good sign, though."

"Ms. Stubbs?" Juliette looked up and saw a short Black woman walking up in scrubs, goggles, and a face mask.

Juliette straightened immediately. "Yes, I'm Mrs. Stubbs."

The woman stepped closer. "I need a quick word."

Juliette walked over and met the woman in a corner of the room.

"I'm Dr. Johnson, one of the surgeons operating on your husband."

Juliette barely managed a nod. "Please. Just tell me. What's happening? Is he okay?"

"Your husband is still in surgery, but if everything goes well, we will have him in recovery soon."

Juliette let out a shaky breath. "How bad is it?"

"The bullet lodged near his right hip," Dr. Johnson explained. "It didn't hit any major organs, but he lost a significant amount of blood. We're not sure if we'll be able to remove the bullet."

With tears streaming down her face, she tried to formulate the questions while she had the doctor there. "Will Grandville survive, and will there be long-term damage from his injuries?"

"We hope so. We'll know more once the surgery is complete and he's in recovery. The next few days will be critical for him. Your husband coded on the table. But luckily, we were able to revive him."

Juliette's knees buckled and she suddenly felt sick. "Oh God ..."

Greta caught her before she collapsed, then helped her ease into a nearby chair. "I'm his sister. He coded?"

Dr. Johnson nodded. "Fortunately, whoever treated him before he got to the hospital stabilized him enough to give him a fighting chance."

Juliette pressed her hands against her face, trying to hold herself together. "When can I see him?"

"Once he's in recovery, we'll let you see him briefly," Dr. Johnson assured her. "After that, he'll be moved to the surgical ICU, and because of COVID restrictions, visitors will be limited. I need to get back into the OR, but as soon as we're done, someone will notify you."

Juliette nodded weakly. "Thank you, doctor. Please... please save my husband."

Juliette turned to Greta, her eyes filled with unshed tears. "I need him to come back to us."

Greta pulled her into a hug. Juliette glanced at the door and saw her cousin hurrying in with little Rafael in tow. Rayshawn was right behind her.

"Juliette, what happened?" Melinia asked, breathlessly.

"Grandville has been shot," Juliette answered, barely audible.

Rayshawn's face darkened. "What?!"

"Yes. He's currently in surgery. We're waiting for an update," Juliette said, hugging Melinia and rubbing Rafael on the head. "How did you guys know to come to the hospital? Did Jabari tell you?"

"No, Julio told me to get to the hospital, but he didn't say why," Melinia explained. "He was watching Jesus and I was so afraid that something happened to him, I almost fainted."

Greta narrowed her eyes. "Rayshawn, how did you know to come to the hospital? I didn't realize you were even in town."

Julio rushed inside, holding Jesus' carrier.

"Chica, you beat me here. I'm so sorry, but I had to get Jesus' bag together." Jesus reached out for his mother and she immediately unstrapped him, pulling him into her arms.

"Julio, what the hell is going on?" Melinia demanded.

"Funny, I have the very same question," Juliette said as she stared down Julio, Melinia, and Rayshawn.

Chapter 48

Till I Die

Melinia swallowed hard, struggling to find the right words to explain why she had arrived at the hospital with Rayshawn. Before she could speak, Julio stepped forward, his voice thick with urgency and regret.

"Ms. Juliette, I'm so very sorry for bringing shame to your facility," he said, his Dominican accent more pronounced in his distress. "I swear I was only trying to help a friend, and I'll do anything you ask of me to make this right. I know the police called you about what happened, and I need you to know that Melinia had nothing to do with any of it. Everything that happened is all my fault."

Juliette frowned, shaking her head in confusion. "Julio, the police haven't contacted me. I'm dealing with a personal crisis right now, and I need to know exactly what's going on."

Detective Finnegan approached the group as Melinia's phone buzzed in her hand. She glanced down. Ms. Zenobia.

"This is an important call." She said quickly handing Jesus back to Julio. "Rafael, stay here with Julio and Rayshawn." Without waiting for a response, she rushed toward the exit, answering as she stepped outside.

"Hello, Ms. Zenobia." She took a deep breath and wiped the tears from her eyes.

"Melinia, I found a detox bed for your friend," Zenobia said. "You sound upset—what's wrong?"

"I'm at the hospital with my cousin. Her husband was shot," Melinia said, exhaling shakily. "But I'm so grateful for this news. I can't thank you enough."

"I'm sorry to hear about your cousin's husband. I'll be praying for him," Zenobia said sincerely. "As for your friend, I called in a lot of favors to secure this bed. She needs to be serious about recovery because once she completes detox, I've already lined up a treatment program for her."

"I promise you, she's serious," Melinia said.

"I hope so. Honestly, I'm doing this for you," Zenobia admitted. "You're a strong young lady who's been through hell and back. I need your friend to get clean because I don't want anything compromising your sobriety. Association brings about assimilation."

"I understand," Melinia assured her. "I swear to you, every move I've made has been legit. I refuse to compromise my sobriety."

"I believe you, Melinia," Zenobia said warmly. "If you need anything, don't hesitate to call. Now, go tell your friend about her second chance."

"I will, Ms. King. Thanks again."

Melinia ended the call, her heart swelling with gratitude—until reality crashed back in. Julio had called her here for a reason. She took another deep breath and turned back toward the hospital, steeling herself for whatever had gone down.

Inside, the tension was still thick. Juliette's eyes were red and puffy, and she didn't recognize the tall white man who stood between her and Julio.

"I'm sorry for stepping away," Melinia said. "What did I miss?"

"Grandville is still in surgery," Juliette said, her voice raw. "This is Detective Finnegan—he's investigating what happened."

Melinia shook the detective's hand, offering a tight smile. "I'm Melinia, Juliette's cousin."

"Nice to meet you, Melinia," Detective Finnegan said, glancing at his phone. "Ms. Stubbs, it seems someone else was with George and your husband. My partner is bringing her in now."

Juliette swept a hand over her braids. "A third person? I don't even know what to think anymore."

Nearby, Rayshawn held a weeping Greta, whispering reassurances in her ear. The sight made Melinia turn to Julio, who was rocking Jesus gently.

"Julio, I have great news," Melinia whispered. "Ms. Zenobia just called—Mimi has a bed in detox. We need to call her."

With tears in his eyes, Julio said, "I need to speak to you and Ms. Juliette privately."

"Why? What's going on?"

"I need to—"

"I'm looking for the family of Mimi Devoux," announced a hospital worker dressed in scrubs as she entered the waiting area.

"That's us," Julio said, jumping up and walking over.

"Where is she?" Melinia asked, panic creeping into her voice.

"Please come with me," the worker directed.

"I have Rafael," Juliette said, stepping up to grabbed Rafael's hand.

Melinia nodded her thanks as she trailed behind Julio, who was holding a sleeping Jesus. They followed the worker into a separate lounge that was empty except for an older bearded Black man dressed in a black suit. The worker nodded at him and abruptly left the lounge, leaving Melinia and Julio alone with him.

"Hello, I'm Reverend Gholsen. Please, have a seat," the man directed.

Melinia and Julio exchanged glances before sitting and turning her attention to the Reverend.

Reverend Gholsen exhaled deeply. "Are you related to Mimi Devoux?"

"I'm her sister," Melinia said automatically. "This is my husband, Julio. Is she okay?"

The reverend nodded solemnly. "I'm so sorry to have to tell you this, but Mimi didn't make it."

The words hit Melinia like a sledgehammer.

"No," she whispered. "This can't be right. I was just with her a couple hours ago."

"I'm sorry," Reverend Gholsen repeated. "Unfortunately, your sister passed from an apparent opioid overdose."

A sharp, keening sound tore from Melinia's throat. "No, no, no," she chanted, shaking her head violently.

"The paramedics did everything they could," the reverend continued gently. "They administered multiple doses of Narcan, but she was unresponsive when she arrived here."

Julio wrapped an arm around Melinia as her body wracked with sobs.

"I'm sorry, but we need you to make arrangements for her body as soon as possible," Reverend Gholsen added. "With the overwhelming number of COVID deaths, the hospital has very limited space."

In a state of shock, Melinia could barely wrap her mind around this news.

The Reverend glanced at Julio before asking, "Would you like to pray?"

"I—I need a minute," Melinia choked out.

"Of course. Take your time," the Reverend said before exiting the room.

Julip sighed heavily, rubbing her arm with one hand. "Chica, I'm so sorry."

"Julio, how did this happen?" Melinia asked, tears streaming down her face.

Julio rubbed his face. "After you left, I checked on Mimi and Jesus. They were both asleep. I was in the kitchen when I heard Jesus crying. When I went to check, Mimi was gone. I figured she went to the store." He cleared his throat. "While I was feeding Jesus, I heard a scream outside. I ran out and found Joe—he was hysterical. He'd gone to the shed to get the lawnmower and found Mimi. She was on the ground, unresponsive, with a needle in her arm."

"Oh my God," Melinia whimpered.

"I called 9-1-1 immediately," Julio continued, his voice thick with grief. "They tried to revive her, but … it was too late."

Melinia pressed her hands over her face, rocking slightly. "I was just telling her about detox… she was so close to getting help."

Julio squeezed her shoulder. "Chica, we both know addiction is a disease. This isn't your fault."

Melinia inhaled shakily, lifting her tear-stained face. It didn't matter if it was her fault or not. Mimi was gone. "I need to tell Juliette," she whispered.

"No," Julio said gently. "I'll tell her. You've been through enough."

Melinia nodded, but she made a silent promise to herself. She would tell Juliette the truth about everything. About the past. About her choices. About Rayshawn.

She just prayed Juliette could survive it.

Chapter 49

Trouble

Juliette's hands trembled as she rummaged through her bag, desperate for something—anything—that would help steady her spiraling emotions. Her breath came in short gasps, her heart pounding like a war drum in her chest. When she finally found the small orange bottle, she sighed in relief. Thank God, she had one Valium left. She popped the pill in her mouth, then looked around, realizing she didn't have any water. Exasperated, she leaned her head back to swallow it dry, and sighed.

Rayshawn stood and walked out of the waiting room. He was gone for thirty seconds when he returned with three bottles of water.

"Here," Rayshawn said, passing a bottle to Juliette and Detective Finnegan.

While Juliette gratefully washed the bitter pill taste from her mouth, Detective Finnegan squinted thoughtfully at Rayshawn and said, "Thanks. You look familiar to me."

The corner of Rayshawn's mouth lifted in a half-smile. "I get that a lot."

Then the recognition sparked in the detective's eyes. "You're Rayshawn Robinson."

"In the flesh ," Rayshawn confirmed.

"How do you know Grandville," the detective asked.

"He's one of my best friends. We grew up together, and I love him like a brother. In fact, he *is* my brother-in-law," Rayshawn said. "Whoever shot him has to pay. If a reward will help get people talking, tell me how much, and I'll have my banker wire the money today."

"We'll let you know if it comes to that," Detective Finnegan said, his voice measured.

Juliette's head spun as she tried to process everything. She had a child and a husband in the OR. She took another sip of water, waiting for the medication to do its job. That was when she heard a commotion near the entrance.

She turned and saw two women walk in—one was stunning, Black, and slightly overweight with a confident stride, the other was petite, white and in a sharp pantsuit. Detective Finnegan straightened. "Ms. Stubbs, this is my partner, Detective Hudson," he said introducing the woman in the pantsuit.

Juliette stood to shake her hand when the Black woman stepped forward, eyes locked on her. "I need to speak with Ms. Stubbs."

Detective Hudson raised an eyebrow. "My partner and I need to speak to you first."

The woman shook her head, her expression unreadable. "*After* I speak to Ms. Stubbs, I'll be happy to tell you everything I know."

Juliette felt a chill creep up her spine. The fact that this woman was pushing past the detectives to talk to her first set off alarm bells.

Detective Finnegan frowned but relented. "Ms. Stubbs, this is Ayana Ali."

"Hi," Ayana stepped closer, her expression filled with urgency. "How's Grandville?"

Juliette studied the girl's face, wondering who she was and whether she could trust her. "I'm sorry, but who are you?" she asked, her tone wary.

Ayana hesitated, clearly taken aback. "I—"

"Because right now, all I know is that my husband was kidnapped, held hostage, *shot*, and left for dead. And somehow, you were involved enough that the police are questioning you. So forgive me if I'm not exactly in the mood for introductions," Juliette continued, her voice tight with anger.

Rayshawn stood and she felt him beside her, but Juliette's eyes were fixed on Ayana.

The young woman's face fell, and she held up her hands, palms out. "I get it, Mrs. Stubbs. You have no reason to trust me. But I didn't kidnap Grandville. I swear to you, I had no idea what George had done until I walked into that condo and saw your husband bleeding out."

Juliette's jaw clenched. "And instead of calling for help, you stayed?"

"I *couldn't* call for help," Ayana insisted. "George—"

"Hold on a second," Juliette held up a hand before turning to the detectives. "Can you give us a moment, please? We won't leave this area, but I need the full story from her and I don't want her to be afraid to tell me everything with you standing here."

Detective Finnegan shook his head. "I'm sorry, Mrs. Stubbs, but we can't—"

Detective Hudson placed a hand on his forearm. "Come on, partner. I need to fill you in on a couple of things. Can you step right over here with me?"

Reluctantly, Detective Finnegan followed his partner several feet away, on the other side of the room.

Juliette turned her attention back to the young lady. "Please continue."

"George wouldn't allow me to leave. He had a gun. I tried—" Her lips trembled as she took a breath. "I did *everything* I could to keep Grandville alive. I cleaned his wound, slowed the bleeding, and kept his fever down. If I hadn't, he would be dead right now."

Juliette stared into Ayana's pleading eyes but was still unmoved. She crossed her arms. "And I'm just supposed to take your word on all of this?"

Ayana's eyes darkened. "No. But you can ask Grandville once he's in recovery. *He'll* tell you."

The young woman's tone caused Juliette to open her mouth, then she thought better of it and closed it. The worst part was—she *wanted* to believe Ayana. If she had really helped Grandville, she had saved her husband's life. But if she was lying? What if this was all just a cover up for her own involvement?

Ayana took a deep breath, and in a softer tone, she said, "Anyway, before George let us go, Grandville asked me to tell you something."

Juliette stiffened. "And what's that?"

"That he loves you. That he forgives you. And that he needs you to forgive George."

A harsh laugh escaped Juliette's lips before she could stop it. "*Forgive* George? The same George who kidnapped and *shot* my husband? That George?"

Ayana held her hands up again. "I'm just the messenger, sis."

"I'm not your *sis*," Juliette snarled. Her hands balled into fists at her sides. She wanted to scream. She wanted to cry. Before she could say another word, Detective Finnegan stepped in between them.

"That's enough," he said, his voice firm. "Ayana, we need to take your official statement. Now."

Ayana nodded but looked back at Juliette one last time. "Just… be careful," she said. "George has it out for you. And after everything I saw—I don't think he's done. Not by a long shot."

Juliette felt a fresh wave of nausea roll through her. She rocked slightly and Rayshawn placed a hand on the small of her back to steady her.

She wanted answers. She wanted to know how her life had spiraled so far out of control. But most of all, she wanted George found.

Chapter 50

Excuse Me

Melinia spotted Juliette approaching the elevators.

"Juliette," she called, her voice thick with emotion.

Juliette turned to look at her and frowned. "Cuz, what's wrong?"

Melinia bit her lip. "I know you have a lot going on, but I really need to talk to you. It's important."

Juliette sighed. "I can't right now. I need to go back to Jolene's room to grab my phone. But when I get back, we'll sit down and talk."

Melinia nodded, watching her cousin step onto the elevator with a security officer behind her.

She returned to the private lounge to wait for Reverend Gholsen with Julio. She was restless, her knee bouncing, fingers fidgeting, her mind racing. What if the authorities traced Mimi's relapse at the boarding house back to Juliette? It could jeopardize everything her cousin worked so hard to build.

And that would be on her.

Melinia knew she had to come clean, tell Juliette everything, and take responsibility for the fallout. She owed her that much.

Across from her, Julio looked like he was on the verge of breaking, his eyes red and glassy. When Jesus had fallen asleep, he'd taken him out to the waiting room and Greta agreed to watch him. Now, with just the two of them there, the silence between them felt suffocating.

"Julio," she murmured, reaching for his hand. "What happened to Mimi is awful, but it's not your fault. I'll tell Juliette the truth—she'll know you had nothing to do with her being at the house."

Julio shook his head, staring down at his hands. "And it's not your fault either," he said. "We tried to help her. But we still lost her. I can't shake the look on her face when Joe found her." He sucked in a shaky breath. "And as much as I hate myself for saying it—I keep thinking, thank God it wasn't you." His voice cracked, and a tear slipped down his cheek. "How many times did you use, Melinia? How many times could it have been you?"

Her throat tightened, guilt washing over her. "I swear to you, Julio," she said fiercely, cupping his face. "I haven't used. Not even when that awful man, Larry, tried to force me before he—" She cut herself off, shuddering. "I fought back. I said no."

Julio pressed his forehead against hers. "I believe you, Chica. I do. But that doesn't stop me from being scared. I can't lose you. I love you and the boys too much."

"I know. We love you too, and we're right here," Melinia whispered. "We're not going anywhere."

Julio nodded and she pulled back, wiping her eyes. "We need to find Mimi's family. I know she's from Detroit, but she rarely talked about her family. Maybe we can use her phone to track down them down."

Julio nodded just as Reverend Gholsen walked into the lounge.

"I hope you've had a chance to notify family members," he said gently.

"We're her family, at least in Cleveland," Melinia sighed. "We'll do whatever we need to get her moved, but we don't know where to start. Can you refer a funeral home?"

Melinia was glad that she now had the money to pay for Mimi's funeral, but she had to take several deep breaths to prevent herself from bursting into tears. She had just found Mimi again, and she felt that finding her was a message from God. She had big plans that she hoped would change their lives, but now all she could do was continue moving forward and find a way to honor Mimi's life.

"Yes," Reverend Gholsen said, nodding. "I'll give you a list. And before you go, let's put on some gloves, hold hands, and pray."

Melinia and Julio bowed their head, gripping hands as the reverend led them in prayer. It didn't erase the grief, but when they finally walked back into the waiting room, something in her felt just a little steadier.

It felt like they had been in the emergency waiting room for hours. Greta, Rayshawn, and Julio sat in tense silence, exhaustion taking a toll on their minds and bodies.

Melinia stared at the floor, lost in thought, when her phone rang. It was Rayshawn's attorney.

"Hello."

"Ms. Gatlin," he said, "the paternity test results for Rafael are in. There's a 99.6% probability that Rayshawn is Rafael's father."

Melinia closed her eyes, exhaling.

"My office will be forwarding you a cashier's check as agreed. We'll also be in touch to make arrangements for Rafael to spend time with Mr. Robinson, including summer vacation and scheduled visits when he's in Cleveland."

"Understood," Melinia murmured. "Thank you. I'll await further instructions from you and Rayshawn."

She ended the call and slipped her phone into her bag, but when she looked up, she met a pair of ice-cold eyes. Greta.

Her expression was sharp as a blade. "Why do you need to 'await instructions from Rayshawn'?" she asked, her voice clipped. "And don't think I didn't notice you two walk in together."

Melinia froze, her mouth opening, then closing. She had no idea what to say.

Rayshawn spoke up first. "Melinia and I have business," he said smoothly. "And this is neither the time nor place to discuss it."

Greta crossed her arms, shooting Rayshawn a glare. "What kind of business?"

Rayshawn's gaze hardened. "Greta, my business with Melinia is none of your concern." His voice was low and measured. "We're no longer married, and I don't have to answer to you. So, you don't have the right to interrogate me."

Greta let out a bitter laugh. "You have some nerve. I don't get to interrogate you? I put up with you for years. Your lying. Your cheating. Don't act like I just woke up one morning and decided to divorce you."

"I had a problem," Rayshawn said, his jaw tight. "I got help."

"Only because I left you," Greta shot back. "And you didn't get help for me, you got help because you had no other choice!"

"The point is, I did the work," Rayshawn countered. "And even after that, you still didn't give me a chance."

"That's why you crashed my wedding?" Greta snapped. "Because you just couldn't stand to see me happy?"

The room fell into stunned silence.

Melinia looked up as Juliette, who had returned unnoticed, crossed her arms. "I don't know what the hell is going on with you two," she said, her voice cutting through the tension, "but Greta—you need to calm down."

Greta turned to her, still fuming.

Juliette grabbed her shoulders. "You cannot get this worked up. It's not good for the baby. Now, calm down."

A thick silence fell over the room.

Rayshawn's eyes narrowed. "Baby?"

Greta tilted her chin up defiantly. "My condition is none of your concern."

Juliette sat down, burying her head in her hands like she hadn't meant to blurt that out.

"So, let me get this straight—you refused to have my baby when I was your husband, but now you're pregnant with his child?" Rayshawn's voice dripped with bitterness. "Every year I begged you for a family, and now you have the audacity to carry another man's child?"

"Thank God Rafael's my son, otherwise, I might not have ever had a child," Rayshawn scoffed.

Juliette's eyes widened. "Wait—what?"

Greta looked like she'd been slapped. Julio stood slowly, a deep frown on his face.

Melinia shot to her feet. "Excuse me, what the hell's wrong with you?" she snapped at Rayshawn. "You signed an NDA, fool! And before the ink's dry, you're already violating it?"

Rayshawn barely glanced at her. "What are you gonna do? Sue me?"

"Damn right, I will," Melinia hissed.

"Excuse me, everyone!" They all froze and turned to look at a petite black female in scrubs, standing with her arms crossed. Melinia noticed a few people who were filming the debacle lower their phones.

"I need you all to lower your voices," she said sternly. "This is a hospital! If you can't compose yourselves, you'll be asked to leave."

The group remained silent and Juliette stood and stepped forward. "We apologize, ma'am. We promise to keep it down."

The woman rolled her eyes and turned on her heels before marching away. A second woman in teal scrubs approached, offering a small smile.

"Ms. Stubbs?" the woman asked, looking at Juliette.

"Yes?"

"Your husband is out of surgery. He's stable and in recovery. Let me take you to him," she said. Juliette closed her eyes for a moment as the group cheered quietly. It seemed to take her a moment before she could gather herself and follow the nurse to a door marked Employees Only.

As Juliette disappeared through the door, Melinia squeezed her eyes shut and whispered a prayer. Please, God. Let Grandville pull through. And please do the same for me.

Chapter 51

Be Ok

Grandville's eyes fluttered open, and for a split second, he questioned whether he was alive or still trapped in some feverish nightmare. The body aches had dulled, but there was a persistent pain spreading from his abdomen. The beeping machines and sterile scent of antiseptic confirmed he was in a hospital.

A figure clad in full protective gear sat at a nearby computer, typing away. The person noticed his movements and turned to him.

"Mr. Stubbs, you're awake," the nurse said with evident relief. "Do you know where you are?"

Grandville's throat was dry so his voice was barely above a whisper. "I think I'm in the hospital."

Walking over to his bed tray, the man poured water into a cup and offered it to him. Grandville slowly sipped from the straw, relieved by the cool water sliding down his throat.

"You are. I'm Nurse Benson. You came in with a gunshot wound. You were in surgery, and you're now in the recovery unit. Your wife is here, and you'll have a few minutes with her before we move you to ICU."

Grandville released a weak sigh of relief. He was alive. He would see Juliette soon. Then a new worry plagued him.

"Where's my son, George?"

The nurse's expression didn't shift. "I'm sorry, I'm not sure who or where George is. Maybe your wife will know?"

Grandville laid there, processing his thoughts and thanking God, when a few minutes later, the door opened. His heart stirred at the sight of Juliette walking through the door, her petite figure wrapped in protective gear. Her eyes shimmered with tears above the mask as a nurse trailed her.

She rushed to his bedside, carefully pressing a masked kiss against his cheek. "Oh my God, I'm so happy to see you, Grandville. We've been looking for you for days. I know that you've been through a lot, but I'm happy that you're here and that we found you. I missed you so much."

"I missed you too, Julie," he said, the smile evident in his hushed voice. "Where's George?"

She swallowed hard, gripping his hand. "Grandville, I don't know," she sighed. "But wherever he is, he won't be able to hurt you again."

"He didn't mean to shoot me, Julie," Grandville rasped, fighting to keep his heavy eyelids from closing. "It was an accident… He snapped when he found out the truth. I need you to represent him and make sure he gets an insanity defense." Grandville stopped, struggling to take a breath.

Juliette gripped his hand tighter. "Baby, don't worry about George. Once we find him, I'll help him."

A tear slid from the corner of his eye. "Franklin is with God now. I saw him." He forced the words out between breaths. "He told me … about you. And Jessica told me … about Greta's baby." His breathing slowed. "I forgive you… Please, tell my twin to take care of my niece."

Juliette stiffened.

Grandville's voice grew weaker. "No matter what happens… I love you. I love the kids." His grip slackened. "I'm so tired… but please help George."

Grandville's eyes closed.

***

Panic surged through Juliette, but the doctor placed a hand on her shoulder. "Mrs. Stubbs, he's stable. His body has been through extreme trauma, and he's exhausted. We're moving him to ICU now, and once he's settled, we'll monitor him closely."

"I'm so scared," Juliette sobbed. "What are his chances?"

"We've done everything we can, but the next few days will be critical," the doctor admitted. "There's also the risk of infection, but we're being extremely cautious."

Juliette asked, "And COVID? What if he gets it?"

"We're taking every possible precaution to prevent the spread of COVID, but the ER is the worst place to be if you're worried about exposure. Grandville won't be able to have visitors in ICU, so I suggest you and your family go home and get some rest."

Juliette shook her head. "Unfortunately, I can't leave. Our daughter is also a patient in the pediatric wing, so I'm staying at the hospital with her. Please keep me informed, and I'll have the rest of our family go home. Thanks so much for saving my husband's life."

"I hope your daughter gets better soon. I'll call you twice a day with updates on your husband. Keep praying, because unfortunately, this journey is not over yet," the doctor advised.

Juliette nodded, exhaustion weighing her down. As she pulled off her protective gear, Grandville's words echoed in her mind. *He knows*. Her worst fear had come true. She didn't know how to face the shame, but she didn't have time to dwell on it now. She had to stay strong—for Grandville, Jolene, and her family.

Stepping out into the waiting area, she found her loved ones in tense silence, their eyes full of questions. "I need you all to gather your belongings and join me outside," Juliette directed.

The group looked terrified but they followed her outside. Melinia and Julio were each carrying a sleeping child, so Juliette headed toward a small park area adjacent to the hospital, equipped with benches. She took a seat, and everyone sat around her, waiting for her to speak.

Juliette took a deep breath. "Grandville is stable for now," she said. "He asked me to tell you all that he loves you. Greta, I didn't mention your pregnancy, but Grandville said God told him that you're carrying a girl, and for me to protect you and our niece."

Greta's lip trembled as tears slid down her face.

Juliette continued. "I heard part of the conversation right before they called me back to see Grandville, so let me say this now. We're family, and right now, I'm asking that we put aside our issues and focus on one thing: praying that Grandville survives. The surgeon said that Grandville is not out of the woods yet. We're going to have a family intervention session to process everything that has been revealed today, but right now, I need your promises that you'll do exactly what I have asked. The devil is busy trying to cause division and confusion among the people who love Grandville the most. Show him that he's a lie and go home and do what I have asked. I need each of your commitments."

Silence fell over the group.

Greta broke down first, pressing a hand to her belly. Rayshawn pulled her into a hug. "Grandville's going to make it," he murmured. "We're going to do what Juliette asked."

Greta pulled away and turned to Juliette. She took Juliette's hands, pulling her up off the bench and into a tight embrace. "Sis, I'll handle the house and

Jabari will help. Don't worry about anything other than my brother and my niece."

Rayshawn hugged Juliette next. "Please keep me updated. I'm family, too. I'll have my driver take Greta to her home. She's in no condition to drive right now."

Juliette nodded. "Thanks, Rayshawn."

Turning, she found Melina's eyes were full of emotion.

"Juliette, I know you heard all of that. But…" Melinia trailed off. "I never meant to hurt anyone. It happened when I was all messed up on drugs."

Juliette reached out and squeezed her cousin's hand. "Melinia, you don't owe me an explanation. I'm not mad at you. Like I said, later we're going to process everything that has happened like a family."

Melinia exhaled in relief, but Julio looked tense.

"Julio?" Juliette prompted. "Did you say you had something to tell me?"

He hesitated. "Yes, Ms. Juliette. I let a friend stay at A New Beginning."

Melinia stepped in. "Juliette, it was *my* decision," she corrected. "Her name was Mimi. She was my best friend when I was being trafficked. We were waiting to get her into detox treatment but she overdosed earlier today at the boarding house. It wasn't Julio's fault—it was mine."

Juliette gasped. "Is your friend in the hospital?"

"Yes," Melinia replied as tears spilled down her face. "In the morgue. She didn' t make it."

Juliette was devastated by the news and concerned about what it may do to Melinia's sobriety, but she kept her composure. She pulled her cousin into a hug. "Melinia, I'm so sorry to hear that." She turned to Julio. "Please go to A New Beginning and check on everyone. I'll arrange for a grief counselor to come a little later."

Julio nodded. "Thank you, Ms. Juliette. Again, I'm so sorry about Mr. Grandville."

"Thanks, Julio."

They hailed down a nearby cab and Juliette hugged Melinia and Julio, paid the driver, then watched as they drove off after safely securing the kids inside.

She walked back into the hospital and headed for the elevator to the pediatric wing. Her phone rang but she didn't recognize the number.

"Hello."

"Hello, Ms. Stubbs. This is Nurse Rhonda. Are you close by?" she asked.

"Yes, I'm getting on the elevator right now."

Juliette rushed down the hallway, her heart pounding as she approached Jolene's room. The past twenty-four hours had left her emotionally drained, but she pushed through the exhaustion. She needed to see her baby.

She noticed Sabrina was inside Jolene's room, talking to Nurse Rhonda. Jolene was asleep, her tiny chest rising and falling steadily beneath the hospital blanket.

"Hey Sabrina. Hi Nurse Rhonda. How's Jolene?"

"She's stable," Rhonda said. The transfusion went well, and she's responding to treatment. The doctor will be here in a few minutes to go over her test results with you."

"Okay, thank you."

"No problem," Rhonda said, leaving and closing the door behind her.

Juliette stepped closer to Jolene's bed, brushing a gentle hand over her daughter's soft curls. "Mommy's here, baby girl. I'm right here," she whispered to her sleeping daughter. After bowing her head and saying a silent prayer of thanks, Juliette turned to Sabrina. She was stunned when her friend's face crumpled and she immediately let out a guttural sob.

"Oh Sabrina, it's going to be okay," Juliette pulled her friend's trembling body in for a hug.

"Franklin's gone, Juliette," Sabrina choked out. "He's gone."

Juliette gasped.

"And the moment he took his last breath, the police called asking if I knew where George was," Sabrina said. "They said he shot someone. Juliette… I didn't know what to say. I know you're dealing with Jolene and Grandville missing, but I need your help. I don't know what to do."

Juliette couldn't find the words to say to her friend—as all she could do was look at her.

After a few moments, she pulled in a shaky breath. "Sabrina, I need to tell you a few things."

As she looked into her friend's expectant eyes, she wrestled with a glaring question. How could she tell Sabrina the truth without causing even more damage to her broken heart?

Chapter 52

Sleep On It

The cab ride back to *A New Beginning* was quiet, the hum of the engine filling the space between Julio and Melinia. Julio stared out the window, his hands clenched into fists on his lap, while Melinia cradled Rafael's head on her lap as he slept. Jesus also slept soundly in his carrier. The exhaustion of fighting for her friend's life and losing, and having her personal business broadcasted for the world to hear weighed heavily on her—physically, emotionally, spiritually.

Once they arrived and brought the kids into the silent house, Julio turned to her with a grave expression. "I'm going to sleep on the couch again, and you and the boys can take the bed. You're staying here tonight."

Melinia nodded, too tired to argue. Julio took Rafael, who was still fast asleep, into his bed, while she trailed him, bringing in Jesus, who was asleep in his baby carrier. She wanted to let Rafael sleep in his clothes since he was so exhausted. But since they'd been in the hospital, she didn't want his soiled clothing on their sheets. She returned to the living room for Jesus' diaper bag and stopped when she heard Julio and Joe talking in hushed voices.

"What do you mean Ms. Mimi died?" Joe's voice cracked. "Man, I tried everything, and it still didn't save her?"

"Joe, this is not your fault," Julio said, his tone heavy. "I'm the one who put you in that position. I'm sorry, man."

Hearing the pain in Joe's voice, and getting a glimpse of his beautiful, gentle heart, she decided to provide some comfort. She walked into the kitchen, interrupting their conversation.

"Hey Joe, how are you holding up?" Melinia gently asked.

At the sound of her voice, Joe broke down, his massive frame trembling as he let go a strangled sob. Tears streamed down his face, and without thinking, Melinia reached out and pulled Joe into a hug.

After a moment, she pulled out a chair and sat across from him at the kitchen table.

"Joe, listen to me. I need you to hear this." She took a deep breath, steadying herself. "I brought Mimi here. She was my best friend. We met in drug rehab and were both victims of human trafficking. I had to leave her to recover and live a sober life for my boys. I haven't seen Mimi in over a year, and she found me the very day we brought her here. I thought I could really help her, but sadly, help came a little too late. We didn't fail her, Joe. Her addiction did."

Joe wiped his face, his breathing uneven. "I know. I was just really fond of Ms. Mimi. I just don't know how to handle this."

"Me too. But, Joe, I'm starting a boarding home to honor her and help people like her. And once I get the home up and running, I'll hire you and offer you room and board."

"Really?" Joe asked, hope in his voice.

"Yes, you can start taking peer certification courses now to prepare. As you get more involved in the field of recovery, who knows, you may decide to pursue a bachelor's degree in counseling or social work. What I want you to take from this conversation is that when you leave here, you'll have a job and a place where you belong."

Joe's face lit up for the first time that evening. "Thank you, Ms. Melinia. I've been worried about what's next for me, so I appreciate that. But right now, I'm going to get some rest. Please let me know about Mimi's homegoing. I want to be there. And thanks for sharing your story with me."

"You're welcome, Joe."

As Joe disappeared down the hall, she let out a deep breath. Julio, who had been silently watching, finally took a seat at the table. He peered into her eyes, and asked, "Were you ever going to tell me?"

Melinia stiffened. "Tell you what?"

"That Rayshawn Robinson is Rafael's father?"

Melinia dropped her head, considering how to respond to Julio's question. "I'm sorry," she admitted. "I should have told you, but I didn't even know for sure myself until today."

Julio leaned back, arms crossed. "It's not about who Rafael's father is, Melinia. It's about trust. Why didn't you trust me enough to tell me?"

She paused, gripping the edge of the table. "Julio, I trust you with my life. I didn't sleep with Rayshawn because I wanted to. The truth is, I was indebted to my dealer and I had to do it. I recorded it for leverage, so they wouldn't kill me. Lovelle kept saying I owed him money. So, I threatened to release the tape. That's when Lovelle put a hit out on me and I ran and joined the crew."

Julio shook his head. "Damn, Chica."

"Now, I finally have a chance to start over. To build something real. You and my boys are the only reasons why I survived, and I promise with God and each other we'll make it through this."

Julio stood up as well and pulled Melinia into a strong embrace, which she willingly returned.

"Get some rest, and in the morning, we'll talk," Julio said.

Later, as she lay in bed, staring at the ceiling, her thoughts refused to quiet. She had lost Mimi but gained Rafael's truth. She had money now, the ability to build the future she dreamed of. But her family now knew the truth—she feared what that meant for her relationship with Juliette. She closed her eyes and whispered a prayer.

"Please, God. Keep Grandville alive. Let Mimi find peace despite her transgressions. And grant me the peace to keep going."

Just as she was drifting off to sleep, her phone rang.

She groaned, reaching for it. "Hello?".

"Melinia, I need to see you first thing in the morning. Please be at my office at 10 a.m.," Ms. Zenobia said.

Her heart sank. "Is everything okay?"

"No, but we'll talk tomorrow."

As the line disconnected, Melinia stared at the ceiling, dread creeping over her. She felt like tomorrow would change everything.

Chapter 53

Pieces of Me

Juliette sat in silence, heartbroken for Sabrina as she watched her struggle with shock and grief. The shock was evident on her friend's face, her body trembling under the weight of the truth she had yet to fully process.

"I can't believe he's gone," Sabrina sobbed, fresh tears streaming down her face. "The love of my life, the man who was supposed to be the father of my children. What am I going to do?"

Juliette had no words. What could she possibly say to ease Sabrina's pain? Instead, she simply reached out, taking her friend's hand in hers. They sat there, shoulders touching, mourning together.

After a long moment, Sabrina wiped her tears and took a shaky breath. "All that I have left is George and my mother, and I might lose George too. The police are looking for him. They're searching my condo as we speak. I have no idea who George allegedly hurt, and I have no clue what the hell is going on."

Juliette's grip on Sabrina's hand tightened. She had dreaded this moment, knowing that what she had to say next might push her friend over the edge.

"Sabrina, I have a lot to tell you," Juliette began carefully, "but before I do, I need you to know that you're an integral part of our village, and we're all here for you. What I'm about to say is going to upset you, but no matter what,

I need you to be strong and understand that I would never intentionally hurt you. After you hear everything, you might not want to be friends with me anymore, and if that's the case, I'll understand. But please let me help before you make that decision."

Sabrina blinked at her, her eyes laced with confusion. "Juliette, what could be worse than my fiancé dying?"

Juliette inhaled deeply. "I've just found out that George kidnapped Grandville," she said, her voice barely above a whisper. He's been holding him hostage. That's why we couldn't find him."

Sabrina's mouth dropped open in disbelief. "What!?"

Juliette reached out instinctively, but Sabrina recoiled, shaking her head in disbelief.

"Sabrina, please try to keep your voice down," Juliette urged. "Jolene is sleeping, and I don't want us to get kicked out of the hospital. I'm supposed to be the only one in here."

"Oh my God." Sabrina's voice cracked. "I can't believe this. Wait… are you telling me George shot Grandville?"

Juliette swallowed hard. "Yes," Juliette admitted, "but Grandville swears it was an accident. He's here in the hospital. He just had emergency surgery, but I was able to see him briefly before he was moved to ICU. He asked me to help George. The only way I can do what he has asked of me is to find him first."

"I don't understand. What would have caused him to do this? George and Grandville only have a working relationship."

Juliette braced herself. This was the moment she'd been dreading. "Sabrina now is the part where you might get upset."

Sabrina let out a bitter laugh. "Please, Juliette, this is already one of the worst days of my life. If there's more bad news, let's just get it all over with."

Juliette exhaled. "Remember when you asked me to find out who George's biological parents were?"

"Yes," Sabrina said slowly.

"You came back to me a few weeks later and told me to hold off, remember?"

Sabrina nodded. "Yes, I remember, but I still don't understand."

"What I didn't tell you is that I actually received the information. I found out who George's biological parents were."

Sabrina stilled. "Well?" she pressed. "Who are they?"

Juliette hesitated, then said as gently, "Grandville is actually George's biological father."

A deep silence fell upon the room.

"What!?" Sabrina hissed, her voice dropping to a loud whisper.

Juliette could see the sense of betrayal creeping in, the questions forming before Sabrina could even voice them.

"When I found out, it pushed me over the edge," Juliette confessed. "I broke down. It contributed to everything that happened with me mentally."

Sabrina's lips parted, but no words came. Juliette allowed the news to sink in.

"Does Grandville know?" she finally managed to ask.

"Yes," Juliette said softly. "But it took me awhile to tell him. At first, I was afraid that the truth would send him spiraling again. So I kept it to myself. But the stress and guilt became unbearable. Grandville did know he had a son who had been put up for adoption, but his mother kept the details from him. He only found out about George right before his mother died."

Sabrina pressed a trembling hand to her forehead. "Who… who is George's mother?"

Juliette's stomach knotted. "George's mother was Grandville's cousin, Gina."

Sabrina frowned. When she didn't say anything, Juliette continued.

"Gina was much older than him and began taking advantage of him. After Gina became pregnant, Grandville's mother moved her in with a family friend. She signed away Grandville's paternal rights. A huge part of Grandville becoming ill was when he found out about George. We were going to tell you but everything happened. I think George found out somehow and confronted Grandville about everything."

Sabrina staggered back a step, her breath coming in shallow gasps. "Oh my God. The police will kill George if they find him."

"We need to find him before they do. A friend of his told me George might try to hurt himself. If we can get to George first, we'll have the opportunity to get him the care he needs before he harms himself or the police get ahold of him."

Sabrina snapped her fingers and straightened up. "I might know where he is."

Juliette grabbed her hand. "Then go. I'm sorry, but I can't go with you. George's friend Ayana said that George hates me. We don't need to set him off. But you—he loves you. You might be able to reach him."

Sabrina's body suddenly grew rigid.

"Juliette, Grandville is going to make it; I feel it deep down in my spirit. And I'm truly sorry about what George did. I think I might know why he's upset with you," Sabrina said. "And once I tell you… you might not want to be *my* friend anymore."

Juliette looked at her friend, wondering what she could possibly have to tell her. "Tell me."

Sabrina sat down again, her eyes glistening with tears. "Just promise me you'll hear me out first."

Juliette exhaled. "I promise."

But deep down, she knew that whatever came next would change everything.

Chapter 54

God's Plan

As Melinia awoke from her slumber, she knew she had to put a plan into action. She decided that she would take her sons with her to meet with Ms. Zenobia. She had already caused Juliette, Julio, and the rooming house enough problems, and she feared that the authorities would come to investigate Mimi's death. The last thing any of them needed was for her minor children to be found in the rooming house with Julio and two convicted felons.

It was only seven a.m., the house was still quiet. Careful not to wake Rafael, Melinia slipped out of bed and moved toward the corner of the room where Mimi had left her belongings. She sat on the floor and opened Mimi's purse. What she saw made her breath catch. A large bag of heroin—Mimi had lied to her about carrying. Her stomach twisted in knots.

Swallowing hard, Melinia pushed the drugs aside and kept searching. She found a cell phone, a key with the number 215 written on it—likely a locker at the Greyhound station—twenty dollars, and Mimi's small makeup bag.

But her eyes kept darting back to the heroin.

Her fingers tingled. Her breathing shallowed.

The temptation clawed at her, whispering its familiar call.

She could almost feel the rush. The escape. The relief.

Then, Ms. Zenobia's words echoed in her mind.

"The devil will test you when you're on the brink of something great."

A shiver coursed through her.

No.

She had come too far to throw it all away. Her boys. Her plans.

With a sharp inhale, she zipped the purse shut and forced herself to stand—just as Rafael stirred.

"Mommy, I have to use the bathroom," he mumbled sleepily.

"Okay, baby. Let's go," she said, relieved for the distraction.

As she opened the bedroom door, she nearly collided with Julio, who was coming out of the bathroom.

"Good morning," Julio greeted them cheerfully.

"Good morning," Melinia replied, steadying herself.

"I overslept, but I'm getting breakfast started now," Julio said.

"I'll help you as soon as I get Rafael situated."

"No worries, I've got it," Julio said, heading toward the kitchen.

After Rafael used the bathroom and brushed his teeth, Melinia said, "I'm going to help Julio in the kitchen. I want you to be a good boy, play your Sesame Street game on the iPad, and listen out for your baby brother," Melinia said, glancing at her infant son, still sleeping in his carrier.

"Okay, mommy," Rafael said.

When Melinia found Julio in the kitchen, a plate of French toast and fried bacon were already sitting on the counter.

"Julio, the food smells delicious! Can I help with anything?" she asked.

"Just sit down, pour yourself a cup of coffee, and keep me company," Julio replied, flipping a piece of bacon in the pan. "Jesus's bottle is already warmed up. You don't have to do anything but relax."

"You're so good to me, Julio," she murmured, pouring her coffee.

"That's because I love you, Chica."

She rolled her eyes. "Whatever, Julio." Then she remembered something. "I forgot to tell you—I have the money you loaned me. I'll give it back before we leave."

"Where are you all going?" Julio asked.

"I have a meeting with Ms. Zenobia at 10 a.m."

Julio frowned. "Well, when are you coming back? I don't want you staying at your apartment alone with the boys if that awful man is still out there."

She sighed. "Julio, I can't keep staying here. This is Juliette's rooming house. With Mimi passing away here, I'm worried the authorities will show up. If they do, me and my boys being here will put everything at risk—including your immigration status. I might check into a hotel with a pool. You know how much the boys enjoy the water. Maybe you can stop by once you get off."

Julio studied her for a moment, then nodded. "That sounds nice. But I'm still worried."

"We'll be fine. I'll call you this afternoon," Melinia assured him.

At exactly ten a.m., Melinia sat across from Ms. Zenobia, who looked up from a stack of neatly arranged files. The short, stocky woman adjusted her cat-framed glasses, her eyes sharp behind the lenses. She pursed her lips, and when she spoke, her naturally slanted eyes bore into Melinia like she was trying to see into her soul.

"Good morning, Melinia," Zenobia greeted, her voice cool but firm. "And I see you brought your handsome young men with you."

"Yes, I didn't have a babysitter," Melinia said apologetically.

"I understand completely. I need to discuss something serious with you, though, so if it's okay, I'd like my assistant to take Rafael for some coloring time." She turned to the boy. "Do you like to color, Rafael?"

"Yes!" Raphael beamed.

Ms. Zenobia picked up the phone. "Kendall, can you to grab the coloring books and crayons? I have a little artist in here."

A minute later, there was a knock at the door, and a young lady in a face mask appeared.

"Who wants to color?" Kendall asked.

"Me!" Rafael said, raising his hand excitedly.

"Great! I have a brand-new dinosaur coloring book and crayons just for you. And guess what! You even get to take them home," Kendall said as she took his hand.

"Rafael, be on your best behavior and remember to keep your mask on," Melinia directed.

"I will, Mommy."

As soon as he left, Zenobia leaned back in her chair, her hands laced together as she studied Melinia in silence.

"Ms. Zenobia, am I in trouble?"

Zenobia tapped her manicured nails against the desk. "Have you done something to get yourself in trouble?"

"No," she insisted. "I've been doing the right things, I swear."

Zenobia sighed. "Are you aware that there was a disturbance at your apartment two days ago?"

Melinia frowned. "No. What happened?"

"According to your neighbors and the police report that was sent to me, a man was pounding on your door, screaming for you to come out, calling you vile names. Your neighbors were concerned for you and called the police."

She studied her before continuing. "A Larry Smith was arrested. He's a known drug dealer."

Melinia froze.

Larry.

Joe had seen someone getting arrested.

Zenobia continued. "Can you explain why a drug dealer would be looking for you? Your association with your friend who needs the detox program hasn't caused you to relapse, has it?"

"No, I swear I'm clean. I'll take a drug test right now," Melinia said.

"There's no need for that. I believe you, Melinia. So where is this friend of yours? I pulled a lot of strings to get her that bed and my people at detox can't hold it forever," Zenobia replied.

Tears welled up in the corners of Melinia's eyes at the mention of Mimi. "Ms. Zenobia, I want to thank you for trying to help Mimi, but unfortunately, she won't be needing the bed. She overdosed last night. When you called to say that you had a bed for her, she was already gone. I just didn't know it yet."

Zenobia's eyes softened and she leaned forward to take Melinia's hands in hers. "My God, Melinia, I'm so very sorry."

Melinia shared the details of her run-ins with Larry and how Mimi made it back to Cleveland. "Ms. Zenobia, Larry was stalking me," Melinia admitted. "He tried to force me to use drugs and rape me. If Julio hadn't come looking for me …" Her voice cracked.

"Wow, Melinia, that's quite a story," Zenobia said. "You should have told me about Larry sooner. You can't take chances, especially with having your boys to worry about."

"You are so right," Melinia said, looking down at her hands. "This morning, I opened Mimi's purse and found the heroin she overdosed on. I think she went back in the bathroom and took it from Larry after Julio beat him up."

"What did you do with the drugs?"

"I left them at the rooming house."

Zenobia's jaw dropped. "You what?"

"They're in my friend Julio's room," Melinia replied, realizing her mistake.

"Call Julio. Right now," Ms. Zenobia's voice was steel.

As Melinia dialed, she prayed.

Prayed that her mistake hadn't just put everyone in danger.

Chapter 55

Shame

Juliette stared at Sabrina, her mind struggling to process what she'd just heard.

"I'm not sure if you realize that Franklin and I met shortly after Jessica's accident," Sabrina began, her voice heavy with emotion. "I was an intern at the time, and Franklin was trying to find a forensic psychiatric team to assist with Grandville's case."

Juliette nodded slowly. "Yes, I knew that. But I thought Franklin hired another team."

"He did," Sabrina confirmed. "But one day, out of the blue, he called me. He sounded …off. He said he was suicidal."

Juliette's eyes widened. "What? I had no idea. I was so distraught back then, I barely saw Franklin—or anyone else."

Sabrina exhaled. "I managed to convince him to meet me at a coffee shop. We talked for hours. I asked him if he had a plan, if he had a weapon, if he had any real intent. After a few weeks, he finally told me the truth."

"Well, why was he suicidal?"

Sabrina hesitated, then said, "Because of what happened between the two of you."

A sharp gasp escaped Juliette's lips as her hand shot up to cover her mouth. "Oh my God," she whispered, turning away. Shame burned through her. She had never wanted Franklin—or anyone—to suffer because of her mistake. "You know?" Her voice was barely audible.

"Yes," Sabrina softly replied.

Juliette squeezed her eyes shut. "You must hate me."

"I don't," Sabrina said.

Juliette shook her head. "I hated myself for a long time. I don't even know how it happened. I love Grandville with all my heart. What kind of woman does that? Especially when her husband is locked up and at his worst? I was supposed to stand by him."

Tears welled in her eyes. She buried the guilt for years, had worked through it in therapy, had convinced herself that Franklin had moved past it too.

But he hadn't.

Sabrina reached for Juliette's hand, giving it a gentle squeeze. "Post-traumatic stress disorder, grief, secondary stress—it all makes people do things they never thought they would," she said with understanding.

Juliette wiped her tears and looked at her friend. There wasn't an ounce of judgment in her eyes. "I've never talked about it with anyone but my therapist. Not even Grandville."

Sabrina's expression softened. "I've known about what happened since before I met you, Juliette. And I give you my word—no one will ever hear it from me."

Juliette let out a shaky breath, grateful for that promise, even as self-loathing curled in her gut.

"When Franklin came to me in that state," Sabrina continued, "I knew right away that I was attracted to him. But he was carrying so much guilt. He said he felt like he had betrayed Grandville, and that he had failed you both."

Juliette swallowed a sob.

"He was overwhelmed," Sabrina continued. "He thought he'd taken advantage of you. He believed he was to blame. He felt he should have protected you, for Grandville."

Juliette nodded numbly.

"He didn't have romantic feelings for you, Juliette," Sabrina reassured her. "But he loved you like family. And he never forgave himself."

Juliette exhaled, trying to absorb everything.

"I ended up referring him to another therapist," Sabrina admitted. "I was just an intern at the time, and I was already interested in him. I felt it would be unethical to treat him myself and unfair to him to jeopardize his ability to receive the care he needed."

Juliette nodded.

Sabrina reached for her purse and stood. "I need to find George," she said. "I'll call you when I do."

And just like that, she was gone.

Juliette sat there, frozen in place.

Both Sabrina and Grandville knew and neither of them had ever said a word.

She had been carrying this shame for years, only to learn that she hadn't been carrying it alone.

She was so lost in her thought, she hadn't noticed the doctor enter the room.

"Ms. Stubbs?"

Juliette blinked up at him, startled.

"The exchange transfusion went well. Jolene is doing much better. If she continues improving, she'll be discharged tomorrow or the next day."

A wave of relief washed over here. "Oh, thank God."

"Do you have any questions for me?"

Juliette shook her head. "No, I'm just relieved she's okay. I can't wait to take her home."

The doctor nodded, his eyes warm with empathy. "I know it's been hard. But I'm a bit concerned about you, Ms. Stubbs. When was the last time you left the hospital?"

"A few days ago," Juliette answered. "Why do you ask?"

"You have other children, don't you?"

"Yes," she confirmed. "Jolene has a fraternal twin, and I also have two sons. And…" Her voice faltered. "I also lost a daughter. She's with God now."

The doctor's face softened as the smile on his lips flattened. "I'm so sorry for your loss. My brother passed away from cancer when I was a child," the doctor said. "My parents were so focused on him that they… emotionally neglected me. Not on purpose. But when you're trying to save one child, it's easy to forget that the others still need you too."

Juliette understood that all too well.

The doctor continued. "I became a pediatric oncologist and hematologist because I wanted to help families like mine. And I want to remind you—your other children still need you, Juliette. Go home for a few hours. Jolene will be sleeping for most of the day."

Juliette hesitated, conflicted.

"I promise, she's in good hands," the doctor assured her.

After a moment, she nodded. "Okay. I'll go."

She leaned down and kissed Jolene before slowly walking out of the room.

***

The drive home felt surreal. Cleveland's streets were eerily quiet, the pandemic keeping most people inside. She pulled into her driveway in record time, unsure of what to expect. She stepped inside and barely made it into the kitchen before her sons bolted from their seats and ran into her arms.

"Mom!"

Jabari and Jonah wrapped their arms around her, their worried faces breaking her heart.

"Hey, my babies," she murmured, squeezing them tight. "How are you?"

"We're okay. We ate sandwiches for dinner. Jenae just went to bed," Jabari replied.

Juliette smiled faintly. "That's good."

Her younger son, Jonah, dropped his head, and when he looked up, there were tears in his eyes. "Mom… is Dad okay?" His voice wavered. "Did something happen to him?"

Unsure of how to respond, Juliette asked, "Why do you ask?"

Jabari shifted uncomfortably. "We were playing video games with Blake when his mom got home from work," he said. "She cleans at the hospital. She asked Jabari's dad's name."

Juliette held back a gasp.

"She said she saw a patient named Grandville Stubbs in the ICU. She wanted to reach out to you. She said you helped their family before, and she wanted to do the same."

Jonah gripped her side, his voice barely above a whisper. "Mom… is it true? Is Dad in the hospital?"

Juliette opened her mouth—trying to find a way to deliver the news about Grandville—when her phone rang. She checked the caller ID. The hospital. Her hands began shaking so hard, she could barely hold the phone.

"Hey, guys," she said, already moving toward the dining room. "I have to take this."

Please, God.

Let everything still be okay.

Chapter 56

Your Love (Déjà vu)

Grandville blinked, trying to bring the room into focus. His body ached in ways he had never experienced before. It had to be dream.

George hadn't shot him.

Franklin wasn't dead.

None of it had happened.

He tried to get up, but he felt pain everywhere. He squeezed his eyes shut, willing his mind to separate nightmare from reality. But when he opened them again, the sterile hospital lights and the rhythmic beeping of machines confirmed the truth.

He was here because of George.

Pain flared through his body as he shifted slightly. He winced, feeling the pull of stitches and the deep throb of his fresh wounds. He heard movement near his bed, then a voice.

"Hey there. I see you're awake," said a figure in protective biomedical gear. "Let me get the doctor. I will be right back."

Grandville barely nodded as the person disappeared.

His nightmare was, in fact, a reality. He was in the hospital. George had shot him. And Juliette wasn't here.

A minute later, the person returned with the doctor, who was dressed similarly.

"Hello, Mr. Stubbs," the doctor greeted. "Do you know where you are?"

Grandville's throat was dry, and his voice was barely above a whisper. "Yes… the hospital."

"That's right," the doctor confirmed. "You have a gunshot wound and you've had two surgeries to repair internal damage. From what we can tell, you're recovering extremely well."

Two surgeries. Damn.

"You've been in a medicated sleep for several hours," the doctor continued. "Now that you're awake, we need to ask—are you up for speaking with the police? They've been waiting to speak to you."

Grandville barely registered the question before his thoughts snapped back to one person.

"Where's my wife?"

The nurse, whose eyes crinkled above her mask in a reassuring way, spoke up. "Due to COVID restrictions, she's not allowed in ICU. But she was with you right after your surgery"

Memory returned in fragments. He remembered her voice, her touch, the way she had cried while holding his hand.

If he wasn't so weak, he would have sighed in relief.

"I would like to speak to her," Grandville whispered.

"We'll call her," the nurse promised. "I'm not sure if you remember me, but my name is Nurse Benson, and this is Doctor Johnson."

"I'm sorry, but I don't remember," Grandville murmured.

"It's okay. How about you speak to the detective before we call your wife?" Nurse Benson suggested.

Grandville winced and nodded faintly. "Okay."

Nurse Benson stepped out, returning with a tall white man wearing PPE over his suit.

"Hello, Mr. Stubbs. I'm glad to see you're awake. I'm Detective Finnegan. Do you remember talking to me?"

"Yes," Grandville whispered.

"We've interviewed Ayana," Finnegan continued. "In her statement she explained that George, who is adopted, is furious with you because he recently discovered that you are his biological father. Is that true?"

"Yes," Grandville said.

"And you believe him shooting you was an accident?"

"It was," Grandville whispered. "I won't be pressing charges."

Finnegan exhaled, but didn't look surprised. "I get that. But we don't need your statement to press charges. According to what Ayana has told us, George is dangerous and out of control. He held the two of you hostage for days. He's unstable, and if we don't find him soon, things could get much worse for him."

Grandville shifted uncomfortably in bed. His body protested the movement.

"I have no idea where George is. But if you find him, please don't hurt him. Please also thank Ayana for me. Her actions saved my life."

"Will do," Detective Finnegan said before rubbing a hand over his face. "Look, Mr. Stubbs, I'll be honest with you. If I find him first, I'll do everything in my power to ensure his safety. But if the other officers looking for him find him and he acts in a dangerous way, they might shoot first and ask questions later. I wish you a speedy recovery, Mr. Stubbs."

Grandville swallowed. The police were on edge. If George resisted or panicked, even moved the wrong way, they wouldn't hesitate to "defend" themselves.

The detective gave his forearm a gentle squeeze before leaving the room.

"Can you please let me speak to my wife?" Grandville requested.

"Okay, we're calling her right now," Nurse Benson said while Dr. Johnson examined him.

"Mrs. Stubbs? This is Nurse Benson from the ICU. Your husband is awake and would like to speak with you."

There was a pause.

Then Nurse Benson put the call on speaker and he head Juliette's frantic voice loud and clear. "Oh, thank God. I was so scared when I saw that it was the hospital calling. Grandville, can you hear me?"

A faint smile touched his lips. "Yes, I can hear you."

A bet of silence. Then her voice trembled. "Baby… you scared me."

"I know," he admitted. "And I'm sorry." He swallowed past the dryness in his throat. "Where's George?"

Juliette hesitated. "I don't know. But we're looking for him."

Grandville exhaled sharply, his chest tightening—not from pain, but from worry. "Julie… you need to help him."

Her voice broke. "Grandville, you can't—"

"He needs help," he insisted. "This isn't his fault. He's sick. He's just… lost."

Emotion thickened Juliette's voice. "Sweetheart, I know. I promise we'll help him. But right now, I need you to focus on getting better. We need you. I need you to fight."

"I need you guys, too," Grandville closed his eyes. "I love you, Juliette."

"I love you, too."

Later, as silence settled over the room, Grandville lay staring at the ceiling. Everything had fallen apart. But, when he was released from the hospital, he would introduce George to the world as his son. He just had to hope and pray that George didn't do anything before that moment arrived.

Chapter 57

If You Could See You

Melinia looked around her living room and sighed. It felt great to be home. Even Rafael seemed happier playing in his bedroom with his toys. Jesus was sleeping peacefully in his crib, his chest rising and falling with soft, rhythmic breaths.

But no matter how much comfort home brought, her mind was still racing. Her meeting with Zenobia had been intense. She could still hear the urgency in Zenobia's voice as she put Julio on speaker phone.

"Julio, I need you to go into your bedroom and get Mimi's purse," she ordered.

"Okay, I'm in my room now," Julio replied.

"Good. Now go into the bathroom with the purse and close the door," Zenobia instructed.

"Uh… I'm in. What now?"

"Take out the bag with the white powder," Zenobia said.

"Yes?" Julio questioned.

"Dump it in the toilet," Ms. Zenobia's voice sharpened.

"Wait… but before I do, can you tell me what this is?"

Zenobia paused, then said, "It's what killed your friend."

"You mean this is the stuff Mimi used? Here at our rooming house?"

"Yes. And it needs to be gone. Now."

Melinia had been holding her breath, waiting for the sound of the running water. When a flush echoed through the phone, she exhaled.

"It's done," Julio said. "I'll clean the bathroom before I start lunch, so unless you need something else, I'm going to hang up."

"I'll call you later," Melinia said, and Zenobia disconnected the call.

Zenobia turned to Melinia, her slanted eyes narrowing behind her frames. "This could have gone badly for you."

Melinia swallowed. "I know."

"You did the right thing by telling me," Zenobia continued. "But, in the future, if you're having problems, I want you to reach out to me right away. Together, we'll come up with a plan, but you need to trust me and the process."

As Melinia looked around her apartment, she gave thanks while marveling at how Zenobia worked her magic. First, Ms. Zenobia contacted a funeral home director she knew and arranged for an appointment to plan Mimi's funeral for the very next day. Then, she called a prosecutor who worked with human trafficking victims. By 2 PM that afternoon, Melinia had obtained a restraining order against Larry. Ms. Zenobia also called her police contact, and Larry was now being held on suspicion of selling illicit drugs laced with fentanyl.

Everything had happened so fast, and now, standing in her apartment, Melinia still felt the weight of it all. But she had no time to waste. She grabbed her laptop and immersed herself in searching for properties. She needed to secure a home before Larry got out on bail.

By the time she finished giving the boys their baths and putting them to bed, she had narrowed it down to six properties, all two-family homes.

One house in University Heights stood out. $240,000. Near her mother. Spacious. Perfect. She clicked to schedule a showing at 10 a.m. the next morning.

With one more chess piece to play, she contemplated how to put her plan into action when she heard her doorbell buzz. She froze. She wasn't expecting company. Was it Larry? Had he gotten out already? She tiptoed to her intercom and pressed the button. Tentatively, she said, "Hello?"

"Hey, it's me."

Relief flooded her as she recognized Julio's voice. "Why didn't you call first," Melinia asked, unlocking the door.

"Because you would have found an excuse to avoid me," Julio said, stepping inside.

"Whatever," she muttered, closing the door. "The boys are asleep."

"I'm sorry I missed them," He said, rubbing his neck. "I couldn't leave the rooming house until now. Ms. Juliette sent a grief counselor to meet with me and the guys, and she couldn't come until this evening."

Melinia sighed. "Maybe I should talk to someone too…"

"You should," Julio said, his voice gentle. "I know how much Mimi meant to you."

"I'm meeting with the funeral home tomorrow. Cremation is probably best."

"I found her phone book in her purse," Julio admitted.

"She still had that thing?" Melinia remarked.

"Yeah and I called some of the numbers. I found her mother's phone number."

"Really? Were you able to reach her?" Melinia asked.

"Yes, and I learned a lot about Mimi."

Melinia raised an eyebrow. "Oh, really? Like what?"

Julio's jaw tightened. "Chica, her family could care less about her dying. To them, she was already dead."

Melinia closed her eyes, bracing herself. "What do you mean by that?"

"Mimi came from a very well-off family. But when she got addicted to heroin, her mother said that Mimi was disowned and became the black sheep of their family," Julio said. "She stole her mother's three-carat wedding band and her family heirloom crystal pieces before running away. Her mother said she would wire the money to have Mimi's body disposed of, but no one from the family is attending the funeral or any memorial we might arrange."

"That's so fucked up," Melinia growled as tears spilled down her face. "I can't believe that Mimi's family would treat her like this. No matter what she did, she was still a person, and her life meant something."

"I thought that was bad," Julio went on, "but then, Mimi's mother thought she had hung up the phone, but she hadn't. I overheard her talking to who I assume is Mimi's sister. She said, 'Your stupid sister overdosed and is dead.' The other person started to cry and then said, 'You know why she got on drugs. You know what he was doing to her, and you didn't do anything to stop it. No wonder she ended up a junkie.' Mimi's mother yelled, 'You know she seduced him, and if you repeat that to anyone, I'll cut you off, and you can end up homeless and strung out like your no-good sister,'" Julio repeated.

Melinia covered her mouth, a silent scream caught in her throat. She already knew what she had to do to ensure that even if Mimi was forgotten by her family, she would be remembered by the rest of the world.

Chapter 58

Love is the Answer

Juliette looked down at Jolene, who was sleeping peacefully, and whispered a prayer of thanks. They were finally going home. She had just received word that Jolene was being discharged and she couldn't be more overjoyed. As she packed up her daughter's belongings, she thought back to the conversation she had with her sons about Grandville.

"Mom, please tell us the truth. Is Dad in the hospital?" Jabari asked.

Juliette stopped what she was doing and turned to face him. No more secrets.

"Yes, baby. Your father was shot."

Jonah gasped, his eyes wide with shock.

"What?! Someone shot Dad? Why didn't you tell me?" Jonah demanded.

Juliette sighed, riddled with guilt. "That's on me," she admitted. I didn't want to alarm you guys. Even Aunt Greta didn't know. But we found him, and he's alive. That's what matters."

"Mom, you still haven't told us what happened. Who shot him? Was he robbed?" Jabari pressed.

"Baby, I don't have all the details yet. But what I do know is that he had surgery, and so far, he's doing okay. He needs us now more than ever. I need you both to step up."

Jabari and Jonah nodded in unison.

"Whatever you need from us, Mom," Jonah said.

Juliette felt grateful for her sons. "I need you young men to help Greta around here and to keep Jenae occupied until I can get home. The doctors said that Jolene is doing better, and she'll hopefully be coming home soon," Juliette lectured.

"Mommy! I'm glad you're home," Jenae said, running up to Juliette and giving her a big hug. "Where's my twin? Is she asleep in your bed?"

"Hey, Ladybug," Juliette kissing her sleepy daughter.

"Now that's some good sugar right there. Your sister's still in the hospital, but she'll be home soon. Tomorrow, you can make a welcome home card for her. Your brothers will help you, but right now, you need to go back to bed. It's very late, and I want you to be rested so you can play with your sister when she comes home."

"Okay, Mommy," Jenae said as she headed toward her and Jolene's bedroom.

Now, she was at the hospital preparing to partially reunite her family again. Her thoughts were interrupted by Sabrina walking through the door.

"Hey, how are you?" Juliette greeted her.

"I'm hanging in there. I heard Jolene was being released. Do you need any help packing?"

"That's thoughtful of you. Everything's packed, but I could use your help getting our bags down to my car."

"Not a problem," Sabrina said as Juliette handed her a pink suitcase.

"I can manage the rest," Juliette said as the two of them walked through the hospital.

"How's Grandville?" Sabrina asked.

"The doctors are saying that he's doing extremely well. I'm hoping he'll be released soon."

"That's good," Sabrina said. "Because I found George."

Juliette froze mid-step. "Where was he? Is he okay?"

Sabrina nodded slowly. "I found him at the ruins of my sister's house—well, where it used to be before the fire. The land was turned into a garden, but there's a cliff overlooking Lake Erie. He was standing on the cliff's edge, threatening to jump."

Juliette clutched her chest. "Oh my God, Sabrina…"

"I talked him down," Sabrina assured her. "I got him into a private hospital owned and operated by one of my colleagues and friends. He's in a locked ward getting the treatment he needs."

"I'm so relieved and I know Grandville will be too once he hears this."

"I hate to ask, but I need a favor," Sabrina said hesitantly. "I need you to represent him."

Juliette didn't hesitate. "Of course. We don't have to report him to the authorities just yet. Obtaining treatment for George will be a huge cost saving to the county and the state. I'll do my best to get George a good deal. Right now, the goal is to get him help, not punishment."

Sabrina nodded, wiping her eyes. "I just never saw this coming. He took my gun and everything."

Juliette understood that feeling all too well. "I felt the same way about Grandville after Jessica died," she admitted. "I never imagined him being capable of hurting someone, and suddenly, I was burying my only daughter at the time, and the love of my life was locked up."

Sabrina squeezed her hand. "I know it had to be hell. I want to apologize to you again for what George did. I had a long talk with him, and he finally understands how unfairly he's judged you and Franklin. He's working through it."

"Thank you for telling me that," Juliette said, both women struggling to hold back tears at the mention of Franklin's name.

"I don't know what to do next regarding Franklin's passing. Should I plan a memorial? Maybe a funeral? I feel stuck. I loved Franklin, but we never discussed what to do in the event of death. Maybe once Grandville is out of the hospital, he can provide me with some guidance. I just want to make sure I honor his wishes and lay him to rest in the way he would have wanted."

After getting the bags into Juliette's car, they headed back to Jolene's room, where Juliette signed all the discharge paperwork and chatted with Jolene, who was ready to go home. She helped get Jolene into a pair of shorts and a tank top, and once she was dressed, they were ready to leave the hospital.

"Juliette, you go ahead and get the car. I will help wheel Jolene down to the front to meet you," Sabrina offered.

"Thanks so much, Sabrina."

As Juliette pulled the car to the front of the building, she spotted Sabrina standing with Dr. Johnson, who was treating Grandville, alongside a nurse pushing Jolene's wheelchair. Her heart nearly stopped. Anxiety surged from zero to one hundred, and she took deep breaths to prevent a panic attack. Reaching into her purse, she quickly grabbed her medication, took a pill out, placed it on her tongue, and washed it down with bottled water from her purse. Had Dr. Johnson sought her out to deliver bad news about Grandville?

She stopped, jumped out of the SUV, and opened the back door. She watched as Sabrina and the nurse helped Jolene into the car, while Juliette waited for Dr. Johnson to speak.

"Ms. Stubbs, I learned that your daughter is being released today, and I wanted to catch you before you left the hospital."

"Please tell me that Grandville didn't take a turn for the worse," Juliette said.

"Mr. Stubbs didn't take a turn for the worse," the doctor replied. "He's doing so well that we're moving him off the ICU and into a private room. If he continues to improve at this rate without any complications, he'll be released about a week from today."

The tears of joy came hot and fast. Her king was coming home soon. She struggled to manage her emotions.

"I want to thank you and the other hospital staff for saving both my husband's and daughter's lives. You're all heroes to me," Juliette smiled at him.

When she and Jolene arrived home, Greta and her children had hung up welcome-home signs and even made a cake. Her daughters were so happy to see each other that they hugged and did their special handshake. It was heartwarming to watch her kids shower Jolene with love, and she could almost see Jessica smiling down at her siblings from Heaven.

As she watched her family and the love they had for each other, she knew that despite all that had been revealed, with love, forgiveness, and understanding, everything in her kingdom would be okay.

Chapter 59

Sunday Drive

Grandville drove down the highway, music blaring. He'd been on the road for a few hours, lost in his thoughts. It had been nine months since his ordeal and his life had changed yet again, but he felt he was a better man for it, despite the physical and emotional turmoil he endured after being held hostage and shot by his son George. True to her word, Juliette represented George and, with Samantha's help, he received a fantastic deal.

The ringing phone snapped him out of his thoughts. "Hello?"

"Hey, sweetie! I'm just checking in. How far away are you?" Juliette asked.

Grandville grinned, adjusting his grip on the wheel. "Girl, I've still got a while to drive before I arrive."

"You sure you'll make it back in time for the opening?"

"I wouldn't miss it for the world. Plus, it gives me another opportunity to see your beautiful face."

"Boy, you better stop! Or I'll have to put it on you when you get home," Juliette teased, her voice full of mischief.

Grandville chuckled. "You just better know that I'm holding you to that promise." But beneath the flirtation, they both knew tonight wasn't about them. Tonight was about family. And legacy. "Despite my plans for you later," he added, "I wouldn't miss the presentation of the Franklin Lowe gift for anything."

Juliette sighed softly. "I'm so proud of my little cousin. She really did the damn thing. The opening of her boarding home for trafficking victims is finally happening. It's already garnering local and national attention."

Grandville nodded to himself, remembering the conversation they'd had about it.

"Yes, the Mimi Devoux Boarding Home of Hope is the perfect name, and Melinia and Julio can use their experiences as trafficking victims to help many," Grandville said. "Following in her big cousin's footsteps, huh?"

Juliette laughed softly. "I know, right? And can you believe how big the yard is? She got permission from the city to host the grand opening outside. Julio's been busy helping set everything up."

Joe had stepped up to take over as manager of A New Beginning. He even started a chess club with the residents.

"Joe's awesome, but I'll never find another Julio," Juliette said.

"Yes, but now that Julio and Melinia are dating, you can forget that. Julio's a genuinely good guy who truly loves your cousin and her kids." Melinia had purchased a duplex for her and the boys, and Julio had moved in with her. She used the other unit as a boarding home.

"Melinia has always been a smart girl and now her past experiences allow her to help others."

Grandville nodded. "She's definitely matured, and it took a lot of courage for her to tell the rest of your family about Rayshawn being Rafael's father. Rayshawn's so excited to have a son, he can barely contain himself. He's always on my phone asking for parenting advice," Grandville laughed.

"I'm also glad that Greta told Rayshawn the truth about baby Glenda," Juliette gushed. "Now Rayshawn has a son and a daughter. It's crazy how much Glenda looks like you, Jenae, and Greta. Her hazel eyes are mesmerizing, and she has both her daddy and her uncle wrapped around her finger."

"Yes, my niece is adorable—a miniature Greta. I credit you for helping to ensure that we all got on the right page. Therapy has helped our family, and we're all so much better for it."

"It took all of us committing to the work. My therapist, Emily, connected us with the right team. I'm really excited about seeing everyone in person again, thanks to the vaccine."

Grandville shook his head, thinking about how it could have saved his best friend's life. "I still can't believe that Franklin died from COVID. The memorial Sabrina organized for him was beautiful. Her choice was to donate his body to science helped develop the vaccine. I know Franklin was smiling down from heaven when our fraternity brothers held our Omega memorial during his funeral service."

"Yes, Franklin's homegoing was beautiful and a true reflection of his life. By the way, Greta called a few minutes ago. Rayshawn rented a stretch limo so we can all ride over to the opening together. Everyone's going to meet here, including Montell and Maria, and Samantha's bringing her husband. My mother's coming to our house to stay with Glenda, Martinez, and the twins while we're out."

"That's good. We're so lucky to have Samantha. She really came through for George by negotiating that deal with the Prosecutor's Office. He's getting the help he needs, and I'll always be in her debt."

"Yes that's my girl. We were a dynamic duo."

"You sure were. So is Sabrina riding in the limo?" Grandville asked.

"No, she said she'll meet us at the opening. She'll be presenting each of Melinia's residents with the Franklin Lowe gift of one thousand dollars apiece," Juliette said.

"My fraternity brothers really came through with raising the money, and it'll go a long way to help the residents with buying essentials," Grandville said. "I thank God for blessing me with my family and friends, because without all of you, I don't know if I would have made it through the ordeal of what has been my life."

"Of course, we love you! You're my king and I can't imagine doing life without you," Juliette said.

"And you're my queen. Thank you for holding me and our family down during some of our darkest times," Grandville lovingly said.

"You don't have to thank me. I did what a wife and mother is supposed to do. I love you with all my heart," Juliette said. The two of them had attended counseling to deal with what occurred between Juliette and Franklin. It took time, but they were able to move forward and learn to trust each other all over again.

Grandville smiled and continued to maneuver the vehicle as he travelled the highway.

"Are you nervous about seeing George?" Juliette asked.

"Yes, a little. I mean, who would have thought that George would end up at Oakhill? He must know how much I love him because I vowed I would never go back there. You and Greta had to convince me to go to Oakhill when they opened the psychiatric clinic that now bears Jessica's name. I thought attending that event would be the last time I would ever be there," Grandville said, gripping the steering wheel tighter.

"Oakhill has helped you, and I'm confident the staff there will help George, too, Juliette said. "I'm grateful I was able to get George into the same program you were in. Hopefully, George won't have to spend as much time at Oakhill as you did."

"I'm praying that he gets to come home soon. I'm going to show him the video that our family made for him. I want him to know that even though we don't know him as well as we'd like, he's family and he is loved. I'm so proud of how well the kids took the news that George is my son."

"They took the news well because we followed our therapy team's advice and told them an age-appropriate version of the truth. I don't want history to repeat itself by keeping lifelong secrets. The only secret I'm willing to keep is that George's Mother Gina was also your half-sister as well as your first cousin," Juliette said.

"You're so right; that's highly-sensitive information that George and the kids never need to know. Except for me, you, and Greta, no one else will ever know that information. Speaking of history repeating itself, I'm pulling into Oakhill right now. I'll make the opening, but if I'm not at the house when you all get ready to leave, just go ahead. Please send me a text letting me know, and I'll meet you at Melinia's."

"Okay, sweetheart, have a great visit with George, and I'll see you later," Juliette said seductively.

"Bye, lover. I'll see you tonight," Grandville replied before hanging up.

He stepped out of the car and turned to face the place he'd sworn to leave behind him for good. But he knew it was what he needed to do for his son. For his family. For his redemption.

Chapter 60

Never Alone

Grandville hadn't seen George since the kidnapping and shooting. Now, standing at the entrance of Oakhill, the very institution where he had once been sentenced, he felt a strange mix of nerves and resolve.

George had pled guilty to kidnapping and aggravated assault and had been sentenced to five years. As part of his plea, he admitted to suffering with mental health issues and was sentenced to serve his time at Oakhill's psychiatric rehabilitation program—the same one that had once saved Grandville's life. If the institution's psychiatrists deemed him stable, he could be released early and reintegrated into the community.

Ironically, the only good thing about COVID for Grandville was that it had accelerated his law license reinstatement. Now, he was one of George's attorneys, granting him the opportunity to meet with his son in a private area, away from the prying ears of the guards.

Taking a deep breath, he stepped through the front doors of Oakhill—and immediately ran right into Ayana.

"Ayana, what are you doing here?" Grandville's eyebrows lifted in surprise.

She smiled, cordially embracing him. "Hey, Grandville. I was just visiting with George. He's super excited to see you."

"So, are the two of you a couple now?"

Ayana let out a soft laugh, shaking her head. "No, but you know I've always had a thing for George, even after everything he put us through. He doesn't need a romantic partner right now. He needs a friend."

Grandville nodded in understanding, appreciation flickering in his eyes. "Ayana, I want to thank you for all that you did to save my life and for standing by George, despite his actions. I'm here today because of the care you provided me. You're going to be one hell of a doctor."

"Awe, thank you," she said, visibly touched. "I'm glad you're okay."

"So am I," Grandville said with a chuckle. Ayana stared at him for a long moment, making him slightly uncomfortable.

"You know, it's trippy to see how much George looks like you."

Grandville chuckled, nodding. "Yeah. Genetics don't lie."

"Listen," she sighed, "I should get going. George is waiting for you and I don't want to hold you up."

"Drive safe," Grandville said, giving her a final nod before continuing into the facility.

After being checked in, screened for weapons, and receiving an attorney badge, he was directed to the visitation room.

As he waited at a small metal table, the door opened and Officer Emerson walked in. Grandville's face lit up at the sight of the man who had once been his favorite guard during his incarceration at Oakhill. Grandville considered him a friend.

"Stubbs!" Officer Emerson grinned, extending his hand. "Man, it's good to see you again! How've you and your family been?"

Grandville stood up, shaking his hand firmly. "Good to see you, too! Juliette and the kids are doing great. Thanks so much for asking. How's your son and wife?"

"The old ball and chain keeps me in line," Emerson joked. "My son is attending Akron University. He made the basketball team, and he credits Rayshawn Robinson for giving him invaluable tips. I want to thank you again for introducing my son to Mr. Robinson, and I want you to know that he still has the signed basketball and jersey that I got from you."

"Glad to hear it. Rayshawn's a solid guy."

"So, I heard you're here as an attorney and that you represent George."

"Yes, that is true."

Emerson's expression turned knowing. "The moment I saw him I knew I'd met him before. Then it hit me—he was at the opening of the Jessica Stubbs Behavioral Health Clinic. I've gotten to know George, and he has confided in me that you are his biological father. He bears a striking resemblance to you."

Grandville nodded. "We didn't know he was my son back at the opening. How's he doing here at Oakhill?"

"A model inmate I've been watching out for him. Nobody will bother him, so don't worry," Officer Emerson assured him. Just then, the door opened again and George walked in, escorted by an officer. The officer unlocked his cuffs before leaving the room. George sat down at the table across from him, dressed in a standard beige inmate uniform.

"We'll be outside the door if you need anything," Officer Emerson said as he walked out of the small room and closed the door, leaving George and Grandville alone.

For a moment, they just stared at each other. Grandville was the first to speak.

"Hello, son."

George's eyes flickered with something unreadable.

"How are you holding up in here?" Grandville asked.

"You already know it's awful here," he muttered. "But I'm making it. How about you? It looks like you've recovered from your injuries."

"I'm doing okay. Thankfully, my body healed," Grandville said.

"I'm sorry for shooting you. I was out of control when I did it. But I'm getting help here for my anger."

Grandville's heart swelled with emotion. "Thanks, son. Your apology means a lot to me."

George hesitated before asking the question that had clearly been weighing on him. "Do really you consider me your son?"

Grandville didn't even hesitate. "Yes. I loved you before I ever met you. I know you didn't mean to hurt me, and while you're here, I need you to work on forgiving yourself."

George's eyes shone with unshed tears.

Grandville pulled out his phone. "Now I want to show you something."

George leaned in over the table and Grandville showed him the video that his family made specifically for him as a welcome to the Stubbs family. As George watched, tears slipped down his face.

"I can't believe they did this for me," George whispered through his sobs. "I mean, I'm here at Oakhill because I almost killed you."

"George, we've all forgiven you."

Grandville leaned forward. "I know you read Sabrina's journals. I know that's how you found out about Juliette and Franklin. But what you didn't understand is that they were both suffering—Juliette with PTSD and Franklin with secondary traumatic stress."

George lowered his head, absorbing the words. "I transferred my anger," he admitted. "I felt rejected. Unworthy."

Grandville nodded. "I get it. But it's time to let that go."

George took a deep breath. "I've been going to therapy. I've even resumed my college classes and transferred my credits to my program here at Oakhill. I'll graduate next year with a degree in culinary arts."

"Son, that's awesome," Grandville cheered, reaching over the table to exchange a high-five with his son. "When you get out, we're going to look into a food truck. You make the best damn waffles I've ever had."

George laughed, wiping his eyes. "I'd like that."

"If you need anything, just let me know or tell Officer Emerson, and he'll get in touch with me."

"I can't believe I'm saying this, but I'm really looking forward to your visits. Thank you for giving me hope," George said, tears in his eyes.

As Grandville stood to leave, he pulled George into a tight embrace.

"I'll see you next month. Take care of yourself, son," Grandville said.

"You too… Dad." George replied.

As Grandville walked out of Oakhill, into the fresh air he looked up toward the heavens and thanked God. Despite the revelations that had threatened to destroy him and his family, he could feel deep in his spirit that his life was right where it was supposed to be. Because for the first time in a long time, his family felt whole.

Chapter 61

Celebrate

Melinia looked around the Mimi Devoux Boarding Home of Hope and smiled. The beautiful space would offer women who had endured the hell of human trafficking the haven they deserved. The living room had comfortable furniture, a big screen 70-inch television, and tasteful decor. She and her mother had a great time visiting antique shops and furniture stores to pick out the inexpensive yet elegant pieces. Her thoughts were interrupted by the doorbell. She rushed to the door and was surprised to see Ms. Zenobia.

"Ms. Zenobia, what a surprise," Melinia said.

"I know I'm early, but I wanted to be the first one here. I was hoping you'd have time to give me a private tour before everyone else arrives."

"Of course! Please come in," Melinia said, stepping aside for Zenobia to enter.

"I heard the doorbell. Who's at the door?" Julio questioned as he entered the foyer. His face lit up when he saw their guest. "Hello, Ms. Zenobia, it's so good to see you."

"Hi Julio. It's great to see you too."

"Julio, Ms. Zenobia came early, and I'm going to give her tour of the home before the opening. Are the caterers good to go?"

"Yes, everything's on track. Ms. Zenobia, I hope you enjoy the tour," Julio said, waving as he walked back toward the kitchen.

Melinia led Zenobia upstairs, watched her slanted eyes widen with excitement at the sight of the resident's rooms. The home featured three large bedrooms, each equipped with two twin beds adorned with matching comforters and drapes. Beautiful pieces of art hung on the walls, and each resident had their own dresser and each room offered large closets for their personal belongings.

"Melinia, this home will be a blessing to so many. I wish I had a welcoming place like this after I escaped prostitution and started my addiction recovery journey. I hope we can partner so I can refer women who need your housing program."

"Ms. Zenobia, I'd love that. I already have my first resident—a woman who was originally referred to Juliette's rooming home. After Julie interviewed her and realized that she had been trafficked, she referred her to me. She moves in next week. I'm also working with the Rape Crisis Center, and they're sending a staff member to hold Survivors group meetings here three times a week. Meetings will be held in the finished basement, and all of my residents must attend if they want to live here. I even set up a small computer lab so the residents have a place to work on their resumes."

"Melinia, I'm so proud of you. I'm sure your friend Mimi would be too."

Melinia's eyes welled with tears. "I wish I could have saved her, but since I couldn't, I pray I can save others in her name. Living right next door allows me to work with my residents while maintaining privacy and independence. My side is an exact replica of this space, and it's a large home we can grow into."

"It's a great setup. Keeping your business overhead low also ensures your earnings will help with your mortgage."

"Yes, but most importantly, I can be a stay-at-home mom. I start my master's program in the fall, and I'll be able to attend classes online."

Julio entered the living room, and asked, "Ms. Zenobia, can I offer you something to drink or a snack?"

"Thanks, Julio, but I am okay right now."

"If you change your mind, I've prepared some tasty hors d'oeuvres for everyone." Julio grinned before kissing Melinia softly on the lips and walking out.

Zenobia smiled knowingly. "I see you two have moved past friendship."

Melinia's cheeks flushed. "Yes, he's been the only good thing that came out of my past with the Sandego Crew, besides Jesus. It took a while for me to realize how much I love him, but he's been extremely patient and supportive. He's amazing with my sons, and he's been instrumental in preparing the home. He's going to prepare all the meals for the residents. We make a great team."

"I'm so happy for you both. You deserve to be loved."

"It took me a long time to believe that. I felt unworthy because of my past. But Julio never gave up on me. I credit you for helping me to see that my past shaped me into the woman I am today. With God's help, I can use my experiences to help others. Just like you have."

"Melinia, you did all the work. Remember, the devil will try to stop you from blessing others. Keep praying and know you can always call me. I still expect you to keep meeting with me each month."

"I wouldn't dream of missing a session. My next appointment is in two weeks."

"Wonderful. Now, let's finish the tour."

After the tour, Zenobia sat at a table outside while Melinia went next door to check on her kids. They were in the finished rec-room in their basement with her mother. She was playing with Jesus on the floor while Rafael played his Switch on the flat-screen. As soon as Jesus saw her, he squealed and ran into her arms.

"This little one is everywhere now that he's walking," her mother laughed. "I'm so glad I have you here to help."

"I'm glad too. I'm proud of you. You're going to change so many lives."

"Thank you, mom. I'm the woman I am today because of you."

Shaking her head, her mother said, "All the glory belongs to God."

One hour later, Melinia greeted her arriving guests outside of the home when a stretch limo pulled up right in front. She watched as Juliette, Samantha and her husband Jared, Greta and Rayshawn, Montell and Maria exited the vehicle.

Juliette walked up with a bright smile, handing her a large bouquet of flowers.

"We're so proud of you, Melinia. Look at this house. It's beautiful!"

"Yes, this is really nice." Greta said, giving Melinia a hug.

"Thank you. Where's Grandville and baby Glenda?" Melinia asked.

"Juliette's mother has the baby," Greta said.

"Grandville should be arriving shortly. He went to Oakhill this morning. Sabrina will also be late, but I expect her soon," Juliette added.

"Great because we have a lot of food, and I'm expecting you all to help us eat it."

Julio emerged from the house. "Hello, everybody! It's so good to see all of you. Please, come on in."

Later, as Melinia stood before her guests, preparing to thank them, Julio interrupted.

"Melinia, I have two surprises. Sabrina, can you come up here?"

Sabrina joined them in the front of the yard, holding an envelope. "Melinia, there are no words to tell you just how amazed we all are at what you're doing here. Memorializing your friend and helping is inspiring. To honor your dedication, I present you with the Franklin Lowe Gift—an annual donation to support your residents. As many of you know, Franklin was my fiancée who lost his battle with COVID. His fraternity brothers and I want to memorialize him by contributing to this amazing cause."

Joyful tears streamed down Melinia's face as she accepted the check. She looked over at Grandville, who winked and joined the crowd in applause.

After she hugged and thanked Sabrina, Julio took her hand. "I have one more surprise."

He dropped to one knee. "Melinia, will you make me the happiest man alive and become my wife?'

Melinia didn't hesitate before shouting, "Yes, Julio! I'd love nothing more than to become your wife!"

The crowd erupted in cheers as Julio lifted Melinia into his arms and spun her around before sealing the moment with a passionate kiss.

Epilogue

Juliette sat in front of the church with Grandville and smiled. Her king looked dashing in a black suit paired with a turquoise shirt, and a matching handkerchief and socks. The bullet that wounded his body was still lodged in his hip but, despite that, Grandville had suffered minimal physical effects from his ordeal.

"Do you remember our wedding day?" he asked.

"How could I forget it? It was one of the best days of my life."

"Mine too."

Juliette looked around and saw many of her family and friends scattered throughout the church. Her mother and her Aunt Mabel were sitting together in a reserved section, and she had never seen Mabel look so happy. She blew them a kiss and smiled even larger when they blew kisses back. She turned her attention to the chaos of Rayshawn and Greta's arrival. Her children, who were sitting behind her and Grandville, exclaimed when they saw their little cousin.

As soon as the couple made it to the front of the church, Rayshawn said, "Grandville, I'm having problems with this tie. Can you come with me to fix it?"

"Sure. Juliette, I'll be right back."

"Okay."

Juliette turned her attention to Greta, who was holding a squirming Glenda, but was interrupted by her children.

"Aunt Greta, can I hold her?" Jabari asked.

"I want to hold her, too," Jonah chimed in.

"Of course, you can take turns holding her. Here, take her." Greta passing Glenda to her oldest cousin, Jabari.

Glenda squealed when she saw her cousins, and her hazel eyes flashed with excitement. Her frilly dress and matching tights, paired with the ringlets of curls framing her angelic face made her look like a living doll. Each of Juliette's kids took turns kissing her, filling the church with love and laughter.

"Girl, I'm so glad I have my nieces and nephews. They're such a huge help with Glenda and she just loves them."

"They love her too. She's such a blessing to our family."

Greta removed her heavy mink coat and matching gloves. Juliette's eyes almost popped out of her head when she noticed the five-carat diamond ring sparkling on her left hand.

"Girl, I know that's not a wedding ring!"

Greta bit her lip, grinning. "It is."

"You and Rayshawn got remarried?"

"Girl, I know it's crazy, but we did. Our wedding anniversary was last week, and we decided to celebrate by getting remarried. Rayshawn has been spending most of his time in Cleveland at his home in Gates Mills. Since Glenda was born, we've been spending a lot of time together. I've had the opportunity to really *see* him. He's a totally different person and Glenda just loves her daddy. I've forgiven Rayshawn and I must admit that I never stopped loving him. I think that's why Derek and I didn't work out. Rayshawn is who I'm supposed to be with."

Juliette was stunned, but she couldn't hide her happiness for her sister-in-law. "Grandville and I would've been there with you if you'd told us."

"I know, but we decided to have a private ceremony with just me, him and Glenda. We thought that it would be weird to have a big ceremony when we've already been married. Rayshawn doesn't really need help with his tie. He took Grandville to the bathroom to tell him the news."

Just then, Grandville and Rayshawn walked back to the front of the church. Grandville stopped to greet Montell, Maria, and Big Joe before reclaiming his seat next to her.

"Rayshawn just told me the news, and I have to say, I'm happy for both of you. Let me see the ring," Grandville said to Greta while Rayshawn settled in next to her.

Greta flashed her ring, and Grandville shielded his eyes playfully. "That's one hell of a ring."

"Yes, he did good. I love it."

"Grandville, I know I didn't do right by Greta the first time around, but I promise you that I'll never take her, Glenda, you, or the rest of our family for granted again. This is the happiest I've ever been. I have everything a man a could want—a beautiful wife, two beautiful kids, and my family. I love you guys, and I'm going to do everything I can to make sure that I'm part of your lives."

"Rayshawn, I'm going to hold you to that promise, but know that no matter what's happened, we love you too."

The wedding march song started to play, and everyone stopped talking to watch Melinia's oldest brother walk her down the aisle to meet Julio and Melinia's children at the front of the church.

Melinia was a vision of beauty in her winter white wedding dress with matching veil, and Julio gazed at her with such love that it melted Juliette's heart.

After the ceremony, Juliette laughed and talked with Sabrina, Samantha, Greta, and Maria at the reception. The twins, along with Rafael were running around playing, and Jabari and Jonah took turns dancing with Glenda, who was having the time of her life. As she looked around the room and watched her cousin and Julio embraced in a slow dance, she saw her King.

And he saw her.

"Excuse me, ladies, I need to borrow my wife for a moment," he said and took her by the hand.

Their journey had been anything but easy, but as they danced, surrounded by love, laughter, and the family they'd fought so hard to protect, Juliette knew—with Grandville beside her, their kingdom would always stand. They were living proof that forgiveness, faith, and family could turn even the deepest wounds into something beautiful.

Author's Note

No matter who we are, each of us faces issues and situations that place stress on our relationships. In those moments of chaos, we must reach deep into our souls to find the forgiveness that is always present in our hearts. The characters in my novel each relied on a scripture to help them to find that forgiveness. I would like to share this scripture with you in hopes that it will help you overcome life's ever-present struggles.

Be blessed, and thank you for reading The Revelation.

Praise for Spiritual Blessings in Christ

Ephesians 1: 3-14 (NIV)

3 Praise be to the God and Father of our Lord Jesus Christ, who has blessed us in the heavenly realms with every spiritual blessing in Christ.

4 For he chose us in him before the creation of the world to be holy and blameless in his sight. In love,

5 he predestined us for adoption to sonship through Jesus Christ, in accordance with his pleasure and will—

6 to the praise of his glorious grace, which he has freely given us in the One he loves.

7 In him we have redemption through his blood, the forgiveness of sins, in accordance with the riches of God's grace

8 that he lavished on us. With all wisdom and understanding,

9 he made known to us the mystery of his will according to his good pleasure, which he purposed in Christ,

10 to be put into effect when the times reach their fulfillment—to bring unity to all things in heaven and on earth under Christ.

11 In him we were also chosen, having been predestined according to the plan of him who works out everything in conformity with the purpose of his will,

12 in order that we, who were the first to put our hope in Christ, might be for the praise of his glory.

13 And you also were included in Christ when you heard the message of truth, the gospel of your salvation. When you believed, you were marked in him with a seal, the promised Holy Spirit,

14 who is a deposit guaranteeing our inheritance until the redemption of those who are God's possession—to the praise of his glory.

If you enjoyed this novel, please share it with others and leave a review on **Goodreads** or **Amazon**. You can also reach out to me directly by visiting my website at www.novelistjjwinston.com

Acknowledgments

In the words of Oprah, “I've come to believe that each of us has a personal calling that is as unique as a fingerprint—and that the best way to succeed is to discover what you love and then find a way to offer it to others in the form of service, working hard, and also allowing the energy of the universe to lead you.”

I have tried to live by Oprah’s words, and my novels have allowed me to use my social work and legal expertise to both educate and entertain my readers. I have been called by the universe to create relatable characters and I’m beyond proud of my newest novel. I hope that you have found the same joy I felt while writing it.

I’m able to sparkle, shine, and offer my service to the world because I’m surrounded by the very best of family, friends, colleagues and Sorority Sisters.

I want to send a special thanks to my husband, Douglas Winston, for being my best friend and my calm in the eye of life’s storms. My children and stepchildren—Julian, Jasemine, and Douglas Jr. —and my grandchildren, thank you for always believing in me and supporting my dreams.

To my sisters and sister-in-love—Jackie, Joyce, Terry, Latrelle, and Margaret—and to my brother and brother-in-love—Julius, Thomas, and Donald—thank you for always showering me with love, encouragement and dedication.

Thanks to my many nieces, nephews and cousins and extended special gratitude to my cousin Beverly Byers for creating my book bundles, bookmarks, and merchandise.

A heartfelt thanks to my editors and writing family, Eryka Parker, author of Beauty Beheld (under the pen name Zariah L. Banks), and Michael Payne, for always pushing me and assisting me with refining my work so it's the best it can be. Your unconditional support and encouragement have been invaluable. I credit my writing success to their advice, love, and counsel as they are both an integral part of my team. The Lit Trio. I would also like to thank Nicole Garner for her copyediting work on this project.

To my dear friends and personal cheerleaders—Judge Tonya Jones, Melissa Stallings, Sunia Marsh, Camille Warner, Pinkey Carr, Renee Bacchus, Tonya Bennett Hardy, and Kim Jones—thank you for your unwavering support.

I also want to express my gratitude to the women of Alpha Kappa Alpha Sorority, with a special emphasis on Alpha Omega chapter and the ladies of Top Ladies of Distinction Cleveland Chapter for always promoting and lifting me.

Franklin's Playlist

1. "If I ever feel better" Phoniex
2. "Please Do Not Lean" Daniel Caesar Featuring BADBADNOTGOOD
3. "Bad Habits" Ed Sheeran
4. "Jolene" Beyonce, Dolly Parton
5. "Let's Fall in Love" Raheem DeVaughn featuring Kenny Allen, H.M.P.
6. "I love you" Billie Eilish
7. "I want you around" Snoh Aalegra
8. "Breathe" Anna Nalick
9. "You can't get what you want (Till you know what you want)" Joe Jackson
10. "Devil is a lie" Tommy Richman
11. "Anxiety" Sleepy Hallow Ft. Doechii
12. "Waffle House" Jonas Brothers
13. "Never Understand Me" Juice WRLD featuring XXXTENTACION
14. "Lights Out" BIA and JID

15. "Sad Girlz Love Money" Amaare
16. "Karma" Queen Naija
17. "Believe" Hiroshima
18. "All Mine" Ralph Tresvant
19. "Save Me from Myself" Eminem featuring 2pac.
20. "Gotta Move On" Toni Braxton featuring H.E.R.
21. "The Way" Lindsey Webster
22. "No Lie" Lalah Hathaway
23. "Wrecked" Imagine Dragons
24. "Clear" Orange Animal
25. "In the Closet" Michael Jackson
26. "Whiskey Whiskey" Moneybag Yo featuring Morgan Wallen
27. "I found you" PJ Morton
28. "Lose Control" Teddy Swims
29. "Fever" Robert Glasper Experiment featuring Hindi Zahra
30. "Good Good" Usher and Summer Walker
31. "Insanity" Gregory Porter featuring Lalah Hathaway
32. "Lost" Maroon 5
33. "Lived and Learned" Timeupteddy
34. "Lose it all" Antoine Dunn
35. "Where you at" Brent Faiyaz

36. "Best for Me" Joyner Lucas featuring Jelly Roll
37. "Freedom" Pharrell Williams
38. "Wake up alone" Amy Winehouse
39. "As it was" Harry Styles
40. "Creepin" Metro Boomin, The Weeknd, 21 Savage
41. "On everything" LaToya London featuring Anthony Hamilton
42. "When I was young" Miley Cyrus
43. "Calling all angels" Lenny Kravitz
44. "Crossroads" Bone Thugs and Harmony
45. "Stick to the Plan" Emmerson featuring Howard Hewett and Lola Brook
46. "Father Time" Kendrick Lamar featuring Sampha
47. "Been Like This" Doja Cat
48. "Till I Die" Machine Gun Kelly
49. "Trouble" Coldplay
50. "Excuse Me" Ro James
51. "Be Ok" Crisette Michele featuring Will. I. Am
52. "Sleep on it" Gallant
53. "Pieces of Me" Ledisi
54. "God's Plan" Drake
55. "Shame" Tyrese

56. "Your Love (Déjà vu)" Glass Animals

57. "If you could see you" J. Brown

58. "Love is the answer" England Dan and John Ford

59. "Sunday Drive" Joe Lanter

60. "Never Alone" Rihanna & Adele

61. "Celebrate" Black eyed peas

www.ingramcontent.com/pod-product-compliance
Lightning Source LLC
Chambersburg PA
CBHW040515170726
48295CB00012B/202
* 9 7 8 1 7 3 5 0 9 0 3 9 9 *